CAMPAIGNING WITH

"OLD STONEWALL"

CAMPAIGNING WITH

"OLD STONEWALL"

Confederate

Captain

Ujanirtus

Allen's

Letters to

His Wife

EDITED BY RANDALL ALLEN
AND KEITH S. BOHANNON

Louisiana State
University Press
Baton Rouge

Designer: *Amanda McDonald Key*
Typeface: *Bembo*
Typesetter: *Wilsted & Taylor Publishing Services*
Printer and binder: *Thomson-Shore, Inc.*

Library of Congress Cataloging-in-Publication Data:
Allen, Ujanirtus.
   Campaigning with "Old Stonewall" : Confederate Captain Ujanirtus
Allen's letters to his wife / edited by Randall Allen and Keith S.
Bohannon.
      p.   cm.
   Includes bibliographical references and index.
   ISBN 0-8071-2256-4 (cloth : alk. paper)
      1. Allen, Ujanirtus—Correspondence.   2. Soldiers—Georgia—
Correspondence.   3. Confederate States of America. Army. Georgia
Infantry Regiment, 21st.   4. Georgia—History—Civil War, 1861–1865—
Personal narratives.   5. United States—History—Civil War,
1861–1865—Personal narratives, Confederate.   I. Allen, Randall.
II. Bohannon, Keith S.   III. Title.
E559.5 21st.A57   1998
973.7′458—dc21   97-50293
                                                        CIP

CONTENTS

CONTENTS

ILLUSTRATIONS

PREFACE

My whole life has been a yearning for a home and some one to love.

WITH those words written to his wife on April 18, 1862, twenty-three-year-old Ujanirtus Allen revealed the essence of his character. Orphaned at age three, he grew up in foster homes and boarding schools. At twenty-one he inherited a substantial estate, married his childhood sweetheart Susan Fuller, and embarked on his dream of life as a family man.

The coming of war only a year after his marriage threw Ugie Allen's life into turmoil once again. He felt more acutely than most soldiers the universal conflict between devotion to duty and longing for home. The young officer's writings consequently reflect both resentment of a situation beyond his control and a staunch determination to play his assigned role. Allen's frustration manifested itself in stinging criticism directed at politicians, fellow officers, duplicitous civilians, and laggard privates. He lamented his inability to procure a furlough and chided his wife for not writing but, at the same time, he encouraged her to persevere in the hope that they would be reunited.

Whether writing about the war or his farm and family, Ugie Allen exhibited a talent for communicating his observations and personal feelings. He was ambitious, pretentious, and quick to take offense at perceived insults and injustices. His letters to his beloved Susie are laced with gossip and abound with vivid descriptions of battlefields and camp life as well as wartime Richmond and the beautiful Virginia countryside. He offered characterizations of individuals as notable as Stonewall Jackson and as obscure as a regimental teamster. With few exceptions, Allen fulfilled his promise to write twice a week, penning at least 138 letters in less than two years. He received a mortal wound at Chancellorsville, Virginia, on May 2, 1863, dying six days later. Susan saved his letters so that their son might some day read them and know something of his father.

Susan Allen's great-granddaughter Ann Strickland Petry learned of the existence of the letters in 1972. Recognizing the richness of their content, she contemplated publishing them, but her father Robert Wilson Strickland demurred, fearing that Captain Allen's words might contradict long-held beliefs or renew old animosities. Three generations had passed, but descendants of the same families whose sons and brothers had marched to war with Ugie Allen still farmed the same land, worshipped in the same churches, and shared a collective notion of gray-clad heroes fighting valiantly but in vain to preserve a way of life. When one of the editors came across a passage regarding his own great-grandfather's 13th Georgia Regiment, "running like the hounds of h——ll were after it," Mr. Strickland's concern was fully appreciated.

For the sake of clarity the editors of these letters have altered punctuation in a few instances. (Allen tended to use semicolons and colons rather than commas and periods.) Spelling has been left alone, and one can almost hear Allen's Piedmont Georgia drawl through his phonetic spelling of "ammediately" or "frunt." Allen frequently used parentheses and underlining; all such marks in the text are his. The editors use brackets [ ] to identify illegible or omitted words. Annotation is included to identify individuals and events mentioned by Allen, and a series of maps should help the reader follow his "peregrinations." Captain Allen's fellow soldiers are listed in a roster of the Ben Hill Infantry, Company F, 21st Regiment, Georgia Volunteer Infantry.

In an era of classical revival, Allen's parents chose for their son a classical-sounding name, Ujanirtus Cincinnatus. (The first name was pronounced you-ja-NIGH-tus, and the nickname Ugie was pronounced YOU-gee.) The derivation of the name is unknown; it may have been a corruption of Eugenius. Allen's contemporaries apparently found it as troublesome as we do, for his name frequently appears in court and military records as Eugene or Ugene.

The editors are indebted to Mr. and Mrs. William B. Petry for permission to publish these letters. Ann and Bill displayed tremendous confidence and boundless patience as the effort to transcribe the original faded pages evolved into a full-scale publication project. We are also grateful that Robert Wilson Strickland preserved his family's lore and relics. Although he expressed reservations about publishing Captain Allen's private correspondence, Mr. Strickland imbued his daughter and grandsons with the respect for their forebears that inspired this publication.

Gardner Allen and Shelly Anderson began the tedious task of transcribing the letters. Bruce Allardice, Frances Towns Allen, Cyle B. Bohannon, Lee Cathey, Lela W. Craft, David Hollis, Robert E. L. Krick, Robert K. Krick, Forrest C. Johnson III, Kaye Lanning Minchew, Frank O'Reilly, and David

Sherman provided supplemental material, helpful criticism, and generous encouragement. Sylvia Frank, John Easterly, and Gerry Anders of the Louisiana State University Press, and copy editor Ruth Laney, deftly guided two novices through the publication process.

These acknowledgments would be incomplete without a word about Susan Fuller Allen Strickland, the "Dear Susie" to whom most of these letters were addressed. Susan was only eighteen when her husband was called to war, and with an infant son she might have chosen to return to her parents' home. Instead, with help from family and neighbors, she struggled to maintain an independent household. She embraced her husband's dream of establishing a model farm, and she clung to that dream even after his death. Neither the privations of war nor the upheaval of its aftermath deterred her. In 1868, Susan married Confederate veteran Wilson W. Strickland, but she carefully preserved the bundle of letters from Ugie, ensuring that future generations would not forget Captain Allen and the Ben Hill Infantry.

Ugie Allen sometimes had bad things to say about his cohorts, but the intent in publishing these letters is not to tarnish or dishonor the reputation of any individual. The collection is simply one young man's observations of the people and events swirling about him during a tumultuous period in American history.

For social historians, Allen's letters offer vivid testimony of the difficulty many Civil War soldiers encountered trying to manage a farm in absentia. (Susan Allen's letters, unfortunately, do not survive, but many of her wartime experiences can be inferred from her husband's letters.) For military historians, the missives offer fresh accounts of important battles, campaigns, and leaders from the point of view of a company-grade officer. These letters also tell a tragic love story that is all too typical of the Civil War era. This book is a tribute to those men and women, separated by war, whose capacity for endurance and sacrifice is almost beyond our comprehension.

CAMPAIGNING WITH

"OLD STONEWALL"

PROLOGUE

How are things back in old Troup County?

ROBERT S. Allen, the son of Robert and Sarah Allen of Burke County, Georgia, was among the settlers who migrated to western Georgia in the decade after the territory was purchased from the Creek Indians in 1825. The younger Allen established a plantation near the community of Antioch in northwestern Troup County. On March 5, 1838, he married Jane E. Wisdom, daughter of Francis and Eleanor Wisdom. Robert and Jane's only child, Ujanirtus Cincinnatus Allen, was born January 20, 1839.

The Columbus, Georgia, *Enquirer* of May 5, 1842, reported that on April 23, at Hathorn's Ferry on the Chattahoochee River, Robert S. Allen had drowned while attempting to save his nephew and three Negro boys when their boat capsized. A wealthy neighbor, John Thomas Boykin Sr., was appointed administrator of Allen's estate. There is no mention of Jane Allen in the estate records. Family tradition indicates that she had died in childbirth prior to her husband's death. What we know of Ugie Allen's youth is gleaned from his father's estate records. He spent his early years in the care of his grandmother Sarah Allen and his aunt Mary Denham.

Allen's formal education began at age five when J. T. Boykin enrolled him at Chattahoochee Academy in Antioch. In 1850, at age eleven, Ugie entered Hearn Academy at Cave Spring, Georgia. After one term at Hearn, he suffered a serious illness and withdrew from the school. He enrolled for the spring term of 1851 at Brownwood Institute, located closer to home at Troup's county seat, LaGrange. The autumn of 1852 found him at the Southern Military Academy in nearby Fredonia, Chambers County, Alabama, where he remained for two years. In 1854, Ugie returned to Brownwood for an additional two years. After a short tenure in a school at Athens, Georgia, he enrolled at Emory and Henry

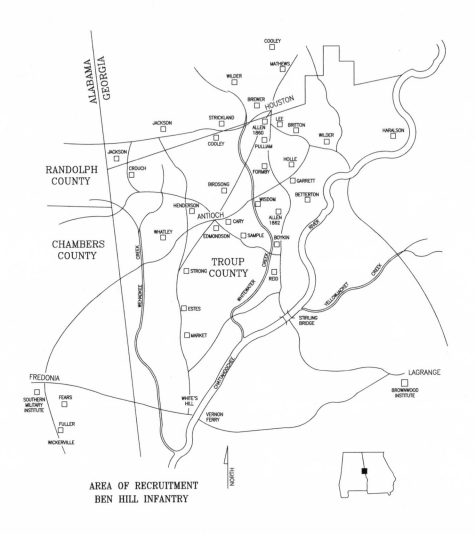

AREA OF RECRUITMENT
BEN HILL INFANTRY

College in Emory, Virginia. His name appears in the junior class in two Emory and Henry College catalogs for the school years 1857–58 and 1858–59. It is not known when and under what circumstances he left the college.

Whatever psychological effects he experienced from being shunted about, Ugie Allen enjoyed considerable material prosperity throughout his early years, inheriting both slaves and cash from his Allen grandparents. J. T. Boykin's meticulous accounts record the purchase of marbles, fishing tackle, innumerable pocket knives, textbooks, and stylish, expensive clothing. On January 23, 1860, Boykin turned over to his ward an estate valued at nearly ten thousand dollars.

It is likely that Ugie Allen met his future bride Susan Fuller during his two years at the Southern Military Academy. Born November 13, 1842, Susan, was the eighth of nine children of William and Stacey Rebecca Fuller of Wickerville, Chambers County, Alabama. Ugie and Susie married at her parents' home on March 29, 1860.

The newlyweds moved into a house near Houston Community, located on the border between Troup and Heard counties, Georgia. When the census taker visited Ugie's farm in 1860, he listed the young man as a farmer with real estate valued at $4,200 and $10,000 in personal property. Allen's farm then comprised 145 acres of improved land, on which he had grown one thousand bushels of wheat, and 175 acres of unimproved land. He owned $150 worth of farming machinery and implements. Ugie's livestock, consisting of one horse, four mules, six cows, and fifty-three pigs was worth $1,150. Eleven slaves worked Allen's small plantation. Polly Allen, a ninety-year-old free black woman originally from Maryland, resided with Ugie and his wife.

In the spring of 1861, Ugie Allen inherited two additional slaves and two hundred acres of land from his Wisdom grandparents. Unfortunately, the outbreak of war made it impossible to build the permanent home he so desperately wanted for himself, his wife, and their infant son born on May 29, 1861.

By April of 1861, Troup County had already sent two companies of men to the Confederate States Army. Pride and patriotism dictated that the men of Antioch form a company. As scion of the area's wealthiest planter and patron of the company, twenty-six-year-old John Thomas Boykin Jr. was the natural choice for captain, though his only military experience had been gained in the cadet corps at Brownwood Institute. "Popular with every member of his company," Boykin possessed, according to one observer, "the dignity and ability commensurate with the duties of his office." The energetic captain and his men, including Second Lieutenant Ujanirtus Allen, named their company in honor of Troup County's Benjamin Harvey Hill, a member of the Provisional Congress and later a Confederate senator.

Private Walton Bell Whatley wrote that the Ben Hill Infantry was "a company almost entirely made up of my kindred, associates, and acquaintances." The volunteers represented a cross section of rural southern society. Most of the company's ninety-odd original recruits hailed from northwestern Troup County, but significant contingents came from neighboring Heard County, Georgia, and Chambers County, Alabama. Nearly every man listed his occupation as farmer. Regulations set the minimum age for recruits at eighteen and the maximum at forty-five, but John Mathews was barely fifteen and Henry Hunt was fifty-six.

In several ways, the officers in the Ben Hill Infantry stood apart from the men they commanded. Ugie Allen had received close to sixteen years of formal education at various institutions but many of the men in the ranks could only "make their mark" on enlistment papers. While John Boykin and Ned Henderson went to war accompanied by their servants, Allen reported to his wife that some of the boys could not afford to pay for their own uniforms. Confronted with complaints from the men about the hardships of military life, Allen scoffed in one letter that many received better fare from the army than they had ever provided for themselves at home.

Such class differences and tensions went unnoticed or unreported by one visitor to the Ben Hill Infantry. In a letter appearing in the July 11, 1861, issue of the Augusta *Chronicle & Sentinel,* a correspondent with the pen name "Antioch" reported that Ugie's company was in camp on Wehadkee Creek in western Troup County. "Antioch" predicted that within a few weeks the unit's "young and energetic" officers would have the company well drilled and qualified "for the bloody fields of strife."

On May 21, 1861, Captain Boykin tendered the company's services to Georgia governor Joseph E. Brown for the period of one year. At the same time, Boykin requested that the state government provide arms for the Ben Hill Infantry. Boykin apparently did not receive a reply, or at least not one that satisfied him, for on June 18, he wrote to the governor again. This time Boykin offered to enroll his company for the duration of the war, requesting also that he be allowed to procure arms from LaGrange's Brownwood Institute. When Brown still failed to respond, Boykin used his father's influence to gain a place in a battalion being raised for Confederate service by former U.S. cavalry officer James Jackson Morrison. The Ben Hill Infantry consequently became Company F, 4th Georgia Infantry Battalion.

April the 9th 1851 LaGrange, Ga.

Dear friend [Robert A. Denham][1]
I now take my pen in hand to write you a few lines to inform you that I am well and so is all at home. There are three boys sick here at Brownwood.[2] One with the mesals and I don't know what is the mater with the other two. I got a letter from P. C. Dean not long ago and he ses that he was well and thare was only fore or five thare that was thare last session. Little Boyd was thare, Johnston and himself. Mr. Ingraham will not take in any borders this year but Peak and his dear beloved James Johnston.[3] Most all of Mr. Bolens family is sick, Sanford and Mistress Bolen and that simple one and Mr. Linches wife. William died about thirteen days ago and they think that none of them will live that are sick.[4] Mr. Smith give us holiday last thursday and friday and I would of come down to of seen you and Aunt Denham[5] but Antie come up to your fathers. I would like for you to come to school up here for it is one of the best plases to go to school in Georgia. You said that you wanted me to send you the speech that Sanford Trout[6] spoke last year. I want you to take cear of it for it is the only one that I have. I want you to send it back to me for I want to speak it myself. Nothing more only I want you to tell me if I have improve in my writing any.
Ujanirtus Allen

1. Ugie's cousin Robert A. Denham (born 1835) was enrolled at the Southern Military Academy in Chambers County, Alabama.

2. Englishman Robert C. Brown founded Brownwood Institute near LaGrange, Georgia, in 1840 and operated the school as a female academy. Following Brown's death, Dr. Otis Smith (born 1801 in Vermont) chartered the school as a university for boys. Brownwood ceased operation during the Civil War and never reopened.

3. John S. Ingraham (born 1812 in New York) was director of Hearn Academy at Cave Spring, Georgia. Dean, Boyd, Peak, and Johnston were Allen's classmates during his brief time there. Between October 16 and November 1, 1850, an unidentified malady confined Ugie to bed in the Posey Hotel at Cave Spring with daily attention from Dr. W. A. Lowe.

4. Daniel Bowling and his wife Rachel owned a plantation near Antioch. Their son William and son-in-law Solomon Linch succumbed to the illness, but other family members recovered. The "simple one" was their eldest daughter Jane. Two of Bowling's sons later served in the Ben Hill Infantry.

5. Mary P. Denham (born 1792), widow of James A. Denham, was Ugie Allen's great-aunt, the sister of his grandfather Robert S. Allen Sr.

6. Sanford C. Trout (born 1839) of Floyd County, Georgia, was another of Allen's Hearn classmates.

Mr. Ujanirtus Allen
Emory P.O. Washington, Va.
Nov 1, 1858

Ugy,

I received your letter a few days ago and was glad to hear from you, but it has been hard work for me to write and now I attempt it. I have no pen and have had the mumps all last week. I know you can sympathise with me, and beside we have a sewing machine and I have not time to do anything now but *sew*. Would you have believed it if it were not so? I would not, or perhaps you will be as I was not long since when I heard that you and your sweetheart were going to marry soon. I was so much surprised that I was going to write you right away but circumstances changes cases sometimes. This is the truth now no joke about it so you must let me know time enough to have my dress made. Virge says you must not expect that philliphenia[1] now from her. She was going to send it until she heard that report but she can not think of sending it now and Fannie[2] says you must pay her's now. She says she reckon you thought they were *too* bold for you which I did not deny as I had just told them unthoughtfully that you like Punck[3] because she was bashful which is the truth is it not? Oh it is not worth while to try to write what they tell me to tell you for I can not begin to do it. They say so much but you cannot immagine how much they were taken down. The last time I was there they were as much surprised as I was to hear you had been writing love letters. I hope though it is not a copy of Mr. Boykin's letter for his letters you know were *real* sensible.[4] I saw your sweetheart today. She is well. She has a new shall that will almost cover her up and is having a new dress made for the marriage. Perhaps unreasonable things hapens when we are not thinking of them. Do tell me are you coming home Christmas? I am so anxious to know. I will be glad to have you come and go with us to Putnam[5] as that is under consideration now. We are thinking of going by private conveyance and John Samples speaks of going to see Mary Farrer as he is out now looking [for] him a wife.[6] He says it is hard work to find one but I do not think so. What do you think of it? Farther says you must study hard and then he said you would not write to him but he wants you to do well. Mother says she expects a great many seeds and flowers when you come and I say you must write soon as you get this and let me know what to say about the report and whether you are coming. Be a good boy now and do as near right as you can and I know you will do well but above all things take care of your health. If it did not agree with me I would not stay there for all that I could learn, for example, look at

T. Sales in the very mist of manhood gone not doubt by imprudence while going to school. So many take their disease then thinking nothing will hurt them. I [would] not risk my health for nothing on earth. It is but a short time to stay anyhow and health above everything else in the world especially when not prepared to die. Are you prepared to die? Farewell, Ugy. Be sure to write. Your friend,
Lizzie

I have not time to correct and punctuate.

1. A small gift or party favor.
2. Virginia and Fannie were the daughters of Augustus and Eveline Reid of Antioch.
3. "Punk" was a nickname for Susan Fuller. Others called her Sudda or Soudie and sometimes misspelled her name Sousy or Sousie. Ugie almost always referred to her as Susie.
4. Despite "real sensible" love letters, John Thomas Boykin Jr. (1835–1901) and Elizabeth Fuller (1836–1914) had married on October 12, 1854. "Lizzie" Boykin, the writer of this letter, and Ugie's fiancee Susan were sisters.
5. Putnam County is in central Georgia. Families such as those in Troup who had migrated west usually maintained ties to their relatives who had stayed behind. Protracted visits were an integral part of antebellum southern culture.
6. Mary Farrer (born 1839) was the daughter of William P. Farrer of Putnam County, Georgia. John Sample found a wife in Troup County. On December 2, 1858, he married Mary E. Formby.

Antioch Troup County, Ga
May 21, 1861

Governor Brown,
Most Excellent Sir,
I as the representative of the Ben Hill Volunteers of Antioch would most respectfully make this offer and also this request of you and also our reasons for so doing. We organized this company some weeks ago for active service for the term of one year, elected our officers and received our commissions and are still desirous of keeping up the company having gone to the expense of uniforming and we beg your Excellency to furnish us with a lot of muskets or some arm for drilling purposes for which we are ready to give bond and security to keep them in good order and return them when called for. Our slave population is large and we are a good way from LaGrange our county site. I as Captain of this company of men offer them to your Excellency's disposal for the term of one year to serve in whatever capacity your Excellency may see fit. Hoping that your Excellency may favorably regard this request I

remain your obedient servant. Accept of my best wishes for your health and happiness.

John T. Boykin, Jr.

C.P. Ben Hill Volunteers

Antioch, Ga

June 18, 1861

His Excellency J. E. Brown

Sir,

When the "Ben Hill Volunteers" formed themselves into a company they did so under the impression that their services would only be required for twelve months—as was at that time the law, many of them felt that they could not well leave home for an undefinite time. Still the organization was kept up and in one week the company will be completely uniformed—at our last meeting a move was made to "go in for the war" when two thirds or more were in favor and I have no doubt now but that next meeting (22 inst) we will resolve to offer our services for the war, and be ready at any moment to march to the seat of war. In the mean time we want arms that we may practice the manual. Can we get them. If you canot furnish them from the seat of Government, I would suggest that you allow us to use some guns now near LaGrange, having recently been used by the students of Brownwood, as I am informed they now have no use for them as the school is pretty much suspended. Please let me hear at once from you on the subject of arms—we are anxious for them.

Your obt. servt.

J. T. Boykin Capt.

1

THE SEAT OF WAR

We are mustered into service at last.

ENLISTMENT day for the Ben Hill Infantry was July 9, 1861, at Antioch. Nine days later the company rendezvoused at LaGrange, where the men boarded a train for Virginia, "the seat of the war." Their route took them north to Atlanta, east through Augusta, then across the Carolinas to Wilmington and Weldon, North Carolina, and finally to Richmond, Virginia, on July 22—a journey of 730 miles, according to their enlistment records.

Lieutenant Allen and his company arrived in the Confederate capital amid the euphoria following the southern victory at the Battle of Manassas. In his first letters home, Allen eagerly recounted wild rumors and exaggerated accounts of the battle. Despite this initial excitement, the reality of army life quickly tempered the patriotic fervor of many volunteers. Allen reported that some members of his company "put up excuses of sickness . . . represent themselves unfit for military duty and go moping about the encampment . . . doing their best to get away." As for himself, Allen admitted that he was "neither well nor unwell pleased or displeased. I live and move in a kind of trance that I can not describe or you conceive."

Weldon N.C.
Sunday, July 21st, 1861

Dear Susie,
This is the first chance I have had of writing to you. We overtook a Fla. Reg. in South Carolina and met with so many delays in consequence that we have

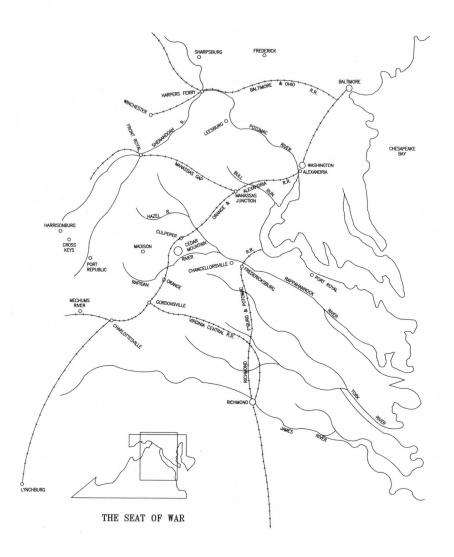

THE SEAT OF WAR

got no further than this place; about eighty five miles from Richmond. I do not know but that we will be delayed here until twelve tonight. We started from Wilmington yesterday evening and have been untill twelve today geting here. We came from W. on, or rather in some freight box cars. Rather poor accomodation of course; but as good as circumstances will admit. I have stood the trip admirably well, in fact better than I expected. Good bye. We are going now. No more time.

Ugie

Camp Georgia[1] (near) Richmond Va
July 24th, 1861

Dear Susie

I wrote last from Weldon N.C. I did not have time to write more. I have delayed writing as soon as I would have done hoping that I could find something satisfactory to tell you. We arrived here last Monday the day after the great battle at Manassas Gap or Junction. We have gained a glorious victory. The whole place is filled with rumors of all kind in reference to the battle. From what I can gather we sustained great loss; say 2000 men the enemy much greater. Some say ten to one. One thing is certain, that we have taken many stand of arms and four batteries. Among them is Sherman's battery the boasted battery of the U.S.[2] About 600 prisners were brought down to this place last night and it is sayed that thare is about 1200 yet to bring. Old Gen Scotts sword and carriege were taken.[3] Thirty five officers were among the prisners brought last night. Bartow of Savanah was killed.[4] I know that his fate will be mourned by evry true patriot. I would go to the city to see his remains today but we may be mustered into service today at 10 AM. We think that we will be furnished with arms that were taken from the Yankees at Manassas. If we go into Morrison's regiment, Mercer, a son of old Jesse Mercer, will be our Col and Morrison Lnt Col.[5] Thare is a great many troops here, but not as many as thare has been. As fast as they could be armed they were sent to Manassas, and they are sending them from here now as fast as they can. Ellsworths pet lambs were all cut to pieces, but only two hundred escaped.[6] The Yankees fought with great bravery and generalship. Our Linchberg Reg was all killed in the charge that captured Shermans battery. You can gather as much information from the papers as I can find out here. I do not state anything that you will not know before this letter reaches you. I can not state anything definite about myself. I am neither well nor unwell pleased or displeased. I live and move in a kind of trance, that I can not describe or you conceive. I hope that my next letter will be more sattisfactory. I do not know where we will be one day hence or what we will be doing. You know that I would like to see you and the little boy.[7] You must bear my absence with a strong [resolve]. Recollect that we display our greatest virtues in adversity. I know that you would like for me to write to you more in detail. I will do it next time—in a day or two. Answer this with a good long letter, care of Capt Boykin. Direct as I have headed it.

Good bye

Your Ugie

1. The Ben Hill Infantry actually camped at the New Fair Grounds about two and one half miles outside Richmond. The men were temporarily quartered in livestock stables until their tents arrived. Camp Georgia was located in Howard's Grove on the outskirts of Richmond.

2. Allen mistakenly calls the batteries of James B. Ricketts (Battery I, 1st U.S.) and Charles Griffin (Battery D, 5th U.S.) "Sherman's Battery." The capture of the two batteries by Confederates was a pivotal point in the battle. William Tecumseh Sherman (1820–1891) was a colonel commanding the 3rd Brigade of Tyler's division, which attempted to retake the key position on Henry House Hill.

3. Winfield Scott (1786–1866), a veteran of the War of 1812 and the Mexican War, was general-in-chief of the U.S. Army. He retired in October 1861.

4. Francis Stebbins Bartow (born September 6, 1816) was a member of the Provisional Confederate Congress but accepted command of a brigade composed of the 7th, 8th, 9th, and 11th Georgia and 1st Kentucky regiments. He was killed leading a counterattack against Federal lines near the Henry House.

5. James Jackson Morrison (1829–1910) organized the 4th Georgia Battalion (later known as the 21st Georgia Infantry Regiment). Exercising his authority to appoint officers, Jefferson Davis passed over Morrison to name John Thomas Mercer (born February 7, 1830) colonel of the battalion. Morrison resigned from the 21st Georgia on March 30, 1862, to organize and command the 1st Georgia Cavalry Regiment. Mercer had resigned his commission as a lieutenant in the U.S. Cavalry at the outbreak of the war. Though he was frequently at odds with his subordinate officers and accused by some of being an alcoholic, Mercer led the 21st Georgia until he was killed in battle at Plymouth, North Carolina, on April 18, 1864. John T. Mercer was the son of Leonidas B. and Lovicia Janes Mercer. Jesse Mercer (1769–1841), to whom Allen refers, was a prominent figure among Georgia Baptists and a nephew of John T. Mercer's grandfather John Mercer.

6. In the struggle for control of Henry House Hill, the 11th New York, a regiment raised among New York City firemen by Ephraim Elmer Ellsworth (1837–61), provided infantry support for Griffin's and Ricketts' batteries. The regiment lost 188 men in the battle.

7. Susan's and Ugie's son was born on May 29, 1861, but at the time this letter was written they had not yet selected a name. When the boy was about eighteen months old, they decided on Ujanirtus Robert Allen, calling him Ugie.

Camp Instruction[1] Richmond Va
July 28th 1861

Dear Susie

I have posponed writing you this letter several days. We are mustered into service at last—yesterday. This was done by calling us up in line and calling our names to which we answered "here." Quite a simple proceding for so much "fuss." I was always under the impression that we were put under oath. It is the rule I think. Yesterday evening an officer came around and gave us orders to be off for Manassas Junction. We will leave here tomorrow or next day if we can get conveyance. Recollect that there are near twenty thousand troops here to be sent to Manassas or some where else. The result of the battle last Sunday is about this: Confederates 500 killed and 1100 wounded; Federals 7000 killed great many wounded.[2] You see that we killed and wounded ten to one. Nevertheless it was a hard fight. The Yankees fought with great skill and bravery. Let me show you the plan of battle: You will understand.

Yankee Forces

35000   *unknown number of thousands*

Confederate forces

15000   25000   15000

W wing   Centre   E wing

Gen Johnson[3]   President[4]   Buregard[5]

You see the arrangement. Let me add that all the fighting was done by the two wings 15000 and 35000.[6] The fight commenced early in the morning and untill three in the evening the fortunes of the day was doubtful. At this time Davis advanced with the centre of the Army which lent such an enthusiasm to the men that they bore evry thing before them. The Yankees were seized by a panic and fled *pell mell* droping guns knapsacks evrything that retarded their flight. They were pursued and entirely cut to pieces. They ran through Fairfax C.H., Alexandria and on to Washington. Many fell exhausted by the roadside. What I tell you is from good authority. Many of them were well drilled and armed. They pited about 10,000 regulars against our West wing among their other men. They thought they were invincible. Many of their officers had checked their bagage to Richmond. They had brought a good supply of fine wines and brandies along with them. Many Congressmen and ladies were along and they expected to have a great time after the victory; but they were happily disappointed thank God! A letter arrived at the post office in this place the other day directed to Gen Scott. I guess President Davis will take care of it for him. Our Regiment will go to Manassas and be armed with arms taken from the anemy. The anemy will attact us again at Manassas or we will advance to the capitol. You have no idea, indeed you can not conceive of the war like preparation that is going on. The streets are filled with soldiers, cannon and artilery trains. Our company is in very good health. We were very much exposed coming and after we got here until a few days ago. Our tents are here now and we are as comfortably situated as we could expect. Our rations are beef, bacon, bread flour meal vinager rice candles soap. This we cook and use as suits our notions. Of course our fair is not epicurian; but hapily we have such apitites that we do not complain. We can have as many vegitables as we want. Cheap. Onions one cent tomatoes one cent rostenears two cents cabage as large as my head, white and firm ten cents. We can get buttermilk at five cents per pint. I neglected to add that we had coffee and shugar included in our rations; some of John Jacksons brown sweetning.[7] I want you and Lizzie to be as cherful and happy as circumstances will admit. Recollect that Boykin and myself are both comissioned oficers and can avail ourselves of more comforts than privates if we get our pay at an early day. We are alowed more baggage, though we have to furnish our provisions. This we have not done yet nor will do unless we are compelled. I would like verry much to hear from you and the *little boy*. I dreamed of you and home last night. This war will not end untill Lincoln's resourses are all gone; money, men and credit. I do not believe that the pride of the North will yield unless compelled to. How long it will be, I do not know. It is the oppinion of a great many leading men that we will conquer a peace in a few months. I can see that our government is making preparations for a desperate struggle, to come soon. If we are victorious in the begining the war will soon end, if not the war will be long and bludy. I heard just now that we captured a body of Indiana cavelry seven hundred and fifty strong last Friday. We have one Congressman among the prisners taken last Sunday.[8] Poor fellow, he came out to see us whiped, and was taken prisner. I am told that he cries like a child. Some of the prisners say if they were loose, they would fight us again, some that they did not enlist to fight the South, only to defend the Capitol, some that their time was out and they were compelled to come and fight this battle. Some say that they are fighting for eleven dollars a month. Some say that the only truth that Lincoln has told them was that they would be in Richmond in July. My dear Susie I would write you a longer letter but I have not time at present. I will write to you again soon and to Mr. Boykin[9] and Berry[10] also. I do not know where to tell you to direct your letter so that I can get it. We will probably leve here soon and I will let you know. Write a long one and have it redy to mail.

Good bye.

Your Ugie

1. Camp Instruction was established at the Fairfield Racetrack, about two and one half miles outside Richmond. Daniel S. Printup, one of the organizers of the 4th Georgia Battalion, preceded the unit to Richmond and arranged for the individual companies to rendezvous at the site which, as indicated in Allen's letters, was also known as the New Fairgrounds.

2. Actual Confederate losses at First Manassas were 387 killed, 1,582 wounded, and 13 missing; Union losses were 460 killed, 1,124 wounded, and 1,312 missing.

3. Joseph Eggleston Johnston (1807–91) became a brigadier in the Confederate army in May 1861, and was given command of troops in western Virginia. In July, when the Federal army advanced from its bases around Washington, Johnston rushed his command by rail to strengthen the Confederate position at Manassas. Johnston was promoted to full general in August 1861.

4. Allen's information regarding Confederate president Jefferson Davis's participation as a field commander at Manassas is erroneous. Davis arrived from Richmond on the afternoon of July 21 and was only an observer. Allen probably refers to the Confederate rally precipitated when Johnston advanced to the front accompanied by the colors of the 4th Alabama Infantry. It was the arrival of Johnston's troops throughout the afternoon that turned the tide of battle in favor of the Confederates.

5. Pierre Gustave Toutant Beauregard (1818–93) exercised field command at First Manassas, although Johnston was in overall command of the army.

6. The Federal army at First Manassas numbered around 39,000 men, while the Confederates numbered 32,000. Only about 18,000 men on each side saw action.

7. John Coleman Jackson (1820–98) was a farmer and a Primitive Baptist preacher in the State Line District of Heard County, Georgia. "Brown sweetening" was crystallized molasses, a substitute for expensive imported sugar.

8. The Honorable Alfred Ely of Rochester, New York.

9. John Thomas Boykin Sr. (1799–1869) became Ujanirtus Allen's legal guardian when Allen's father died in 1842. The tone of Allen's letters indicates that Mr. Boykin assumed the role of surrogate father. (Allen refers to John T. Boykin Jr. as "Boykin" and to John T. Boykin Sr. as "Mr. Boykin" or "Mr. B.")

10. Littleberry B. Rowland (1830–1908) helped to manage Allen's farm prior to enlisting in the Ben Hill Infantry on February 23, 1862.

Camp Instruction (Near) Richmond Va
July 31st 1861

Dear Susie

This will be carried to you by Lieutenant Waller who is compelled from bad health to return home for 12 or 14 days. Besides being unhealthy he wants more recruits for the B. H. I. We have a fine company of men already and want more of the same kind.

Susie if you can get me up a good shirt or two I would like for you to send them to me by Lieut W. He will take great pleasure in bringing them. I can buy shirts here of course; but they cost money, a comodity that I have *not* got. You know that I am Lieutenant now and it will take evry red cent that I have to furnish me an outfit. In fact it will take more. Besides payday will come about the last of August and I can do or at least I am going to try to do without money untill then.

My dear Susie let me tell you that I am well and as well pleased as I anticipated. You may probably hear that the company is not well situated and healthy. Let me tell you when the news of the battle at Manassas reached us some of our bold men became *weak in the knees* and wanted to sneak back home. They put up excuses of sickness, rumatism, constitutional dibility reported a parcel of falshoods to the surgeon of the encampment and represented themselves as unfit for military duty and go moping about the encampment and are doing their best to get away. These men will limp with rumatism and grunt and sigh many times before they accomplish their object. Now I have no doubt but the status of the company has been represented in a very unfavorable light in their letters home. Let nothing distress you my little woman, your boy will tell you the truth.

I have been out sightseeing today. Richmond is situated on the James river as you know. And like Ancient Rome it might apropriately be called the seven hilled city, without we choose to include the surroundings or suburbs, when we might well say twenty hilled. It is by no means as pretty as our own Augusta. Still it is a nice city. The streets are all well McAdamised with fragments of granite or round stone taken from the James. (Get out my book on roads and railroads and refer to McAdamised roads and you will understand me better). The drainage of the city I have no doubt is as good as any in the Confederacy. You are never anoyed by the stench of filthy sewers. The Capitol grounds are situated in the heart of the city. They are seeded down with clover and other grasses and beautifully layed off with gravelled walks. It is quite shady. This combined with the seats interspersed in the grove make it a pleasant lounging place. Today fatigued with walking I threw myself upon the grass near a fountain and was lulled to sleep by the music of its falling waters. In these grounds is a statue of Henry Clay cut from pure Darian marble. Thare is also an equestrian statue of Washington by Powers said to be the best piece of art in America. It is placed upon a base of marble and granite about forty feet high, and is said to have cost the state of Va one hundred forty thousand dollars.[1] Susie I want you to write to me at this place, in care of Capt Boykin 2nd Independent Regiment Ga Vols. New Fair Ground near Richmond Va. It may be ten days before we leave here. The railroad is so crowded that it is difficult to get transportation. I know how glad I would be to hear from you.

Your Ugie

This is a poor scribling. I sit upon the ground and write upon a camp chest.

1. The Washington statue, which still stands, was designed by Thomas Crawford of Philadelphia and unveiled amid much fanfare on February 22, 1858.

Camp Instruction Near Richmond Va
August 2nd 1861

Dear Susie

Although I sent you a letter by Lieut Waller two days ago, I embrace another oportunity and send this by Ornan Whatley who is discharged on account of Rhumatism which renders him unfit for duty. According to Northern accounts the yankees lost 1200 killed at Manassas we not one tenth; in fact we do not know accurately what our loss was. The arms taken are being sent to Richmond. We will be armed with them tomorrow, so I understand. I heard today that there was a battle between the advanced gard of our army and the anemy at Falls Church in seven miles of Washington City; the anemy were defeated. There has been a battle in Masouri which you will here of before this reaches you.[1] Of course you take out my papers and read them now, especially the *war news*. What has become of Haywood Lodge and our Cousin Esther Craig?[2] Do you read the Cultivator?[3] How does my crop look? I would like to see my corn. I do not expect much from the new ground unless the season is extreamly faverable. You know that my corn culture this year was rather an experiment. I regret that I can not watch it in all its faces. How are my hogs. I told Berry to try and keep them up and to feed, exchange wheat for corn, or see Mr. Boykin and buy corn for them and the Negroes if necessary. I will write to Berry tomorrow or tonight if it is not too late when I finish this. Are the peaches ripening. They sell here at 5 and 10 cents apiece. I never see any but what I think how fond you are of them. Susie I am well with the exception of a little cough. The health of the company is remarkably good. When you write to me you must tell me evrything about yourself and the little boy the family and farm. Answer this as soon as you get it. Direct thus: Mr. U Allen, Richmond Va, Care of Capt Boykin, Camp Instruction, New Fair Ground.

I can not say anything definite about the length of the war. It is the opinion of many prominent men that it will finish before Christmas. Some think that the pride of the Northern people will not suffer them to acknowledge our independence soon, not under several years. I wrote to you that we were under marching orders. We will join the Grand Army at Manassas as soon as transportation can be procured. The men are very anxious to be in the next battle. Some think that the next prominent event will be an attact on Washington City. I do not know; your facilities for judging are as good as mine.
Good bye
Ugie

I sit on the ground and write upon a trunk. Susie I enclose a letter to Berry. Send it to him as soon as convenient. Of course you will read it.

Aug 3rd 1861
I recieved your letter just now. You cannot amagine the pleasure it gave me write; write; write!!! soon, a long letter.

1. At Carthage, Missouri, on July 5, 1861, Confederates under Missouri governor Claiborne Jackson repelled an attack by General Franz Sigel's Union troops.

2. Allen's reference is to a serialized novelette entitled *The House at Haywood Lodge: A Story of the South* that appeared from February to June 1861 in weekly issues of *Southern Field and Fireside,* a "literary and agricultural journal" published in Augusta, Georgia. The novelette was written by Mary Edwards Bryan (1842–1913), a former literary editor of the *Georgia Literary & Temperance Crusader* and frequent contributor after 1860 of novelettes, essays, and poems to *Southern Field and Fireside.* "Haywood Lodge" was the New Orleans home of Doctor (and Colonel) John Haywood. "Cousin Esther Craig," the step-daughter of Dr. Haywood, is the central character of the story.

3. The *Southern Cultivator* was a popular agricultural periodical published at Augusta, Georgia.

Richmond Va
Aug 8th 1861

Dear Susie
Crouch & Black arrived here Monday all well (this Wednesday). They brought me the second letter that I have recieved from you since I left. Mr Crouch told me what you said about writing and my absence. You can not regret my absence any more than I do myself. O what a delerious shout of joy will go up all over this beloved country when this fratricidal war ceases. It seems that evry household has sent forth its dearest idols to repel a foe that led on by fanaticism and lust for "beauty and booty" would scatter misery, desola-

tion and want in its path regardless of no higher law than that dictated by its own fiendish hart. I fear this war will become one of extermination. I can not divine the future. I know of nothing that I can say only Hope! Hope!! Hope that golden chain that ever binds us to the future; dazeled by whose beauty we forget the present with all its harsh realities. You want to know how we do, get along etc. Let me begin at the begining. Revelle is beat at daybreak when we all get up and call the roll. Then cooking comences by those whose time it is to cook for their mess; the others sometimes drill untill breakfast at sun up. We find it is quite exausting to drill hard at this hour. At 6 AM there is a drill of the battallion which last untill everything is almost overcome with heat, say eight or nine oclock. Then we lie about and try to keep cool until diner or drill the company if they do not do well. In the evning we have another company drill; then dress parade at five, which lasts about half an hour after it is formed. (I know you do not understand this nor have I room to explain it.) Then super. Then talking reading writing fiddling dancing chewing smoking untill nine when the roll is called. At ten the drum taps, after which no lights are allowed only to the comissioned officers. In a previous letter I told you something of our rations. Let me add that oficers have nothing furnished them. It does not pay much money to be an officer. Our cooking is very good considering evrything; however good health and an all consuming apetite make us relish it better than it deserves. The boys are improving very fast in the culinary department. There is quite a contest among them for the honor of making the best biscuit.

We recieved our guns today the majority of them were loaded with a half ounce ball and three buck. I have a cartridge of this description drawn from one of them which I shall keep or send to my friends as a trophy of the victory of Manassas. You know that we are under marching orders now. It is uncertain when we will leave here; perhaps in one two or three weeks. I have not drawn any pay yet. When I do I will send you some money. You won't make a fortune geting all my money as you said. I know that you are tired traveling about from one place to another. But my dear little woman strive to make yourself contented and happy. We will learn that the sands of life do not always flow smoothley. Ours are not the only fond hearts separated; Ours is not the only home left desolate.

Tell the negroes that I say that I am well. It will give them great encouragement to know that I have not forgotten them. When you write tell me all the news, especially concerning our own affairs. You spoke of going over my crop. How did you like it. How much corn will I make? How much cotton? I

know that you revel in fruit and rostenears; and I hope watermelons. What of Ethan Allen?[1] Last but not least kiss the dear little boy for me.
Good bye,
Ugie

1. Allen had expressed his sense of humor, as well as an interest in history, by naming his spirited stallion Ethan Allen after the Revolutionary War patriot.

Richmond Va
Aug 14th 1861

Dear Susie
I recieved your letter by Lieut. Waller today. I anticipated his return and did not write to you last Sunday. He gives us an idea how things are in "Old Troup"; many are very encouraging, some are not. He says that some of the boys have written back that they at one time had nothing to eat for forty eight hours and that if they ever get home they would never leave it, were treated worse than negroes, etc. Shame upon any one that would make such statements; the richeous contempt of the whole company falls upon their deserving heads. It is an old adage that some men would grumble to be hung. The greatest disafectants have always been men of no social standing, and whose fare here was better than they provided for themselves at home.

I have told you in a previous letter what were our rations. We recieve eighteen ounces of bread or flour and three fourths pound of meat. This is more than people alow negroes; besides rice, beans, peas, or dried peaches more than we can consume. We have Western bacon, pickled pork or the finest beef that I ever saw. Two of evry mess cook each day. They have as good and many cooking utensils as they could wish for, furnished out of the company treasury. Here is another source of discontent. Thoughtless fellows, they spent all their money coming and soon after they got here, and now grumble because the company treasury is not divided among them to squander. Besides this military decipline is too strict for them. They grumble and say that they are free men and are being imposed upon, evry time they are not alowed to do as they please.

You do not know the pleasure that your good long letter gave me. The money was acceptable also. I have been down to the treasury department twice this week after money on my salery, but it is empty. I thought that I would have sent you some before this instead of you sending it to me. You

may expect some when I get it. However you need not say anything about it to aney one. I want to send you some and pay Mrs. Boykin[1] some also. This will not be much; but I intend to save and send home evry cent that I can. How thoughtfull you were in sending me my cap and pillow and other things. I did not need the knit drawers having suplied myself with good woolen ones. I have some good woolen undershirts. I do not know that I will need the flanell shirt that you spoke of unless it is your desire that I should have it. Make it; send it on anyhow. It is said by good authority that we will have a winter campaign. The weather is quite cold here now. You say that I see something new evry day. You are mistaken; evry day is the same rutine that I wrote you in my last letter. We are two miles from the city and its attractions are so little that I only visit it occasionaly on business. You must not consider yourself under any obligations to affiliate with Mrs. Cary or patronize the Dr if they do not act as becomes a person in their position.[2] Black told a great long tale about the Dr and that Mr. Boykin had discarded him etc. Waller says that he heard nothing of it, and that he manifested great interest in the wellfare of the company. We have some cases of cold and measels in the company. All doing well now. I have no war news to write. We get our news from the papers as you do. Soldiers know nothing of what is going on. They come here now and stay untill they recieve orders like this. "Capt. ———— company will be ready to march at ———— o'clock with rations for ———— days in their haversacks." Let me add that these orders are sometimes recalled before the given hour. Some say that thare was 12000 troops sent away from here last week; I do not know as thare is four or five encampments here besides ours. I think of my boy often; but not a name. I had rather name him Bartow than after any other patriot hero that this war has developed. I should have said developed themselves in this war. Circumstances do not make men like Bartow. My dear woman name him after me if you want to. We have made no exertions to get Uncle Wisdom off; but I expect we will exchange him for Cousin Robert.[3] Uncle Wisdom stays with me and I know he can not stand the hardship of camp life well. It is not just to keep him here if he can be got off. I will write again next Sunday.
Your boy
Ugie

Tell Berry to make old man House[4] give up those rails if they are mine. Where do you find timber to make the boards and ladders you spoke of. I would give anything to see my crop especially the corn. How much corn and cotton does Berry think I will make. Do the best you can with the hogs untill the fields are open. I have so much confidence in Berry that I have almost forgotten the little menutia of my farm. How do the negroes do? When you write tell me of yourself, my boy, home and then the gossip and news generally.

1. Cynthia Hawkins Boykin (July 4, 1805–July 25 1887), wife of John T. Boykin Sr.

2. Dr. Henry Hamilton Cary (1820–99) was from Vermont, and his wife Mary Jane Prouty (1828–72) was from Massachusetts. Cary had practiced medicine in Antioch since 1847, but the couple's neighbors apparently questioned their allegiance to the Confederacy.

3. Hamilton McGee Wisdom was the brother of Ujanirtus Allen's mother Jane. At age forty-seven, Wisdom enlisted in the Ben Hill Infantry. He became ill soon after the company arrived in Virginia and was discharged in October 1861, replaced by his son Robert Allen Wisdom.

4. James M. House, his wife Cinderella, and their ten children lived on a farm adjoining Allen's.

Richmond Va
Sunday Aug 18th 1861

Dear Susie

Perhaps you think that because I promised to write to you today that Sunday is a day of rest; but it is not this way. Sunday is not regarded only in battalion and company drills. We have "dress parade" as usual and general inspections instead of battalion drill. A general inspection is an inspection of arms, acutrements, clothing, and quarters. We came near having a battle in camp a few days ago. Thare was a regiment of Louisianians from New Orleans and a part of a Regiment of Texans here. Some of their men got to fighting each other, and the quarrel became general between the two parties. Each flew to arms; the Texans drew themselves up in line of battle and the excitement was such that three companies from our Regiment was detailed to stand gard around them all. Next morning the Louisianans were sent away. The Texans left for Manassas this morning.[1]

We recieved orders this evening to march at seven tomorrow morning, for the same place. Our camp is in a perfect uproar. We are busy packing up evrything and cooking having been ordered to provide two days rations. It is the opinion of a great many of our boys that we will be in a battle in a few days. We do not know for certain. Evry soldier is being sent away that can. Whether thare will be another attact on Manassas or an advance of our army I can not say. I am confident that one or the other will take place. Write to me at Richmond care Capt Boykin 4th Battalion Ga. Vols. I will write again as soon as we reach our point of destination. We have several sick men who will be left behind. Of course we will leave nurses. Uncle Wisdom will be one. He wants to go on with us; but all hands agree that he must stay with the sick. Boykin is down with the diarrhea. I expect he will remain here a day or two longer. I am as fat as a young bear, and saucy as a fox.

We sent in uncle Wisdom's petition to substitute cousin Robert today. I expect Uncle Wisdom will come home before Cousin Robert comes, that is if his petition is granted. I will leave forty dollars with him to carry to you. You can keep it or let Mr. Boykin have it just as you choose. If neither of you want it nor have a special use for it; pay Mrs. Boykin. I want her payed before anybody else. Tell Mr. Boykin so. Perhaps Garrett will want pay cash for his wages.[2] My dear Susie; with a kiss for the boy let me say

Good bye,

Ugie

1. The Texans were part of a contingent that eventually became the 1st Texas Infantry Regiment. The Louisianans, with a reputation for brawling, larceny, and other misdeeds, became part of General Richard Taylor's 8th Brigade.

2. When Susan Allen became administrator of her husband's estate in 1863, she was required to file annual financial reports with the county ordinary. Her accounts indicate that she paid $61.95 to Antioch mechanic Wright Garrett for repairing a cotton gin (work he had completed in 1861).

2

THE MANASSAS FRONT

We are perfectly ignorant of what is going on. . . .
It is come day, go day, drill, cook and eat.

AFTER a month's training the 4th Battalion left their Camp of Instruction on the Richmond Fairgrounds and moved north by rail to join General Joseph E. Johnston's army near Manassas, Virginia. Unfortunately for the Georgians, the orders to strike tents came during a driving rainstorm. Captain Thomas C. Glover of Company A of the 4th, a prewar physician, asked permission to leave men stricken with measles in their tents. Colonel John T. Mercer refused the request and eventually placed Glover under arrest for protesting orders. In the ensuing dispute, most of the battalion's officers sided with Glover. Hard feelings between Mercer and his subordinates degenerated into a bitter feud during the Seven Days' campaign, when company officers accused their colonel of being intoxicated at the Battle of Gaines's Mill on June 27, 1862. According to regimental historian Charles D. Camp, the rift in the unit "grew and spread and lasted until death claimed the principal, Colonel Mercer."

Autumn of 1861 passed without significant military activity. It was a critical time when volunteers were still adjusting to army discipline, facing the threat of disease, and coping with the rigors of marching and the hardships of camp life. Ugie Allen faced additional difficulty when he became embroiled in a rivalry within the Ben Hill Infantry. Both Captain Boykin and First Lieutenant Dempsey Eugene Dawson suffered from ill health. Dawson died of typhoid fever on November 21, and Boykin remained in command only nominally until his resignation on May 21, 1862. Allen's letters reflect growing resentment of the malcontents who failed to meet his standards of soldiering. He found the behavior of the company's other lieutenant, Leroy T. "Dick" Waller, particularly galling. With Boykin, Dawson, and Waller frequently absent from the

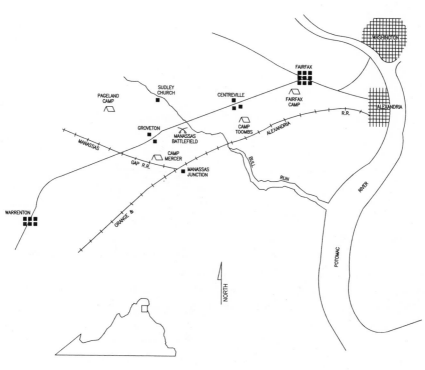

THE MANASSAS FRONT

company, Second Lieutenant Allen often felt the burden of command without the respect and privileges of office.

Camp Mercer Va
Aug 23d 1861

Dear Susie,

When I wrote to you last we were about leaving Richmond. We left Monday morning and arrived here Tuesday evning about sundown. After leaving Richmond we reached Manassas Junction Tuesday, we stayed thare untill late in the evening and after a march of about three miles northwest of thare we hauled up in an old field tired and hungry, about sundown. I can not say that I was hungry and if I had been, I had several friendly biscuits in my haversack. Most of the boys eat up their rations just because they had nothing else to do coming along in cars. I think by the time we are out a while longer some of our men will learn how to cherish a haversack on a march. I said that we hauled up in an old field; it was we and nothing else for we had been provided with rations when we left Richmond to last untill next morning, and our tents did not arrive untill about three oclock that night. So kindling a fire and cuting brush and spreding our blankets upon them we slept. I never slept sweeter in my life. I slept so sound that my tent was pitched over me and I never knew it. Who could not sleep on a good soft bed of leaves with two blankets? It would be "deth in the pot" for me to sleep thus in the open air with a cold dew falling, about home. It is very singular how a man can become hardened so as to endure such things. The next day I was on duty, as "Officer of the Guard" and up all night, yesterday lofered about taking a snooze occasionally, slept last night and write to you today. What I will write I do not know. I did not think of leaving Richmond so soon or sudenly I must confess; but we stayed as long as is customary. Uncle Wisdom did not stay with the sick at Richmond nor do I know whether he will come home soon or not. His application has not been sent from our Regiment to the Adjutant General yet. Our Regiment or rather Battalion (for ten companies make a Reg. we have only nine) is now under Gen Johnson and evrything will have to take a new start. I am afraid to send you the money that I spoke of untill I know whether you get my letters regular, or see some one going home. However I shall take good care of it; as I can not buy anything but rations such as the men eat unless I pay an exorbitant price; though these are good enough for a hungry man if well cooked. The four commissioned officers buy provisions. Uncle Wisdom, Dawson Sr., John Terry, and Bagby draw rations and mess with us. I am the hartiest eater among them, and with a few exceptions have been the healthiest man in the company. My whiskers grow prodigeously. I have at least seventeen on my chin and seven on each cheek. We have a great many cases of measels in our company though none of them bad ones. We take evry possible care of the sick. Those that were left at Richmond were carried to private houses to be nursed.

If you see Mrs. Brewer you may tell her that Johny[1] was under me on guard duty the other night and acted nobley, so much so as to elicit the praise of the oficer of the "Grand Rounds." Poor boy he will never stand a campaign. Him Tip Horsley and George Terry, aught to be sent home. You must not say anything about this for you know it would distress their friends.

Thare is something going on or will bee soon. It is rumered that our outpost and those of the anemy have been fighting today. Five Regiments were ordered from this vacinity today, on to Fairfax. So I hear. The telegraph has been working rapidly all the evening. I hear this, do not see. Our Colonel is very strict about going out of lines. Boykin and Lieut Waller went to the battle ground today. It is eight miles north of here. I will go when I have an opportunity and give you the particulars of my visit etc. My dear I have not heard from you in a long time, not since Waller came back. I hope that you are contented with your lot. Hope that you do not get weried passing about from one place to another. You are fighting a greater battle than I will ever fight. My struggle will only be a theme for a moment and be forgotten. Yours will be recorded near a throne of Eternal light around which rejoice cherubims and seraphims.

> Take the pearly shell far from its home on the lea;
> Where ever it goes, it will sing of the sea.
> So take the fond heart, from its home and its hearth;
> It will sing of loved ones, to the end of the earth.

How strikingly true are these little lines. My heart sings of you and my dear boy. Sometimes gay sometimes sad.

Direct your letters to Manassas Junction 4th Ga Battalion care Capt Boykin. Write amediately, I know you will.

Ugie

1. John C. and Mary Ann Garrett Brewer and their seven children were Susan and Ugie's neighbors. Their son John H. was eighteen when he enlisted in the Ben Hill Infantry on July 9, 1861.

Camp Mercer Va
Aug 26th AD 1861

Dear Susie

I recieved your letter of the 15th inst. yesterday. It was just eight days on the road. I wrote to you last Thursday, and gave you all the news about our situation etc. I recieved Berry Rolands letter on the same day that I recieved yours. You want to know who is in my mess. I anticipated your question and answered it in my last letter. You want to know if you must make me a matress tick. It is a good idea; but do not make it untill I write to you to do it. I do not know whether I could carry it or not. Thare is only one wagon alowed to each company on a march. I do not know but what I may have to abandon my trunk. An oficer is alowed eighty pounds of bagage if the government can furnish transportation: but in war evry thing yields to necessity. I will let you know if I see proper. I have sent to Richmond for a camp bedstead. I can tell you that we do not know when, how, where we march or move untill the order is given to execute. Tomorrow we move again. We are cooking two days rations (Sunday night about ten) and will go about ten or twelve miles nearer Washington City: Somewhere near Fairfax Courthouse I expect. All that I can learn is this: that we are to go to Page's land near a turnpike. I hear that our picket gards and those of the anemy have been fighting for several days. I can not say that I know what is going on outside of our own regiment; and I have heard that Gen Bouregard said once that if his coat knew his secrets, that he would burn it up; but some important movement of one party or army will develope itself before a month. I cannot say that our army is advancing on Washington. O that I was gifted with the eyes of prophecy that I might looke beyond the vail that o'er shadows the mystic future.

I am sorry that you can not get a wheel and cards.[1] It would save a great deal these hard times. The negroes must be clothed, wheel and cards aught to have been bought by me long ago. It would be a good plan to buy the winter clothes and make provisions for shoes as soon as posible. Consult Mr. Boykin about it. We have a great maney cases of measels in the company. We left seven in Richmond, and will not be able to leave here with more than fifty. None of our men are dangerous; but they can not walk and carry their gun and knapsack. I shall help them all I can. Uncle Wisdom first, then others. I am very well with the exception of heart burn occasionaly; which is caused by imprudence in eating poor cooking. Boykin is going back to Richmond tomorrow I expect. You must direct letters to Richmond or Manassas as before. Do not forget the "4th Ga Battallion care of Capt Boykin" etc. I can not hear from you too often so let evry churished message reach me. Pray do not distress our friends by saying that thare is much sickness among us. Tom Green, Billy Bennett and Joe Rodgers are all well.

I would not have you hurt any persons feelings that do not come, but whose chance was not equaly as good or better than mine? You can tell any one that wish to impress the community with their patriotism that thare is plenty of hard fighting to be done soon and Virginia is the field to show it; and that staying at home and saying they want to come will never conquer their anemies. We will never have peace untill our foes are conquered by the mite of our strong arms. I heard just now that Gen McClellan[2] has crossed the Potomac with near one hundred thousand men. These men are to be driven back. The scene of Manassas is to be enacted again with thrice the bludshed. We must conquer in the next battle let it cost what it may. My dear love let me close. I will write again when we get settled. Be of good cheer.
Good bye
Ugie

12 M Aug 26th 1861
P.S. I have just recieved your letter of the 17th and break this open to acknowl-edge it. We are packed up ready to move as soon as the wagons come. You said that you thought of getting Mot Brit[3] to stay with you a while. Do so if you can and wish. Be shure and write as often as you said. I have been doing so. Whip that saucy boy for me. Are you pleased with Bartow for a name. I expect we will pass by the battle ground. It was Bartow that won the battle of Manassas Plains. I do not want anything. Keep that money or give it to Mr. Boykin. I have seventy dollars on hand. I will write to Mr. Boykin and Berry as soon as we get settled again. Ought to have writen before now.

1. Cloth was among the critical imports cut off by the Federal navy's blockade of southern ports. The South's few textile mills were pressed into production of cloth for uniforms and tents. Spinning wheels and cotton cards became scarce and valuable as southerners became dependent on production of homespun cloth for their needs. Georgia governor Joseph E. Brown proposed a plan whereby the state would distribute cards at cost to the needy. Susan Allen eventually obtained both wheel and cards. Her records indicate that by war's end she was selling surplus homespun cloth.

2. George Brinton McClellan (1826–85) assumed command of the Union Army of Virginia on July 27, 1861.

3. Martha Brett and her three-year-old son John lived with her mother while both her husband John H. Brett and her father Henry Hunt served in the Ben Hill Infantry. Both men were discharged in January 1862—Hunt, who was fifty-six, because of age and Brett because of illness. On his journey home, twenty-seven-year-old John Brett got as far as Chattanooga, where he died on February 5, 1862. Hunt returned home and joined the local militia.

Aug 28th 1861

My dear Susie

You see that I have not headed my letter only with the date. I told you in my last letter that we were on the eve of marching. We left Camp Mercer about 2 oclock PM and marched at a steady gait for twelve miles. The men were very much fatigued, you know, but could have done much more if it had been necessary. I stood the trip finely, although I carried a gun very near all the time so as to relieve Uncle Wisdom and some others. We are now in a section of country called Pages Land in the North East corner of Prince William County. We are on the West side of the Railroad runing north from Manassas Junction, eighteen miles from the Potomac River and twenty five from Alexandria. This is all that I can tell you of our whereabouts only that we are in an old field covered nicely with grass. I think that we are north west of Manassas Junction. We are the north east wing of our line of battle. Our line of battle is about twenty miles long; so I understand. We do not know anything of the movements of the anemy. When I say we, I mean us "small fry." Perhaps Bouregard and Johnson does. They do if they can possible find out. Our Battalion is in poor fighting order just at this time. We left a great maney men at Camp Mercer, some sick others to nurse them. I think that we can turn out between thirty five and forty men able to do duty. I have fattened evry day since I left home. None of our men are seriously ill. Ol Fears and John Higginbothem are both sick. It is easier to say who are well, than sick. Uncle W and Boykin are both well or about. Boykin was rite in saying he wanted no more men because our company is under great disadvantage in maneuvering in the battalion drill, the other companies being smaller. You do not understand this. Besides we are not allowed any more transportation (one wagon) than if we had sixty or seventy men. It is rumered that McCleland is on this side of the Potomac with a large army. Where he will attact us we do not know. This is only rumor. I do not know it to be so. The fact is you hear more war news than we do. For instance you have been duped about Davis and the body gard. I have seen Davis once since I left home. I not only saw him but "shuck" hands with him. Now what do you think. Let me tell all. The President presented in the name of a fair lady, a banner to the Texas Regiment. When he had presented it and was returning to the city from the fair ground hundreds of soldiers ran and "shuck" hands with him. This is quite customary. I once (forgive me) held the paw of that Hungarian "Orangoutang" Lewis Kosouth[1]

We passed over the battle ground in coming to this place. I saw the ground where Bartow fell. Noble son of my native State, posterity will crown you with the laurels that thou hast so bravely won. You do not know the depravity of the human hart. Would you believe that the Hydra headed monster party spirit still lives and seeks to persecute his memory.[2]

Yes, pay Mrs Boykin that money. You know what I said in my last letter. We are all going to have our measures taken and send home for a winter suit of clothes. I do not need anything particularly; but will want you to send me several little tricks; so as to pass through winter comfortably if we have to stay. We all pass the time in talking of the war and things at home, when we are not drilling. Tell Cousin Robert to stay at home untill his father comes. He will come if we can get him off. If we do not succeed, then stay with his mother.

Dear Susie, you are not more anxious for me to come home than I am myself. I can give you nothing to hope for. It is almost impossible to get a furlough: and I do not have any idea when the war will end. Let us wait patiently, a while longer and see how things develop themselves. Perhaps it will not be long before we can form an idea of the future. Endeaver to be contented and happy if you can. You and Lizzie must cheer each other. Pray do not both of you despond at once. If I could just slip home and hear you both talking as I know you sometimes do I would be glad. Cheer up! Cheer up! I will have no oportunity of having my ambrotipe taken. I wish I could. I would like for you to write just as often as you can, you do not know the pleasure your dear letters give me. Tell evrything about evrything.
Good bye Susie
Ugie

1. Hungarian nationalist Lewis Kossuth (1802–94) had addressed the citizens of LaGrange during a tour of the United States in 1852. Kossuth's visit emboldened the young ladies of LaGrange Female College to defy their professors by attending his address attired in their finest crinolines rather than the prescribed drab school uniform. The local newspaper reported that Kossuth created a great excitement and was the talk of the community for weeks afterwards.

2. Allen probably refers to a highly publicized dispute that arose between Francis S. Bartow and Georgia governor Joseph E. Brown. The controversy revolved around the legality of Bartow's company "the Oglethorpe Light Infantry" taking to Virginia arms owned by the state of Georgia.

Page's Land N.E. Va[1]
Sep 4th 1861

Dear Susie

I know you have been looking anxiously for a letter from me for several days.
I aught to have writen last Sunday but I was on guard duty (oficer of the
guard) and did not have one moment to spare. Since then I have not had one
moment in the day that I could call my own; at night no candles; for we could
not get aney for love or money. I authorised Ned Henderson to pay fifty cents
for a candle for me and he could not get it. We have sent out in the country
and bought some. The men have had no candles isued to them since we left
Camp Mercer. We are all doing as well as aney one could expect in the eating
department. We buy mutton at nine cents, eggs 25, butter 25, chickens 25 to
40 butermilk 40 cents a galon, hams 16. We have fine beef. You know how
our mess is arranged. Both of our black cooks are sick. The privates of our
mess are sometimes sick and frequently on duty; then we hire some of the
boys to cook for us. We do not pretend to say that evrything equals home; but
we are blessed with good health and all consuming apetites. I mean our mess;
for thare is much sickness in the company. Two thirds of the company are
unable to do regular duty. Measels and diarhea. I do not think that we have
any serious cases here. We have not heard of our Richmond boys lately; and
are looking for them. About half of our sick left at Camp Mercer were
brought up last Saturday. You have probably heard of Mr Tho's Reid's death
ere this.[2] Poor fellow. But the soldier who dies from sickness is no less to be
honored than he that dies upon the battle field. Ol F. is better. John H. is
about [well]. I have told you in a previous letter that we were in the NE corner of Prince William county about three miles from where it joines Loudon
and Fairfax. I do not know when [we] will leave here; probably not very
soon. I hear that our troops will take Alexandria soon. We sometimes hear
vague reports of picket skirmishes. I may sum up the whole by saying that we
know nothing and never hear anything. Permission to leave camp must always
be obtained from the Colonel. If we could go where we pleased, what would
become of the Regement (Battalion). Other regements know no more than
our own. It would not be prudent for our generals to devulge their policy. I
have no idea but that our army and this country is full of spies. I had no idea
when we left Richmond but that we would have had a battle before now.
Child like I just thought so; had no reason for it either.

Winter is coming on; the boys are all thinking of trying to get blankets
shoes etc. from home. Infact are oblige to; or do worse. Boykin has writen to

his father to get cloth for another uniform. The people ought to make them up for nothing; and then let each soldier pay into the company treasury the cost of the cloth and cuting. By doing this the boys will have a good suit of clothes at a small cost and our treasury would be full. Blankets and shoes must be bought and sent to the men also. I do not know that I want anything but blankets and shoes. I have 4 pr of cotton and 2 wool socks. If you have me a pair already knit you may send them when the uniforms are sent. I will have Mr Boykin to send me some blankets (about four good ones) when Cousin Robert comes. If not I will have him or Berry to buy them and you can line some of them and send with the other things. It will cost nothing to send anything to the soldiers if it is done properly. Do not send me these things only as I have told you; for they would never get to me, and even if they did the freight would be twice their value. If you send me anything with the uniforms, be certain to mark it. I will tell you about that tick in my next. My pillow and cap are the best institutions in the company. Myself and Uncle Wisdom sleep upon the pillow evry night. We spread down about three blankets and cover with one; put our coats and the pillow under our heads and sleep sound. I have not slept without my pants (and sometimes coat and vest) more than a dosen times since I left home. The nights are always cold and the ground damp. The boys do not have more than enough to keep them warm now; and if the people do not provide for them they will certainly suffer. They will be paid off soon; but what good will the money do if they can not buy comforts. I fear that many will spend their money foolishly, and suffer when winter comes. The plan that we propose is the only safe plan. Let the people buy these things and send to them. Buy with the company treasury if they are not able to give; and then let each soldier pay into the company treasury what was paid out for him. I think I will write and have Hollie to make me a good pair of winter boots.[3] Perhaps I may get some; but I see no prospect now. Be shure and write what your relief society is doing and proposes to do. Do your part in evry respect. I do not think of paying what I subscribed at Whites Hill[4] that day; and you must feel free to contribute. I will share evry cent of my wages here with the men if necessary. They are our strength, the pillows upon which we hope to build a nations freedom. I am so sorry that so maney of our men are unfit for duty. I do not know how other regements are. If we do not whip in the next battle you may set it down that the war will be a long one. If evry man felt like I do about it (I do not know how I will act) thare would be neither a prisner or messenger of defeat.

I dreamed of you and home last night. All was pleasant and happy; but I awoke only to realise more forcibly my sad situation. I need not say my own only, but that of my country. Canons have been heard firing in the direction of Washington City today. I do not know but some how or other I have a presentment that some stiring event will take place soon. I have not seen a newspaper in near two weeks. You know that I miss them. I would certainly read the advertisements now. Boykin recieved a letter from his father today stating that Govner Brown had ordered all the malitia under arms. This is only war news that I have heard in three weeks. If the Yankees land on our coast; I want them to send Georgians back to *wool them*. We would certainly do it if we got half a chance. I am not an aspirant for ofice; but would like to command a regement on such an occasion. Appropos I acted as Adjutant of the battalion yesterday. An adjutant ranks as a first lieutenant. Col Mercer is a superior officer. Lieut Col Morrison is not very good; but is quite populer. Our battalion is in the seventh brigade; commanded by Brig. Gen Critenton, a son of senator Critenton of Ky. You know his father was the great compromise man; he now votes men and money to subjugate us rebels. The seventh brigade is composed of our battalion, one N. C. one Ala and one Mississippi Reg.[5]

I have not recieved a letter from you in a week. I do not know what is the matter; but none of our boys have recieved any for several days. We usualy recieve from twelve to twenty daily. I know that I will recieve one tomorrow. Am I not writing too long a letter? Will you read it over again and again as I do yours. Is thare any news that you want to know? I have writen all that I recollect. I have no opportunity to have my ambrotipe taken. I want you to have yours and the boy's taken and send it to me by the first one that passes. I expect that Bob Strong has gone home from Richmond and will come on soon if those recruits do not come. You need not tell any one about the sickness in the company unless it becomes generally known. It might scare those recruits. I can not say that we want them so very bad though. We want stout ablebodied soldiers. Just let some of those fellows have an excuse not to come to this company and you will see that they never join any. My dear Susie you must write me a good long letter when you recieve this. Tell me of yourself, the boy and home. Tell me of Lizzie, Mrs B and the children. Give my respects to Berry and all enquiring friends, Mrs Jackson & Lee.[6] Any arrangement that you can make about having some one to stay with you, make it. My whole desire is for you to be contented and happy. Get a relation, friend or hire some one. What is the news from George. Did he come home on a furlough. How is your Pa, Ma, Jesse, Jimmy and the rest of the family.[7] You want me to say something about coming home, don't you? Can't say anything yet. Goodbye
Ujanirtus Allen

1. Pageland Lane intersects the Warrenton Pike a short distance west of the Manassas battlefield.

2. Thomas B. Reid died September 2, 1861, at Manassas, Virginia, leaving his widow Angeline and a three-year-old son. He was the first member of the Ben Hill Infantry to die in service.

3. Frederick Holle (1820–1907) was born in the principality of Hanover. He married Artemisia Lucinda Britton in Troup County on May 3, 1855. Holle manufactured boots and shoes in a workshop on his farm near Antioch.

4. The settlement of White's Hill was in the West Vernon District of Troup County, about six miles south of Antioch.

5. George Bibb Crittenden (1812–80), the son of Senator John Jordan Crittenden of Kentucky, commanded the Seventh Brigade, composed of the 21st Georgia, 21st North Carolina, 15th Alabama, and 16th Mississippi regiments. The Seventh Brigade was assigned to Brigadier General Richard S. Ewell's division. Crittenden was promoted in the fall of 1861, and Brigadier General Isaac R. Trimble assumed command of the brigade.

6. Leroy Jackson (October 26, 1826–March 19, 1904) and his brother John Coleman Jackson were sons of Samuel Jackson, who came to Heard County about 1840. "Lee" (as Allen refers to Leroy Jackson) married Martha Lucinda Gamble about 1847. The Jacksons migrated to Tallapoosa County, Alabama, after the war.

7. Susan's parents were William Fuller (1802–81) and Stacy Rebecca Welborn (1806–62). James Madison Fuller (1825–63), Jesse Gunn Fuller (born 1831), and George Melton Fuller (born 1840) were her brothers. George was a member of the 7th Alabama Infantry stationed at Pensacola, Florida.

Pageland Va
Sep. 5th 1861

Sir [J. T. Boykin Sr.]
I have delayed writing to you longer than I should. But you know our facilities for writing any thing worth to be called a letter are very poor. It is quite probable that if I do not write tonight I will not have an opportunity to write in several days. For a day or two it has been rumored that we would move from this place on the next. Our Col. has orders to move near the Stone bridge on Bull's run: and as we have heard that about sixty Confederates were killed by "Old Abe's" hirelings just beyond thare; we think it quite probable that we will pitch our tents thare tomorrow. I do not state this to be a fact about our men being killed; but as I say only heard it. We hear rumors of skirmishes evry day or two, and are priviledged to believe or disbelieve, just as we like for we have no oportunity [of] finding out the truth or the lier. I heard several days ago and so wrote home that our pickets were around Alexandria: if they were how came some of the anemy near Centerville. Ten days ago I heard that Gen McClellan was this side of the Potomac with seventy five thousand men. Four days ago I heard that some of our oficers were near enough to the Federal capitol to look into it with their glasses. To tell you the truth, you know and can find out as much war news as we can. Though I believe that "somebody will be hurt" soon. I do not believe that the Yankees

will let us sit here and do nothing even if we were disposed to. You have heard of our disasters in N. C. before now. North Carolina had better have stayed in the Union if she can not do better than that. The idea of two little shaby vesels taking two forts with a regiment of men without having to kill more than a half dosen is preposterous.[1] What a great moral effect this affair will have upon the North! How maney more battles such as Manassas will we have to fight if one state is alowed to act this way. If Butler's[2] version of the battle is true, I think we had better disown the state and kick her out of the Confederacy. The fact is I am mad when ever I think about it. We have a rege-ment of North Carolinians in our brigade and four or five of the men have deserted evry night for the last week.

A great maney of our men have been sick with measels and diarhea lately. We have had no new cases lately; that is within the last three days. Two thirds of our men are unfit for heavy duty. We will not carry any sick or convalesent soldier with us tomorrow. I hear that no man is to go that can not double quick several miles, and then fight a battle.

I recieved a letter from Rowland a few days ago saying that evrything was working well. I am glad to hear that I have such a fine crop. I would like to know how much corn I would make. Of course we can not judge very acura-tely about the amount of cotton. I think it would be a good idea for farmers to gin their cotton as fast as they pick it out; even if they did not sell it. We must not sell one pound of cotton untill Lincoln or someone else raises the blockade. I think that I will have to buy a new gin this fall, if I can see a pros-pect of paying for it. Perhaps I might get one on a years credit. My gin house runninggeer need some repairs before I can gin aney. Roland will see what is the matter with it. What is the prospect for money among the people next fall. Quite poor if we can not sell our cotton, I expect. Billy Edmondson[3], Pulliam[4], and Acel Winn[5] are all owing me on some accounts. See them if you can find it convenient and get their notes for the money. They are all under obligations to pay as soon as they can. You know what I owe and what I have to pay with. I would like to settle up evry thing if it is possible. I owe Lee Crouch $12.50 besides what I owe you and Wilder.[6] It will be a great deal for me to pay all; but I want to do my best. I can save something from my salery. Get everything for Susie that she wants and can not get. In other words see that she needs nothing conducive to her wellfare or happiness. I would be glad if you would get me about four good blankets and send them to me when the uniforms are sent to the boys. Or just so I can get them by winter. I do not mean fine blankets; but good heavy fellows. An india ruber blanket would be of good service if I could get one but I know I can not. It would be

good to spread down to make my pallet on. The blanket next to the ground is wet evry morning from dew or moisture rising from the ground. Those of us that have not been sick have increased in waight condsiderably. I have not weighed; but I think I have gained ten or twelve pounds. Other companies have suffered as much from sickness as ours. We will write again in a day or two. With many feelings of regard for your maney favers permit me to remain
Your Friend
Ujanirtus Allen

Give my love to Mrs. Boykin and Lizzy. Direct your letters to Manassas Junction care of Capt Boykin 4th Ga Battalion, Col. Mercer.
U.A.

I am on guard duty today and have no better facilities than my lap and a blank book to write this upon.

1. On August 27, 1861, Union forces occupied Fort Clark on Hatteras Inlet, North Carolina, without Confederate resistance. The following day Fort Hatteras surrendered after a heavy bombardment. Capture of the two forts gave the Federals a significant advantage in controlling blockade runners.

2. Benjamin Franklin Butler (1818–93), the most notorious of the North's political generals in the eyes of many southerners, commanded Federal infantry in the expedition against Hatteras.

3. William P. Edmondson (born 1830) was an Antioch merchant. Allen refers to Edmondson as "Billy" or "Billy E." and to his wife Sarah Birdsong as "Mrs. E." In the latter part of 1861, Edmondson paid Allen $1,200 for a tract of land, probably the farm at Houston. Susan Allen resided with the Edmondsons for a brief time in 1862.

4. Joseph D. Pulliam (May 6, 1837–September 7, 1899) and his wife Ann E. Wilder resided north of Houston in Heard County. Pulliam was a corporal in Company K, 56th Georgia Infantry.

5. Acel Winn (born 1824), his wife Sarah Brooks, and their four children lived on a small farm near Antioch.

6. James and Nancy Weston Wilder's large family were Allen's neighbors in Houston Community. Allen owed money to their son Mitchell Wilder (born 1825).

Fairfax Co. Va
Sep 8th 1861

Dear Susie
You see from the heading of this letter that we have moved again. I do not recollect whether I told you or not in my last letter that thare was a probability of moving nearer the anemy. I know I did in Mr Boykins letter. The fact is time has passed so swiftly since I last wrote; that I did not know untill this evening that today was Sunday. I was oficer of the guard yesterday up all night last night and today we came down here: so you see that two days of the half

week have passed almost imperceptibly. It makes no diference whether we are on special duty or not we are so busily engaged that we do not notice the flight of time. We left our old camp this morning about nine and reached here about two hours by sun. I did not feel much like walking; but I had rather have walked several miles ferther than to have come so slow. We only came eight miles. We are now at Centerville between bull run and Fairfax. We are between Manassas and Washington City. We came back the road that we traveled when we went from Manassas to our old camp untill we passed the battlefield then turned to the left crossed Bull run at the stone bridge and are now encamped upon the same spot where the Yankees camped the night before the battle of Manassas. Let me give you a rough sketch of our routes. We are about twenty miles from Washington City. I do not know how far we are from the anemy. Some say only twelve miles. We frequently hear rumors of skirmishes but never find out the truth.

We have thirty four privates and noncommissioned oficers along. We brought no sick or convalescents: no baggage but blanketts and rations. I do not know what is up now: but may learn before long. I will write again soon. Accept my love and let me close; for you know that I am very much fatigued. Kiss the boy for me.

Ugie

P.S. I have not recieved a letter in a long time from you. We are hard run for writing material. Inferior paper sells at fifty cents per quire: and cant get any at that.

Centreville Virginia
[September] 11th AD 1861

Dear Susie

I recieved your letter of the 1st Aug. day before yesterday; and as I had just mailed one to you, I answer it now. I have been writing to you twice a week regularly, with one exception and then I wrote a long letter. Your letter of the 1st was the only one that I recieved in about ten days; I had wrote about three or four in the interval. My dear you must continue to write twice a week, whether I recieve your letters or not. I have only two sheets of paper left, and if I can not make a rise soon, you will have to wait untill I can recieve some from Richmond. If I was going to be hung I could not produce an envelope. Do you have a daily mail at Antioch? How do you get your letters? Does Mr.

Pitts[1] send them to you evry oportunity. Do you recieve my letters regularly.
Mr. Boykin or Berry must hire some hands to work on the screw.[2] It was my
intention to hire as many workmen as possible so as to be at less expence and
trouble. If I did not I intended to tell Mr. Boykin of it before I left. I am so
glad that your Ma is going to stay with you. Tell Berry if the workmen do not
do as they aught, that is if they spend their time in talking to turn them off. I
would be glad if he would stay about as much as possible. I will send you
twenty dollars in this letter and will send some more after a while so as not to
run too great a risk in sending you money. I have sixty dollars on hand now,
and about one hundred and twenty owing to me. When I can get it the Lord
only knows. The workmen I have no doubt will want some money cash. Tell
Mr Boykin that it may be a good idea to buy negro shoes as soon as possible. I
would be glad if I could furnish money to pay cash for them and winter
clothes so as to get them as cheap as possible. Perhaps I have some clothes that
would answer for the boys. Will I have to buy any bacon? I wrote to you in
my last letter that we were at this place. I have found out that we are twenty
five miles from Washington. I do not recollect whether I wrote to you that
we brought only fighting men, with forty rounds of cartridges. Some of our
sick came along any how. Some have been taken sick here; they will be sent
back to camp Wright. I do not have any idea that we will be in a battle soon
or late. In fact I can not find out anything. Though I know that thare will be
some hard fighting before this war ends. Both parties are making all the preparations possible for a mighty strugle. When they do come in contact thare
will be such a din of arms that the whole universe will tremble. We will have
to whip the North time and again before we can have any peace. Defeat with
us is utter ruin. We would be disfranchised, dishonored, murdered and our
property taken away from us. The mind of man is unable to concieve the deso-
lation that would cover our country. Thare is only one alternative and that is
to fight. Fight for all that is near and dear, our country, our lives. Never yield
as long as there is one of us able to draw a sword. I have one petty hope left
and that is that England and France will interfere as mediators. And I can not
say that I have seen anything in their conduct as yet to authorise such a delu-
sion. We will probably be able to tell what course they will pursue by Christmas. Nothing but interest will cause them to do this. What does it matter
with them how much we fight. They have all the hatred that can exist
between monarchies and republics; and only rejoice at our downfall. They
never will interpose unless their interest (which I hope is) is greater than their
antipithy. We will soon see if cotton is king.

As the end of the year draws near I feel more forcibly the situation of my country, and of course my own identified with it. We are separated by circumstances it seems, over which we have no possible controll. Indeed my dear Susie long before you wrote those words "we can not live thus," had I sought to know whether I should desert my country in the hour of her peril, or her whom I had before the alter vowed to love cherish and protect. Here we might very apropriately ask whether I can better fulfill my vows and do my duty at home or in the field. It seems that you are tossed alone on lifes troubled waters. Hope and struggle bravely. Gen. Johnson has recalled all persons on furlough and issued an order prohibiting the granting of them to any one for the present. More than half of the company are wanting to come home about Christmas. I am coming if there is any possible chance.

Susie you must not trouble yourself one moment about those reports. You know what I owe and who I owe. As for the others, language fails to express the point or depth of moral degredation to which any one has fallen who would concieve and circulate such. Treat that arrogant young gent as best suits your mind. You know the source of his weekness. No such blood courses in my vains. I have not had an opportunity to have my ambrotipe taken since I left Richmond. Tell Berry to repair the old smokehouse for the present. I will write to you or some one else the names of those who are needing clothes. My dear, let me close. It is now at least two oclock at night. We have poor facilities for writing and no time only at night.
Good bye
Ugie

I will write again at the end of the week.

1. Littleton Pitts (born 1822) was a merchant and postmaster at Antioch. Pitts was elected ordinary of Troup County in 1864. After the war he moved to LaGrange, became a banker, and continued to be active in local politics.
2. The screw was a massive device with a threaded wooden pole used to pack cotton into bales.

Camp near Centreville Va
Sep 15th 1861

Dear Susie
I wrote to you on the 11th. Have recieved no letter from you since I wrote; did not expect one, because you said in your last that they would commence the screw on the next day, and I did not think that you would have an oppor-

tunity to send to the office. We have a mail evry day or at least should have. The boys do not recieve as maney letters as they should. Be careful in directing your letters, for thare is much carelessness in the diferent postal departments. Direct thus: Manassas Junction Va, Care of Capt Boykin, Company F 4th Ga Battalion, Col Mercer Commanding. I think they will come then if they will come atall.

We have a regiment now, but I do not know the number of it.[1] I will probably recieve a letter from you in a day or two. We are doing about as well as a person could expect. Our sick boys are coming in evry day or two. We have one man, Wiley Mobley, a son of "old man Mobley" who we do not have any idea will recover[2]. We left him sick with the typhoid fever at Camp Mercer: he has been geting worse ever since. Bobby Strong has been and is very sick. So is Jack Young. I have had a cold for several days but am doing well now. We will leave this place this evning or tomorrow. I do not know where we will go to: but think we will go on near Fairfax C. H. I will send you a map of the seat of war so that you can follow us in our perigrinations. Perhaps some of your friends would like to refer to it. I will try to get you a map of the battle-ground. If I had seen it more I would try to give you an idea of it with my own pencil. I have seen nothing that could delineate only the positions of the seventh and eighth Ga. Regiments.[3] I hope to be able to give you a verbal description of the next battle. We took twelve Yankee prisners yesterday. We recieved news yesterday of a great victory at Luriville (don't know where it is, suppose somewhere ahead) a few days ago.[4] One battalion with one piece of artillery and a company of horse routed three regiments of infantry one of cavelry with several pieces of artilery killing fifty and wounding many more, without loosing a single man. Very near all of the Confederate army is ahead of us. Susie you will find or have found this a remarkably stupid letter. I hope I will be more interesting next time. Give my respects to all, especially your Ma, who I recon is staying with you. Be asshured of my love, and kiss that boy.
Ugie

Tell me what reports those were or what were those reports.

1. Ten companies constituted a regiment, according to nineteenth-century military organization. A unit with less than ten companies was designated a battalion. On August 28, 1861, Captain John B. Akridge's company from Chattooga County, Georgia, became Company K of the 4th Georgia Battalion, and the designation was changed to 21st Georgia Regiment. It was a source of irritation to the men that they had to accept a higher number (21) than other regiments that had enlisted much later.

2. Wiley Mobley (born 1836), son of James and Eliza Mobley, died of typhoid fever on September 11, 1861.

3. During the Battle of First Manassas these two regiments held positions in the initial Confederate defensive line on Matthews Hill before being driven, with heavy losses, back to Henry House Hill, where the northern advance was checked. Their colonel, Francis S. Bartow, was killed on Henry House Hill.

4. Allen undoubtedly refers to the skirmishing which occurred on September 10 and 11, 1861, in the environs of Lewinsville, Virginia, a settlement located only a few miles west of Washington, D.C.

Camp Tatnall Near Fairfax C.H.
Sep 18th A.D. 1861

Dear Susie

This is my usual time to write; and I write. Not that I have any very special news: but know that it will give you pleasure to hear from me. It is about ten days now since I heard from you. Boykin recieved a letter from Lizzie last night; but no news from you. Do you recieve my letters regular? Let me know if you recieved one with twenty dollars in it. The boys have all quit paying postage, thinking that their letters will be more apt to reach their friends: and if they do not, they will loose nothing but the time and paper. If my letters do not go regularly or I get out of specie I shall do so too. It is quite dificult to get specie here: when I mail this I will have five cents left. I dislike to frank my letters because you might be put to some inconvenience in geting them out of the office. Most any person would cary your letters to you I guess. Tell me how you get your letters to and from the office? Does Mr. Pitts always send them to you, as soon as he has an opportunity?

I like to have forgoten to tell you where we are. Day before yesterday we moved from near Centreville to about a half mile of Fairfax C. H. Today we moved back the same road and are about three miles of Fairfax, on the road that leads to Centreville. You might take that map I sent you and mark and number all our camps. The one we left today was on the right between the forks of the road and Fairfax. We are now on the left as you go from C to F about three miles from F. Some think that we will stay here some time, but I don't. We move evry Sunday or get ready Sunday to move Monday. I mean cook. We can strike tents, load wagons and be on the road in a half hour. I do not know what is the object of [these] moves.

Susie my dear, I would like for you to send me several course towels when you get a good chance. I wrote to Mr Boykin about some blankets, and other things. Perhaps you saw the letter. I forgot to mention negro shoes, and several other things. No doubt he will provide evrything as he does for his own negroes. Write to me how you are geting along in evry respect. I see that Liz-

zie will have some company and of course will like to stay at home more. I
want you to be satisfied; or in other words I want my absence to bear as lightly
as possible on you. My dear I dislike to have you going too and froe as you
have been doing. Write to me all about yourself, our boy and home.
Good bye.
Ugie

Camp Toombs Va
Sep 22nd 1861

Dear Susie
You need not infer from the heading of this letter that we have moved again.
Our camp is named Toombs instead of Tatnall as I last wrote you. I do not
[know] whether we will move again soon or not; in fact I see no place to
move to unless we are attacted (which is not probable); or there is a great forward movement of our army. I understand that both parties have agreed that
their picketts should not kill each other. I do not believe it; though it is quite
current in camp. It looks a little like they did not want to hurt each other, if
they did make the agreement. Susie I believe that if England or France was to
interpose the least bit: the north would grant what we ask willingly, and the
war would end. Without some power interposes: her pride will not let her
yeald, as long as she can raise men or money. I know that the north hate us
and our institutions with all the hate that their puritanical fanatical bigoted
minds can concieve: and would gladly blot us out from the face of the earth:
but this war is opressive, and has already asumed such proportions as was
never dreamed of by their leading spirits.

Susie my dear; I have just this minute [received] your letter of the 12th
Sep. It has been ten days coming, and is the first I have recieved in two weeks.
No one can concieve but yourself the inexpressable pleasure that it gave me.
Immagine that for two weeks you recieve not a word or letter from me. See
me going confidently, and anxiously enquiring evning after evning and always
recieving the cold, gruff no! I know my dear, that you have written. Boykin
has recieved a letter a week ago of about the same date of yours. I invariably
write to you twice a week. I have never failed to do this since we commenced
a regular correspondence, but once, and then wrote a long letter, and stated
the fact. This was about three, four, or five weeks ago. Boykin says that for the
last three weeks he has averaged a letter evry two days. You do not recieve my

letters for you ask me about blankets and other things that I wrote to you about when we were at Camp Mercer, if I am not mistaken. Did you recieve a map that I sent you? Did you recieve a letter containing twenty dollars? As soon as I can get some money worth speaking of in your hands I will feel much better. My wages or salery will amount to one hundred and sixty dollars at the end of this month. If I get it will send you some. I do not intend to mail any more. Besides I think I will quit paying postage. I have about thirty five dollars on hand. It may be a little doubtful whether we get any pay soon or not. The men's pay has been due ever since the lst of August and they have recieved nothing. If I was at Richmond I could draw: if there was anything in the treasury. The government has been paying soldiers with Confederate bonds bearing eight per cent. I want you to give as liberal as any one to the society as soon as I furnish the money. I have already writen to you on this subject. My dear your hart would bleed if you could see the misery and sufering that our poor soldiers are doomed to undergo. I may probably write your society a few lines. If I felt myself equal to the task I should certainly do it. Some active measures must be taken soon; for I think we will have frost tomorrow morning. I wrote to you to send me about four good blankets. I do not know that you have recieved my letter, and mention it again. Sugest that you line one or two of them. I wrote to Mr. Boykin about them also. I do not know that I will want those legans. I like the idea of having a tick with a hole in the midle so that I could fill it with straw, and take it out when we were passing about. Uncle Wisdom has writen to Cousin Robert to bring one. He is bent on having him to stay with us. I mean Waller, Dawson and myself. Uncle Wisdom has writen to him to come on; for he cannot leave untill he gets here. Susie I do not know what to say about the way those wicked people are doing. Only that they will never find their match or just deserts this side of Eternity. I just know that those that know us best & those people of the community who are of any standing, those who are not of the same ilk, do not believe the backbiters, liers, the vile slanderers. Cheer up my dear and pay no attention to them. Show yourself above them and their mean gabbling. Never condecend to quarrel with them. Recollect that the slanderer never strikes at any but a superior. I have talked to Jeff Sample about that original report. I would be glad if you could have heard us discuss the family at length. He told me many things. He said that such talk only had an affect among those ignorant of the source.

Let me tell you what to send me. Several pair of drawers, a good silk handkerchief or two. I would not ask for socks but I see you have them already knit. I have five pair; two thick ones. I think I have enough shirts with the exception of overshirts. If I had a good flannel one it would answer a good purpose. If you send me any more clothes than I need I will give to the boys who have no one to provide for them. I would not care if I had some extra things. I know who need charity. I want you to send me several quires of paper and a quantity of envelopes to write to you and that bad boy. Send my blotter or bloting paper of some description. I do not recollect writing for my rule. My little woman I think you are trying to joke me. I would be glad if you would send me a book that I see Richards has advertised. "Bayonet Exercise and Skirmish Drill."[1] He sells for cash. Get Mr. Boykin or Berry to get it for you. I would like the best in the world to have a good oil cloth or indea ruber blanket; but I do not think you can get one. If I was in Richmond I could supply myself with all these things; but no one is allowed to leave here unless pronounced unfit for service by a board of surgeons. This is all I think of now. Probably I will think of something else in the course of this epistle; if it arrives at the dignity of an epistle. I use the word epistle as is costomary and not according to its original meaning. Thare are several things that I wanted to mention to Berry. One is about that crib. Could he move that work house from the Ridley place. This would probably be more trouble than profit if he was very buisy. If the crib is not large enough, I would prefer that the new ground corn be pened to itself; as it is said not to be as good for horses as old ground corn.[2] I am so rejoiced at making a crop of corn, that I will not be very mealy mouthed about it. Is my horse geting well of his lameness. Sugest to him (that is the horse) that he must not forget his best friend.

We sometimes hear some very bad reports that are circulated about us. Somebody wrote home that evrybody in the company was in the habit of playing cards on Sunday except themselves and one other. We do not know who it was; but suspicion a fellow from the lower district with it. You all must not let such reports disturb you. I forgot to add that it was said that thare were not but two or three temperate men in the company. Poor whiskey sells at two dollars a quart here. At this price I dont think that our company will ever become very intemperate unless we make a rise of some of the "rhino" soon. This suggest to me the idea that our men want clothes more than money. We cannot buy anything here but tobacco.

Give my respects to all enquiring friends specially to Mr Boykin's family and Berry. Remember me kindly to the negroes. Direct as before. Write to me frequently. I shall continue to write if I only write my name whether you recieve my letters or not. Recollect that I write twice a week and do not become so discouraged. I would give anything if I could see you and the baby. Let us hope and not dispond. Hoping that this letter may soon reach you and that I will soon recieve another from you; my dear I bid you Good bye
Ugie

P.S. You must prepare for paying postage. For we can not get specie; besides it is the opinion of a great many that letters franked are more shure to reach their point of destination. And if they do not, of course there is nothing lost but paper pains and perhaps a few brains.

1. R. H. Richards (born 1830 in New York) was a LaGrange merchant. The book to which Allen refers, *Skirmisher's Drill and Bayonet Exercise,* was compiled and translated from the French by R. Milton Cary. West and Johnston Printers in Richmond published the volume in the summer of 1861.

2. "New ground" refers to newly cleared land under cultivation for the first time.

Camp Toombs Va
Sep 25th 1861

Dear Susie

I recieved your letter of the 15th yesterday, which was Tuesday the 24th. As some of our clerical friends would say, this is my day in course: though I do not know that I shall finish my letter tonight for I am much fatigued and it is owing to the train of thought that I get into. I was oficer of the guard yesterday and set up the whole blessed night last night.

Susie just as I finished the above lines orders come that the men "should cook up three days rations and be ready to move without tents at any hour:" We are going on towards Washington I expect to fight or do picket duty: that is to stand picket guard. If we have a fight you will hear of it long before this letter reaches you. I will close up this letter and go to sleep, and write to you again tomorrow or the first opportunity. We may start tonight. It is now nine P.M.

Good bye
Ugie

Camp Toombs Va
Sep 26th 1861

Dear Susie

We were all made glad yesterday by the sudden apearence of Mr Pitts and Dr H.[1] and glad tidings from dear ones at home. They brought everything safely except the boxes; which they were compelled to express in Richmond, and will be here inside a few days. I also recieved your letter by mail that you sent the day before he started. I was just in the act of replying to your last letter when he came. What a great difference in the tone of the one I had commenced yesterday and what I shall now write. That is if I can even write. My hand is half chilled this morning. I may probably send you what I had written.

Let me see what was your first question. I think the last was about coming home. However it makes no difference as you wrote some very important news about geting married. Now if you are serious about this and want a soldier I shall certainly interpose my claim. Knowing that I am quite as handsome if not so gallant as any in the army. You will probably be surprised at the extent of my ecquaintence among the fair sex: one old lady that asisted in giving us breakfast in Augusta. She was quite suprised to learn that I was over twenty and had a wife and baby. Now some of the fellows if they had an opportunity would recomend themselves to the woman by posing as single men. Now I shall allways adopt a diferent course unless I find that it is not as popular as theirs.

Let us pass from matrimoney to money. Let Lee Jackson have that old wagon for ten dollars, if he wants it. Again I must sow a large crop of grain and if I have to buy seed I am as willing to buy from Billie E. as anyone provided evrything else is equal. You must consult Mr. Boykin about this and renting and sowing grandma's old place.[2] I am compelled to sow or cultivate some of it if nothing hapens and I get no negroes shot. I think it would be best to sow much and rent the rest to some responsable man; so that it could be taken care of. Now Uncle Wisdom will want some if Mrs. Sale[3] does not take her negroes away. I have been waiting for Uncle Wisdom to go home or I would have wrote to Mr Boykin about this before now. If I am not mistaken he has very near all of it planted in cotton. This I am afraid will be in my way. If it is, I will have to plant it (some of it) in cotton or corn and sow up at home or sow a late variety of wheat. I must write to Mr B about this. Let me whisper a secret in your ear: the more you consult him the greater pleasure he will take in befriending you. I shall never be able the longest day that I live to repay the debt of gratitude that I owe him. He is truly a model man. Uncle Wisdom is sick at Centreville. I am afraid that he has the typhoid fever. Cousin Frank[4] is down thare waiting on the sick of his company and Uncle Wisdom would not go to Pageland. At least nobody knows that he is at Centreville but this company. We send all our sick to Pageland and when they get able to do duty they are sent back. We have about fifty men able for duty here. Thare are some, cowardly fellows at Pageland that never intend to come to us as long as they can skulk around it. Our men have begun to find out such scamps and mark them. An army is a great school for studying human nature. We have some of the best soldiers in the Confederate army in our company. It may not be proper for me [to] say what I have said but it is the fact and others disclose it. We are not worse; but better than other companies. Payday has come and gone and no money for the soldiers yet. The men of our regiment are somewhat indignant. They say that the government might soon strike enough Confederate bonds to pay them, not that they want much money here; but want to send it home to buy their winter clothing and to their families who are compelled to pay cash for anything they buy. I accidently found out that the governmnet is not to blame but our brigade quartermaster, who has not given bond. The other regements were paid before our brigade was formed. Did I write to you that our regiment was formed; but I did not know the number?

We hire our washing done at six and a quarter cents a garment. As for patching we have no use for it . Though some of our boys clothes are geting a little seedy. Let me tell you what I shall nead. One good pair of pants and a coat lined and paded well. Thank your Ma for me for her present. Do not forget the Misses Brewer[5] and Mrs. Jackson[6]. Miss Beuna[7] is kniting me those socks on the strength of a cotillion that we danced when I was a young man. I hope that I am worthy of the many acts of kindness shown me.

That painted cloth that you spoke of is a good idea. I wrote to you about other things in a previous letter. Do not send those blankets that we have if it can be avoided. I will see if Mr. Pitts can not buy on the road home. If you are lucky enough to get some before he gets thare it will make no diference for they will be worth almost any price. I can not bear the idea of not having sufficient cover this winter. Anything to keep out cold. I am cold now. Susie we are expecting marching orders evry hour. You need not put yourself to any inconvenience to send those things before all the other things are sent though if anything is ready thare is no reason why you should not send it. Our sick are improving, though several are very bad off. Wiley Mobley is dead. Three of our men that we left at Camp Mercer have disapeared. They were sent to the hospital at the Junction. Boykin wrote enquiring about them and they wrote him that their names were not recorded on the books. I expect they went in and did not record their names. The mail will leave in a few minutes. I will write again in a day or two.
Good bye dear.
Ugie

P.S. Write often and such letters as your last. May heaven protect you.

1. William Reid Hurst (born 1830) practiced medicine in Houston Community. He apparently had no official connection with the Confederate army, but the people of Antioch and Houston sent him to Virginia to attend the sick of the Ben Hill Infantry. Hurst married Sarah Rowland, sister of Littleberry Rowland, in 1854. After the war he moved to DeKalb County, Georgia.

2. Allen and his Uncle H. M. Wisdom had jointly inherited 200 acres from Eleanor Wisdom (1790–1860). On July 18, 1861, the day they departed for service, they recorded a deed whereby Allen purchased Wisdom's interest in the property for $1,500.

3. Eliza Sale (born 1793) was the widow of Adolphus J. Sale. Allen's Uncle H. M. Wisdom married her daughter Charity.

4. Francis L. Wisdom, son of H. M. and Charity Wisdom, enlisted as a private in Company I, 2nd Georgia Regiment, from Marion County, Georgia. He was elected captain of the company on October 8, 1863.

5. Elizabeth, Martha, Mary, Nancy, and Catherine were the daughters of John C. and Mary A. Brewer.

6. Martha Lucinda Gamble, wife of Leroy Jackson.

7. Buena Vista Henderson (May 9, 1847–September 30, 1924) was the daughter of John and Emily Young Henderson and the sister of Lieutenant Edward M. "Ned" Henderson. She married W. R. Lord on November 23, 1872.

Camp Toombs Va
Oct 2nd 1861

Dear Susie

The box arrived safe last night. Evrything was all right even the rule which you persisted in sending and had slyly hid. My dear you are the best woman that ever was. Those were Boykins clothes were they not? This suggest to me that I have enough flanel knit shirts and drawers. A flanel overshirt is what I want you to send me. You see I have one and another will do unless it is quite convenient to send. I have enough socks now; three cotton and four woolen pair. Recollect that I will send to Richmond or Augusta by Mr Pitts for some blankets. A great maney of the boys are agoing to do the same. Today we were all payed some money, and of course are in fine spirits. I might have said that spirits are in the boys, as they have drawn whiskey instead of coffee. The government has commenced giving a gill of whiskey daily to the men instead of their rations of coffee. What do you all do for coffee? What can you expect of an oficer when the government gives a ration of whiskey to each soldier. Appropos, I have not chewed two ounces of tobacco in three weeks. I am not saying that I have quit the filthy habit or am going to; but would like to and hope that I will. The truth is, my dear, I am compelled to use but little. The order concerning the three days rations etc. was revoked yesterday. I do not know what our prospects for a fight are. At one time we thought that we would go into a fight the next day. Evrybody thought so. Our pickets were driven in or retreated on purpose from our stronghold this side of Washington. The anemy sent out some regements and destroyed farm houses and evry-thing that they could lay their hand on; but they dared not come out and risk a battle with us. I saw about forty women and children whose homes were burned, and they driven forth upon the world with nothing but what they wore. No one can immagine the deeds of horor that these vile cretures perpetrate. May the Almighty ruler of the universe sheild our beloved country from the horor of civil war into which it is fast murging. Our president is up here. I guess he is looking about to see what is to be done next. Susie, he is one of the noblest men that ever walked. I would like for you to see him. I am anxious to see Beauregard. The whole army worship him. The government has paid us one months wages and each private a little over sixteen dollars. I will send Mr Boykin some money to pay taxes and other purposes; and give Mr Pitts some to buy me some blankets and other things in Richmond or Augusta. It is not the falt of the government that we are not paid. I understand that we will be paid more soon. The soldiers can contribute a great deal to the comfort of their families by remitting their wages home. They do not have an opportunity to buy many foolish things. Our board cost more than a person would expect.

Our sick list is increasing. You must understand that evry man that is not able to do full duty is considered sick and is so reported. Evry one that is not reported sick that does not do duty is put in the guard house if a private and subject to court martial if a commissioned oficer. You see the army regulations are very strict, and our colonel follows them to the letter.[1] An oficer can no more shield his men from duty or the law than he can fly. In other words he has no power over them. To return to the subject, sixty odd of our company are sick. Though I hope none but Jack Young seriously. I heard this evning that they are expecting him to die evry day. Uncle Wisdom has the typhoid fever, so he wrote me today. He is at Centreville attended by Cousin Frank. He is better situated than any of the company. I will write again when Mr Pitts leaves; about Saturday. Good bye, my dear. I hope you are well and happy. Write me a good long letter. Kiss the boy for me. Give my respects to all enquiring friends, especially to Mr Boykin and your Pa's families.
Ugie

1. A correspondent from the 21st Georgia wrote to the editor of the Rome *Weekly Courier* on September 15, 1861, that Colonel Mercer was "a strict disciplinarian—some think too much so—as he has had regulars to deal with who usually require harder treatment than the class of citizens who are in the present service."

Camp Toombs Va
[Oct] 4th 1861

Sir [John T. Boykin Sr.]
Mr. Pitts thinks of starting back tomorrow, and I will send this letter by him.
We are near Fairfax C. H. waiting patiently for something to turn up. I have
no doubt that thare is always more excitement among you all about the war
than thare is with us. You see, we are perfectly ignorant of what is going, and
hear no news, and of course become perfectly indiferent. It is come day, go
day, drill, cook and eat. About a week ago we were expecting a battle; but no
Yankees came and of course no fight. I have no idea what is the policy of our
generals. The President is up here with Beauregard and Johnson. Not long
ago I thought that we would have a forward movement, but our pickets have
retreated back several miles within the last week. This retreat of our pickets
was made in order to draw the anemy out I think. This makes me believe that
we are still acting on the defensive.

We have more than sixty men unfit for duty. Bill Reid and Estes, two of
the men that we lost sight of, came up a few minutes ago. They were sent to
Culpeper about sixty miles from Manassas. Uncle Wisdom has the tiphoid
fever, though I hope not bad. I heard from him yesterday. He is at Centreville
in the same hospitle that cousin Frank has some men. I should have said that
he was boarding at a hotel and not in a regular hospitle. He is very well
situated.

I have been waiting some time for him to go home in order that you could
make some arangements about cultivating that place of Grandma's. I would
like to sow as much wheat and oats as I could conveniently and I think it
would be best to sow that or a part of that place. The principle obsticles to my
doing this is that I would derive no benefit from the pastures and the oats
would be too inconvenient. Do you think it is best to sow it or cultivate it; or
sow a part and cultivate a part. What I do not use I would like to rent to some
clever responsable man. I have not got enough land up at home to sow and cultivate unless I was to curtail my force by hiring Bob or keep a shop.[1] I would
like for you to do about that place just as you think best. Uncle Wisdoms crop
will be somewhat in my way if I sow it. I had better risk your judgement than
my own. I do not have any idea that thare is or will be any chance to sell it
soon. In fact I hear that you can not sell anything and are compelled to pay
cash for evrything.

I wrote to Mr. Wilkerson about that note and told him that I must have
the money this season.[2] I would be glad if you would write to him that I had

instructed you to collect it; you need not let on that I have requested you to write. Using a rather military phrase, this will flank him and place him in a cross fire. Of course we can not pay our debts unless we sell our cotton.

I will send you sixty dollars in Confederate notes. You can pay my tax with it and if thare is anything left pay it to Mrs. Boykin or as you see most fit. It is geting to be rather tight times about money. I understand that we will be paid all that is due us in a few days, though I do not know how true it is. Each private has recieved ($16) sixteen dollars, and each oficer one month's wages. I will send by Mr. Pitts to Richmond for blankets and some other things that I need. If you have already bought them for me, someone else will take them off your hands.

Give my respects to Mrs. Boykin and Lizzie, and accept the best wishes of Your Friend

Ujanirtus Allen

1. Allen contemplated "hiring out" his slave Bob, a skilled blacksmith.

2. In 1854, Jesse Wilkerson had purchased a 200-acre tract from the estate of Robert Allen for $1,500. He still owed $735.30.

Camp Toombs Va
Oct 5 1861

Dear Susie

Mr Pitts starts tomorrow; I write you a few lines tonight. Let me tell the war news first. We have orders this evning to send all our sick and surplus baggage to Manassas. If we do not fight or go upon a forced march now, I will neither prophesy or write you any more war news soon. Several of our sick boys were too bad off to go: C. C. Whatley, Ramsey and Henry Crenshaw. We will probably send them tomorrow, if they are able to go. We have found the boys that we lost sight of. You asked me in a letter not long since, if we went uniformed all the while. No. We wear anything, just so we have a military button or stripe about us. The men go in their shirtsleves all the time. We have as many colors as Joseph's coat.[1] You need not send me any coat. I will send fifteen dollars by Mr Pitts to bye me some blankets in Augusta. I have sent sixty dollars by him to Mr Boykin and retain thirty. If thare is any more than will buy my blankets Pitts will give it to you or Mr Boykin. I hope we will draw more money soon. I send a letter to Mr Boykin. I am looking for one from Berry. Susie I cant write you a long letter tonight, for the boys are all talking about fighting tomorrow, or some day soon. If we have a battle you will hear of it before you get this letter. Mr Pitts will be able to tell you all how we are situated, how we do and evrything else. I will write if anything new turns up. Write me a long sweet letter as usual. I think of nothing else at present. Kiss the boy for me.

Good bye

Ugie

P.S. I have not heard from Uncle Wisdom since I last wrote. We are not allowed to leave camp.

1. The story of Joseph's multicolored coat is told in Genesis 37:1–33.

Camp Toombs Va
Oct 9th 1861

Dear Susie

I recieved two letters written, one on the 26th and the other the 29th, the latter sent from your Pa's with Lizzie's day before yesterday, Monday. I fear that I am never able to interest you as much as your letters do me. However I have often told you that I was a poor correspondent. You say that Thos Britton is coming soon. Horace the prince of Roman poets says: Dulce et gloria est pro patria mori (it is sweet and glorious to die for ones country) but I will asshure you he will soon tire of playing soldier and die of homesickness. Thare are stouter harts than his in this company that pine for home. The polar star of the wanderer's dreams, "How pleasures bright when they take their flight." I think we will send Lonny B and several others home.[1] Sergt Joe Green left here this morning discharged for disability. Some of the boys prophesy that he will take the consumption. I would have sent this letter by him if it had not been for one thing. I had not writen it. I had nuralgea in my face so bad last night that I could not write with any satisfaction. I am very well pleased with that cloth. Exchange for a coat of it by all means, though do not cut it untill I tell you. You have no chance to make a fit; besides I will make an effort to come home about Christmas. The fact is I am compelled to. I am not satisfied to stay away for any length of time with the present arrangement. I am going to write George[2] not to write so much discouraging news home. Walk eight miles a day if it is necessary and fight like blazes if he can get a chance. You need not infer from the above that I am in a very belicose humer. I am discouraged dishartened, mad. Old cloven foot has had the best of me ever since I heard of Joe Brown's election.[3] Ever since I heard that the liberties that we are fighting to perpetuate are usurped by a petty tyrant aided by a fanatical rable. A feeling of mingled sadness and anger pervades the brest of evry Georgian in the army. Thare is greater danger from Brown and his adherents than Abraham Lincoln. He has set at nought a time honored precedent, a precedent laid by the immortal Washington, and claimed the sufrage of the people for the third time, and they foolishly have given it to him.

We heard heavy guns firing all day yesterday and today. I have not heard what it means; it may be on the Potomac. I am not able to give you any sensation news; even if I was I would not give it; for I expect I have frightened you half to deth several times by my imaginary bloody battles. We are standing face to face with the anemy. If we dont fight soon I shall certainly believe that all hands are tierd of the fun, and peace will soon follow. I am looking forward anxiously to the course that other nations will pursue towards us.

Mr Boykin must pursue the course he thinks best about sowing wheat. I would like for it to be sown soon. Tell Berry to put my fatning hogs up as soon as possible. I wrote to him that I wanted evry pound of meat that they would make. It is time they were being put up. You have never wrote me anything about baging and rope.[4] Has Mr Boykin bought his? Is thare any in the market.

I would like the best in the world to have your's and the boy's ambrotipe. I expect it would make me think of home too much. I know he would not look naturel to me. I have seen Lizie's and the childrens. The children look well: but Lizzie looks like she was not in good health. Mr Pitts declares that you look better than you ever did. He flatered you very much. My helth is very good at present; in fact I think I am fatning considerably for the last week. Uncle Wisdom is very sick. I will go to see him today if I can get off. Susie when you write tell me evrything that you can think of. You do not know the pleasure that your letters give. Let me know when you go to your Pa's so that you can get my letters. Don't insist on Jesse's coming to live with you.[5] I would not be satisfied because it would not be voluntary on his part. Ugie

1. Thomas J. (born 1837) and Leonidas A. (born 1842) were sons of the widow Mary Lucinda Walker Britton. Lon enlisted on July 9, 1861, and Thomas joined the company on October 4, 1861. Allen's critical assessment of the Britton boys proved incorrect. Lon served through the war; Thomas was killed in action.

2. George Melton Fuller (born February 23, 1840) was Susan Allen's brother. He was a member of the "LaFayette Guards," Company A, 7th Alabama Regiment, organized at Pensacola, Florida, on May 18, 1861.

3. "Old cloven foot" is a reference to the devil. Joseph E. Brown won his third of four terms as governor of Georgia in October 1861, defeating Judge Eugenius A. Nisbet by 46,493 votes to 32,802.

4. Jute or burlap bagging and rope were used to bind cotton bales.

5. Jesse Gunn Fuller (born July 29, 1831) was another of Susan Allen's brothers. In May 1862, he enlisted in Company I, 47th Alabama Regiment.

Camp Toombs Va
Oct 12th 1861

Dear Susie
I recieved your letter of the 3rd yesterday. I find it is much better for us to acknowledge each letter according to date: for if I was not to write; your letter was recieved, you would not know whether it was the one writen a week or a month ago, unless I was to accidently give some other landmark in my reply. It was my understanding that Thos B & Cousin Robert were not to start untill Mr Pitts got home. This would have been much the best, on account of Mr P buying many things for the boys in Richmond. We recieved a letter from him yesterday. He did not buy any blankets in Richmond. They were selling at $12.00 a pair. I told him not to buy me any if $15.00 would not get two pair. He will hand you the money.

The great muss that we were looking for has turned out so far to be nothing. We all nead such excitement sometimes to cure our sick. You would be surprised to see how many men get better when they hear that thare is a probability of a fight. You might be surprised also to see some well men get sick. The latter are few of course. I do not know whether the health of the company is improving or not; because I do not know how our sick are, only those that are with us. We have some very sick men, some that we fear will never recover. Uncle Wisdom is very low with the fever. I got a chance to see him day before yesterday for the first time. He is as comfortably situated as any one can be. I can say this much about health; that the men look much better and are in much better spirits. They are more cheerful laugh and talk more. Seven eights of the sickness, is billious.[1] We pay more attention to sanitary improvement than we ever did before. Our camp is swept out evry day and the trash and waste from the cook places carried away. The tents are suned whenever the weather permits. The men have a day evry week for washing their clothes and themselves. These are orders from brigade headquarters.

I think that Haywood Lodge was a failure.[2] The story should have been about one fourth longer. Esther Craig was too interesting a character to get lost in such a country and enlightened an age as this. Perhaps John went off to the war and thare was no one to look after her. Better luck to our authoress next time; if she does not use a goose's quill. I form my opinion from what you wrote me.

Monday, October 13th 1861

Susie,

I wrote the above day before yesterday. We have sent no mail from this regiment for two days. I hope we will tomorrow. Cousin Robert and Thomas got here yesterday; and I answer both of your letters in one. I think that you will recieve a letter from me about those clothes before you all send what you have made up. I have writen in reference to evrything that you wish to know of, except the comfort. I brought mine along. Cetch an ancient wesel asleep. Though the next time I go to the wars I will be better prepared. However I am thankful that I [am] about as well off as some others.

Oct 15th 1861

I have fifteen minutes to write to you in. Sometime tonight we go back to Centreville. A battle is at hand. This morning we were woke up by the beating of the long roll. We fell in lines and went forward nearly to Fairfax. And were ordered back. Cannon have been firing off and on nearly all day. They are now throwing up breastworks beyond Fairfax and also at Centreville. Our sick are all sent back. Some were sent off on litters tonight. Boykin is sick. We sent him to Centreville. Uncle W is better. The whole army is on the qui vive. I do not know when we will fight. But am confident that it will be before you get this letter. I think of nothing more to tell you now. Goodbye my dear.
Your boy
Ugie

1. In the nineteenth century, gastric distress, or "biliousness," was attributed to excess bile in the system.
2. Allen again refers to the novelette *The Household at Haywood Lodge* (see n. 2, page 18). Others apparently shared his opinion that the work was too short, as the authoress intended in 1861 writing a sequel that had "been from time to time demanded by the public."

Camp Near Centreville
Oct 17th 1861

Dear Susie

I drop you a few lines tonight to let you know how things are going on. The anemy are advancing on us certain. I hear many conflicting reports about their movements and those of our own army. Some say that they are advancing from towards Leesburg, Washington, and some point below the latter. I do not know the position of our army now. I can see about twenty thousand troops around this place. This is all I know. We are under orders to be ready to march on thirty minutes warning. No soldier is alowed to go more than a half mile from camp and only for a short time. Notwithstanding this, this morning I went to the village to see Boykin and Uncle Wisdom. Boykin is doing well, walking about. Uncle is much better.

We consider a battle inevitable. When, and at what perticular spot I do not know. We have left and burned Fairfax Station though some of our troops are beyond Fairfax C. H. I promise to write to you often. At least evry other day. If we do not move about or fight so as to prevent me. Though I can not ashure you that you will recieve my letters. Evrything in our postal arrangements is turned topsy turvy.

Thos Britton never gave me Berry's letter untill about three days ago. I will write to him when I can. Tell him that no man of our company has ever went to sleep on his post. I will try to answer your letters more in detail soon. Give my respects to all.
Good bye Susie.
Ugie

P.S. While I was away this morning myself and Dr. Hurst made a coffin and assisted by Lee Crouch and John Mathews buried one of our dear soldiers, Henry W. Crenshaw, who died on the 14th. Those men would have been put in the guard house and myself arrested and court martialed if we had been found absent from the regiment. I state this to let you know how things go here. The people at home are ignorant of our situation and slander us by saying that we are not doing our duty towards our men. Direct your letters to Manassas Junction, care Capt Boykin, Co F 21st Ga Volunteers, Col Mercer commanding.

Camp Near Centreville Va
Oct 19th 1861

Dear Susie
I sent you a few lines yesterday, and will mail this today if I finish it before the mail leaves at 12 M. It is raining a little this morning, and we are buisy packing evrything unnesesary for our present comfort to be sent to Manassas. We send the arms of the sick men, a great many clothes some tents and in fact evrything that would retard our progress on a march. My trunk is packed with evrything

that I have including blankets, ready to move at any moment. I do not know where the yankees are what they are doing or what they intend to do. I hear that Beauregard has fallen back with his corps (core) of the army from Fairfax. You must understand that the army of the Potomac is divided into two corps one under Beauregard the other Smith[1], the whole under Johnson[2]. We belong to Smith's corps. We are throwing up breastworks in four places here at the vilage. We keep our guns in order all the while. Did I write you that we are ordered to be ready to strike tents load wagons and be in lines on thirty minutes notice. I hear some cannons firing accasionaly this morning. If I knew anything definite I would write it to you. Of course we hear a thousand and one rumors, but do not know what to credit. We hear that the anemy are at Fairfax station and C. H. Then we hear that thay have advanced but little. I have not seen Boykin or Uncle Wisdom since I last wrote but they are doing well. Cousin R passes backward and forward evry day. Another one of our dear comrades died night before last: Benny Robinson. All of our sick except three are at Sudley Church[3] near where the Yankees crossed Bull run on the 21st July. We have no control of our sick. We can not even detail a man to wait upon them either in camp or in the hospitles. We are not allowed to leave camp to go to see them. I have seen Uncle W twice since he left camp once with permission once without. Lt Waller has seen our sick once since we left Pageland. We have some well men about ten of the company besides others that are at Sudley detained thare to cook and nurse the sick about 300. They do not do as they aught. John Bedington is the only one of our company thare that is worth a cent. He has a hart as big as a house. He cooks for about forty sick men and bares the curses of as many more who are able but two lazy to cook for themselves. We intend to have him away from thare if it is possible. We hear that he is imposed on by the men about cooking. Billy Bennett acts a noble part waiting on the sick. We do not see those things but hear them. Thos Briton who returned from thare yesterday is my author. We have six very sick men Gus Ramsey, Cicero Whatley, Doler Cooley, Mr Vance, Tommy Haralson, and Williams. These are dangerous. When our men get the fever they seem to loose all spirit and linger along untill they die. The doctors say this is the nature of camp fever. But I have no doubt much of it is the result of their situation, surrounded as they are by sick and dying away from home and friends. It is noted fact that men in the army do not have the simpathy for each other that they do at home. Admit that they do; and they can not manifest it on evry occasion. Be careful how you give any statement that I make in my letters. People do not comprehend our situation and surroundings.

I recieved your very pleasant letter of the 11th this morning. I do not know where to begin answering it at. I will begin by saying that some questions are answered in letters on the way to you. I see that you all have sent your boxes. We will not endeaver to get them from Manassas, even if they come untill all this excitement passes over. I do not expect them in several days yet. Evrything else might go for a season if I could only get the ambrotipe. That bad boy; I do not know what you are to do with him. I shall be mad with Prophitt if he has made you as black as some of your ambrotipes.[4] I anticipate its arival with a great deal of pleasure. Before I forget it let me thank Jim[5] for his present. Tell him that I highly apreciate such manifestations of kind feeling from him and the others. I acord to you the palm in writing letters. You certainly write more or as much in two as I do in four pages. Write me one a mile long and I will violate one order here: not to leve camp more than a half mile and only for an hour. I infered from what Mr Boykin wrote, and so did Boykin that Lizzie was not in good health. Though I confess that he is no better proof against homesickness than myself; especialy when he is sick. Comparitively speeking I think I can do tolerably well as long as you are satisfied and happy, and my afairs flow smoothly along. This is becoming a very serious consideration with me; one that I have felt a delicacy in mentioning. I do not see what in the world I am to do. I dislike to throw you upon anybody; I can not do it. I can not think of any arrangement for you to stay at home. What can you suggest? I sometimes think that I aught never to have come. At others; that I am doing my duty and can not desert my country in the hour of her peril. I do not know whether Mars and Venus well agree or not. I am not such a military spirit that I have forgoton or will forget you and the boy. Not long since I heard a man say that if he ever got home again he would be a model husband. He had always thought that he was doing well; but if he got home he would do evrything that his wife even hinted or sugested without ever being asked. And that his whole time should be spent in a way conducive to her pleasure. Besides this I have heard several young fellows say that they intended to marry as soon as the war ended. I think that a very good arrangement about sowing wheat. I am satisfied with Mr Boykin's judgement about anything. Berry writes me that I will not make more than 15 bales of cotton. How does my cotton compare with his. This is less than I ever dreamed of and of course am anxious to know if it averages with evrybody else. I want my meat hogs as fat as corn and good care can make them. We are expecting the anemy evry day. They are coming; no doubt about that. I will write frequently. Good bye

Your boy,

Ugie

P.S. Direct to Manassas Junction, Care Capt Boykin, Co F 21st Reg Ga Volunteers, Col Mercer Com'd'g

1. Major General Gustavus Woodson Smith (1821–96) was a senior division commander in General Joseph E. Johnston's army in northern Virginia in the fall of 1861.

2. For a time, both the Confederate army defending Richmond and its Federal counterpart were known as the "Army of the Potomac." The name Army of Northern Virginia did not gain wide acceptance until June 1862, when Robert E. Lee assumed command and began to use it.

3. The wartime Sudley Church stood two miles north of the intersection of the Warrenton Turnpike and the Manassas–Sudley Road. A new church building replaced the war-torn structure in 1873.

4. Pleasant G. Prophitt had established a photography studio in LaGrange in 1853. Ambrotype images were produced by using a light-sensitive collodion coating on a glass plate.

5. Jim (born 1826) was one of Allen's slaves.

3

SUDLEY CHURCH HOSPITAL

But the soldier who dies from sickness is no less to be honored
than he that dies on the battlefield . . .

ILLNESS depleted the ranks of the 21st Georgia in the fall of 1861 as the men took their turn at picket duty, labored on fortifications around Centreville, Virginia, and prepared for the coming winter. With thousands of susceptible recruits thrown together in camps, such diseases as measles, typhus, and typhoid fever were epidemic. Rheumatism, harder to diagnose and easier to feign, was also a common complaint. Diarrhea and dysentery persisted throughout the war, often weakening soldiers to the point that they succumbed to other diseases. Treatment was usually little more than confinement to hospital—with occasional doses of opium, calomel, or quinine—until the disease ran its course. Soldiers stricken with the more serious ailments might be unfit for duty for several weeks.

Ugie Allen was one of many members of the 21st Georgia who fell ill after only a few months of service. His symptoms, including "fever of a bilious type" and skin irritations, suggest that he probably suffered from typhus.

The gap in Allen's correspondence between December 21, 1861, and January 30, 1862, suggests that he managed to return home, although there is no mention of it in his service record. His plea for Susie to maintain strict secrecy about the matter hints that the leave might have been unofficial. A little more than a week after his return to the army, Allen received orders detaching him "on recruiting service to Troup County, Georgia." Once again, he left Virginia for home.

Camp Sudley Church
Oct. 28th 1861

Dear Susie

I wrote to you about eight days ago, and have not had an oportunity of writing since. I know that you will be very much distressed by my not writing if Boykin has not wrote the cause. The next day after I wrote my last letter I was buisy on the fortifications at Centreville and the next our regiment was out on picket guard and did not get home in five days; that is Saturday evening; that night I could not write owing to company in my tent. Yesterday, Sunday, we moved camp and I was detailed to come here and take charge of this place which is the hospitle of our regiment. I am now purched upon a box and write upon a table for the first time since I left home. I have been on the trot all day and it is now late at night and I fear that I will not be able to write all that I wish. However it is a gratification to be able to write to you after so long an interval even if I only say that I am well, greeting you with my familiar fist on the envelope.

I am comfortably situated here. I board at a private house and sleep in a tent. Last night I had not assumed command and slept at a private house on feathers. You aught to have seen me nestling down among them. I know I acted like a child. Who could have helped it when for three months they had touched nothing but a common gray blanket. I do not know but that I sleep as sound here as I do at home. It may be because I am geting used to it. I don't believe I do unless fatigued. Much is owing to circumstance.

The regiment is still near Centreville. Sudley Church is where the Yankees crossed Bull Run on the 21st July. Uncle Wisdom is discharged and will come home as soon as practicable. Boykin is about well, has come back to camp and will go to duty tomorow. He said that he was agoing down to Manassas today after our things. I hope he will. I am quite anxious to get them. The men all are grumbling for theirs. So we thought it best to send for them Yankees or no Yankees. I shall go to Manassas tomorrow myself to draw rations for the hospitle. Thos Briton has the measles. Our company has thirty sick men here and several in Richmond. These are not all sick but are unfit for duty. My dear excuse this short note. I will write again in four days from now as I will go to Manassas again then.
Ugie

P.S. Will tell you about being on picket in my next letter.
Ugie

Sudley Church Virginia
Nov 4th 1861

Dear Soudie
I received your letter of the 20th tonight which found me in quite different circumstances to which you anticipated or hoped for. I am quite sick and have been for some days though I hope and think nothing serious. I have had fever of a billious type and been badly salivated and have suffered very much with my throat but I hope I am now improving. Don't suffer any uneasiness about me, for if I get dangerously ill I will write you immediately. I feel something better tonight than I have felt. The health of our company is bad at this time, at least half sick at this place. No recent deaths amongst us. Our sick are generally convalsecent and I hope will get well soon. We have had some white frosts which I hope will be an advantage to our sick men.

I received a lot of clothing and such like articles from home this evening. They all came up right except some few things I reckon Capt Boykin kept out at the Regiment. I was more than glad to hear that your Mother was improving the last I had from you stated that she had had a stroke of Palsey and I awfully feared the consequences. I hope she may entirely recover soon. Mr. Wisdom will bring this letter to you and he can tell you all and more than I think to write to you. I hope to hear from you so soon as you get this and hope to be in such health as to write more next time.
Your affectionate husband
E U Allen

P.S. Sousie I write this for Ugy and say to you not to be uneasy about him for he shall have the necissary attention and I dont think he will be confined long. Give my respects to Lizzie and receive the same for yourself.
W. Reid Hurst

Remember me to Sallie when you see her. W. R. H.

Sudley Church Nov 10th 1861

Sousy

I again write to you from this place. I am yet quite sick and have been ever since I wrote to you before. I can't say that I am improving much, very little if any. I am at a private house and with a clever family. They do I guess all in their power to make me as comfortable as possible. Henry Rowland has been quite sick in the same room with me. He is getting about again. Dr. Hurst has been staying with us all the time. You need not fear but that I get as good attention, in the way of nursing as I could wish so far from you. I have not yet despared but still hope I may get well and see you again; you shall hear from me often while I am sick. I think I forgot to mention in my last that I received the Ambrotype sent by you and am really proud of it. I dont know any news to write you more than I suppose the health of our company is improving a little. Thos Gilham died a few days ago; good bye for this time. Kiss the babe for me and write to me often.
Your affectionate husband
U Allen by W. Reid Hurst

P.S. Sousy when you see Sallie tell her that I have had an attact of fever, which reduced me very much in a few days, but I think with care I shall soon get over it. Give my love to Sallie & Berry and his wife and accept for yourself my warmest regards.
W. Reid Hurst

Sudley Church Hospital Virginia
Nov 16th 1861

Sousy,

I received your letter of the 6th this evening. The contents were duly appreciated. I am glad to inform you that I am improving fast. I think if I take no back set I shall [be] up in a few days. As soon as I get able to travel I shall come home and if I only come on furlow. Now I shall quit the army right away and come home to attend to my own concerns and be with my own dear Sousy. I have had a very severe time of it I assure you, but now am mending fast I think. I think I shall be able to start home by the first of December and can get there by the 7th or 8th of December. By that time I think you may look for me. Boykin was down to see me yesterday. He is well. The health of our company is still improving. No fighting news since I wrote you before that is reliable. Write to me again as soon as you get this for it does me a great deal of good to hear from home. Write often. Kiss the babe for me.

Your affectionate husband

U. C. Allen. Written by my friend W. Reid Hurst

Sudley Church Hospital

Dec 1st 1861

Dear Susie

I wrote you a letter about eight days ago, and would have wrote sooner if I could write as I used to, and not get tiered. The fact is I have not been noticing the days of the week or month and the time has passed off much faster than I was aware. I am able to go up and down a small flight of stairs to the table without help. I find it much easier to go up than down for I can crawl up. I sometimes think that I am doing well; at others I almost dispair of ever recovering. I have been out of doors twice. I went out this morning to see two fine hogs. They are about twenty one months old and will weigh near four hundred pounds; and will weigh much more when thoroughly fat. They are of the white Chester variety or breed that you see spoken of by my papers. You think I am geting better; dont you? The weather is cold windy & rainy in other words bad and I have been afraid to get out. For my liver is still torpid and, my face still a little swolen, my scalp tender and my ears sensative and one still running. I should have been out more if I had my overcoat which I loned out to be returned several days ago.

I have wrote to you about resigning, coming home and furlough etc. I understand that nobody can get a furlough unless they are sick and it is recommended by the surgeon. I am looking for a reply to my last letters. These I hope you have replied to in detail. I feel like hearing your opinions and feelings freely expressed. I suffer much anxiety on your account. I frequently fear that no one takes any interest in your welfare or my negroes and farm. Mr Boykin has never writen me a line since I left home. I know nothing of the prospect the people have for paying debts or any business tranactions. I do not know whether it is proposed that my cotton shall lay in the gin house or be gined and packed. I do not know what the people are doing about their cotton. I do not know whether my crop will pay store accounts and other debts or whether my plantation will absorb the pecuniary reward of my sufferings.

Now about those reports. First, the intercourse between me and Boykin has been as pleasant and agreeable as ever in our lives since we left home. Second, I have never known whiskey to sell at more than eight dollars a gallon. I do not know what price it has rose to since I left the regiment. I can clear myself of drinking much twelve dollar whiskey. I left home with sixty dollars. Paid over fifty for sword and uniform sent seventyfive home by Mr. Pitts and now the government owes me three months wages. If I drank much I certainly eat but little. I have taken a good many drinks since I have been in service; but I feel responsible to no person but yourself for it, and my creditors for what it cost me. Indeed I have bought none except when I was on picket and since I have been convalescent. I have not seen Boykin since he came to see me when I was sick. I understand that the regement goes on picket about evry two weeks. I hear that some men (not of our company) went to sleep on their post, built fires and left their post when last out and will probably be shot. I hear rumors of an advance on the part of the Yankees; but do not know what faith to put in it.

I am going to the regement to see them all as soon as I can. I shall apply for a furlough or sick leave then or resign. Much depends on circumstances and your reply to my last letter. I shall quit the defence of my country only when circumstances require it. I shall always consider a mans first duty is to his family and next to his country.

They are breaking up this hospital and sending the men to Culpepper. I hear no prospect of winter quarters from good authority. The fact is we can not go into winter quarters untill the anemy does and they think they can stand a southern campaign. My dear I am much fatigued writing and will quit. Accept my love and kiss the boy.
Ugie

Second Ga. Hospital[1]
Richmond Va
Dec 11th 1861

My Dear Susie
I know you are uneasy about me. I would have wrote sooner: but I expected to have had a sick leave before this time, and of course would have got home before you could recieve a letter. I applied to the surgeon for a certificate or recomendation for a leave of absence, and he gave me one for thirty days. I

wanted to get it through as soon as possible, and caried it to the Brigadier Gen'l myself. My face was (and is) bloated by the eracipulas[2] and he told me I was too good looking a fellow to grant such a furlough to: and only recommended one of ten days. I told him I cared nothing for his ten days as I knew I would not be put to duty in twice that length of time. So here I am; and expect to stay here or rather at a private boarding house just as long as I can find it agreeable. The brigadier Gen'l and his ten day furlough may go to grass. I am getting tiered of being snubbed by these arrogant [page torn].

I arrived here this morning. Boykin and Waller left for home this morning. I have not seen them. I may apply for a sick leave here. I do not know that I will or if I do, with what success. If sick leaves are not made for sick or convalescent men God only knows what they are for. I think I would improve very fast under faverable circumstances. The last few days exposure has been a great disadvantage to me. The last letter that I recieved from you was dated about the middle of last month. I will send you some money. I am not as flush as you might supose, from my last letter. I am out over seventy dollars since I was taken sick. I have a very bad headache from riding on the cars. Let me close. I know these few lines are more agreeable than none. I will write regular. I think of you and that bad boy often. Kiss him for me.

Your boy

Ugie

P.S. I have not sent any money to you in this letter.

1. The Second Georgia Hospital, also called General Hospital No. 14, was in a warehouse on the west side of 20th Street, between Main and Franklin, in downtown Richmond.

2. Erysipelas, a bacterial blood infection also known as the Rose, or St. Anthony's Fire, caused symptoms similar to those of a staph infection—fever, swelling, and irregular red blotches on the skin.

Second Ga. Hospitle
Richmond Va. Dec 14th 1861

Dear Susie

I wrote you a letter four days ago and sent it by Billy Strong who left for home the next morning. I am now boarding at a very nice private house (five dollars a week) and am geting along swimingly. I have an all consuming appetite. Am doing well. I went up on Main Street yesterday and into a restaurant and ate a dollar and fifteen cents worth of ham, fish, eggs, oysters etc. I often wished, when I began to improve, that I could have you to prepare me something to eat. This reminds me of a good joke (or rather fact) that we have on Thos B.[1] He is a little sick and has no appetite. You know he talks rather long and as he is always talking about it; the boys say "he is longing for just a little milk and mush." Poor soldiers they can not have evry thing they want or is even necessary. O you rebels, who dare take up armes against your country, this glorious union; you ask for furloughs and milk and mush! but nary time do you get either. The fact is and I will confess it to you, I sometimes feel much mortified at my ill success. Not that I am pining or sighing like a home-sick school boy, for I can dash evry thought of home and evry one, save you and my boy, from my mind. But I have been denied a privilege which is some-times alowed others and would have contributed much to my benefit without injuring the service. Tell me is thare any diference to the service whether I am in Richmond or Ga, when off of duty?

I have just been rereading the letters recieved from you when I was sick. They give me great pleasure. In the last letter you write me or at least the last I recieved, you write that you had hired McCommock.[2] I never wrote to you about hiring him because I was undicided in my mind what to do. I hope he will do well and you may be happy in the course you have chosen. You are right and have pursued the best plan I know of: but I fear that he is unfit for the position that he holds. You know it will take quite an intelligent and busi-ness fellow to carry on my farm scatered as it is, when he has no one to look after him but an unexperienced woman. I will have to buy another mule or trade my horse for one or work the horse alltogether. If the horse can stand the work it is best to work him. I don't want ever who attends to my business to have any excuse, or he will rue the day that he went on that place. For as certain as I live if anybody impose on you or our little estate in any maner I will make them repent it. Would I flinch from being revenged upon anyone under such circumstances. If a person represent themselves as capable of doing certain things and demand a renumeration according and prove them-selves incapable; what recourse have you or I to get justice? To their con-cience? No, they have none. To law? No. Nothing remains but to pursue the most primitive mode of acquiring justice; which is to be revenged. "Sweet is revenge; especially to woman, pilige to soldiers, prize money to seamen."

I do not know what to say about the Yankees. We are waiting for them to come and cannot go into winter quarters. It seems providential that the win-ter has been mild so far. If it had not been more mild than usual the soldiers would have sufered much. They are doing better than you might expect as they have built little turf chimneys to their tents, which they can even cook as well as warm by. Soldiers can do very well in good weather. I often compare a soldier's life to the character in the story and tune "Arkansaw Traveler."[3]

I have been looking for an epistle from Berry for sometime. When you write tell me how evrything is geting along. Will I make enough meat? The weather has been so warm I do not expect you have killed and my hogs are quite fat. I truly regret to hear of your Pa and Jesse's misfortunes. I hope that, as your Ma is improving faster than you or the Dr. first thought, your fears about her walking will never be realised.[4] Please remember me kindly to all, as well Mr. Boykin's family. Of course I include Lizzie. Jeff Sample and Lee Crouch arrived here yesterday morning. Jeff has an extremely violent attact of the feaver. I mean what I say. He is quite sick. George Terry is so low that he can not be moved from camps. With these exceptions I think the boys are doing well. Sam Rowland came down when I did. He has the fever though I do not think he is seriously ill. I have not seen him since he came. He was sent to one hospitle and me another, and I have not been able to find him. He is at none of the Ga Hospitles. I am going to as many of the general hospitles tommorrow as I can find. Good bye my dear Susie. Kiss our sweet boy.
U Allen

1. Thomas Britton.
2. Robert McCormack had worked as an overseer for Susan's father in Chambers County, Alabama.
3. "The Arkansas Traveler," a popular nineteenth-century fiddle tune, is ascribed to Sanford C. Foster. The lyrics describe a conversation held in 1840 in the Boston Mountains of Arkansas between a squatter and a group of prominent state politicians.
4. Susan's mother Stacey Fuller suffered a stroke in October 1861. She died in February 1862.

Richmond Va
Dec 19th 1861

Dear Susie
I recieved your letter of the 18th November when I was at the Regement and have not heard from you since. I know that I am anxious to hear from you by this time. I wrote to Ned Henderson (or Lieut. Henderson I should have said) this morning to send my letters down here. I would tell you to direct yours here: but I know several would come here after I had left. I know you will hear of the deth of T. J. Sample before this reaches you. I had him put in a zink coffin and will not bury him in some time hoping that they will come after him amediately. I am informed that some of the family is necessary for his removal. I wish that I was able to pay a just tribute to his memory. I would be glad if I could find something that would interest you. Like the rest of the world seems to be doing I am joging along liesurely pursuing the even tenor of my way. Thare is no war news at all. You have probably seen an account of

the excitement in England about the Mason and Slidell capture.[1] I do not put much reliance in such excitements. We have nothing to hope for from that quarter only such as indeed is strictly to their interest. Slave holders have no friends thare.

You will not recieve this before Christmas holidays. I would be glad if I could be with you all. How sad it is to compare our as well as the situation of the country last Christmas and now. It will not be long before Boykin and Waller will be poling off from home for Manassas. I expect to turn my face in that direction before long. I would like for them to take up winter quarters before I do. You would like for me to be looking the other way wouldn't you? I will when I find it will avail me something. Susie my dear, I cant write untill I hear from you. It is true I might say something about my business at home. But what good will it do, I do not think that you are all burdened with numerous financial transactions. I do not even hope to be paid by those that owe me and of course can not pay those that I owe. However I will leave all this to Mr. Boykin, as he is somewhat interested. It is a great pity that I am not at home for Mitch Wilder to dun.[2] I do not know what the poor man will do unless he pounces on Mr. Boykin. I hope to be able to send you near two hundred dollars soon after Christmas, however you need not hint it to anyone, for I know that you and Mr. Boykin would be almost run mad by creditors, especially our cousin M. W. I thought that I could have been at home before now, or I should have written to Mr B and Berry. You must write often and tell me evrything. I know that I can not give you the same pleasure in writing that you do me. Kiss our dear boy for me.
Your boy
Ugie

1. On November 8, 1861, the USS *San Jacinto,* commanded by Captain Charles Wilkes, stopped the British packet *Trent* off the Cuban coast and seized Confederate emissaries James Mason and John Slidell, who had run the blockade and were bound for Europe.

2. Allen's irritation at being dunned by Mitchell Wilder stems from the fact that Wilder's stepmother Mary had owed Allen $26.05 since December 1860.

Richmond Va
Dec 21st 1861

Dear Susie
I send you these few lines to inform you that I have an idea of trying to get a furlough in a few days. If I do I will spend some of the Christmas holidays at

home. Now mark the request that I am about to make of you: keep this a profound secret. Do not breathe it to anyone, not even the family. I have good reasons for making this request, or would not do it. Promise that you will. Good bye
Ugie

Camp near Manassas
Jan 30th 1862

Dear Susie
I am here at last after being delayed in Richmond one day and wading about two miles in mud last night. Capt Boykin has been sent back to R on the sick list; diarea and cough. He will be back soon. Thare are not less than twenty applications for furloughs in our company now. You may look out for them. I will send this letter by some of the boys who will start today. It is now raining. Our camp is about three inches deep in mud. I understand that the roads are from two to twenty feet deep. Lieut Henderson is sick in Richmond. Allen was sent off yesterday.[1] Col Mercer is very sick. Col Morrison is absent in Richmond. None of our men are sick [except] Billy Bennett. Some few are off duty. It is cold and disagreeable today. We are not as pleasantly situated as I expected to find. The officers have nothing but their tents to stay in. I can tell my situation in a very [few] words; mudy, wet, cold, and almost sick from fatigue. John Terry and Thos Britton start home in a few minutes. I wish that I could write twenty pages. I will write tomorrow or next day. This is not a letter. Write me a long letter.
Your boy
Ugie

1. This is probably a reference to Captain Boykin's servant. There was no other soldier named Allen in the Ben Hill Infantry.

Camp near Manassas
Feb 1st 1862

Dear Wife
According to promise I write again today. It is quite late and I fear Morpheous will draw his folds around me before I say as much as I would like too. I said it

was late, and so it is; for I have been ever since morning troting and writing for some of our men who are going home on furloughs. Seven go and forty seven bore the surgeons with applications. The medical director of the division of the army is about closing down on the furlough sistem so as to not grant any only to men sick in bed.

I told you that Capt Boykin was in Richmond, so is Lieuts Henderson and Waller. I look for Boykin and Waller back in a few days. Boykin told me that the surgeon told him to remain untill he was entirely well; but he was not agoing to remain much longer. I saw Robert Hunt and Jesse Gunn both in Richmond. I also saw Robt Denham. He was just convalescing from a atact of pneumonia. A great many of Capt McCoy's men are sick.[1] He has lost several more men than we have, probably four; Capt Ferrell has lost more than him.[2] Both of them are now at home on furloughs. The 14th Ala is in very comfortable quarters and I predict great sanitary improvement. Our men have tolerable pine pole cabins about half of which are covered with boards the others are covered with the tents which do much better. They have no floors and are generally muddy; I might have said sloppy. However the most industrious have put up beds to sleep on and boxes for cupboards and are doing well. Nothing has been done to our own quarters; but I will commence halling logs and geting boards tomorrow. I am in one of our marques and with the aid of an extempore chimney would make out to survive a few days, if I could have more room than two feet square. The tent is filled with beds boxes trunks etc. which I can occupy if I sit. However if I wish to stand I must go out of doors ancle deep in mud, put my hands in my pockets, look as unconcerned as a downeast Yankee and whistle dixie to keep my courage up. I am siting in the space spoken of now and write this letter on my lap holding both ink and candle. Our boys are all in good health and enjoy themselves finely as thare is no duty to do. They eat beef and talk of the war and furloughs. John Higginbothem tells a good joke on Ol.[3] He says that Sue[4] wrote him that his sweatheart was passing and saw some of his clothes hanging out in the sun and burst out crying. Probably you will not appreciate this as much as the boys do who have left sweathearts behind. I would like for you to let me know where George is so that I can write to him. Sam Rowland has applied for a discharge. I have defered signing it untill the captain comes. This I think is the proper plan for me to pursue. As he will soon be here and would not give his own signature if he was here. I find that thare is no earthly chance for me to get away without a surgeons certificete. Lieut Branch[5] of Capt Borders[6] company has resigned five times and it has not been accepted. They consider that thare is a moral obligation devolving on the oficers to stay with the men that they brought into the service. I have a thousand and one things that I would like to tell you about many things that I did not have a definite idea of when I left home. The boys are surprised that so many reports are in circulation about them individually and the company. Ol Fears has never killed a hog though someone at this time unknown to me did. John Higginbothem has had no dificulty with the Colonel nor has never been in the guard house. Some of our, or I might have said Capt Boykins bitterest anemies are soon coming home. Our suspicions are well confirmed by many circumstances. It is growing very late and I must close. Goodbye my dear. Kiss our boy for me. I would be proud if I could be with you.

Your boy

Ugie

1. Hunt, Gunn, and Denham were members of Captain Daniel H. McCoy's Company C, 14th Alabama Regiment, "Tom Watts' Greys." The Greys were one of five companies recruited in Chambers County that served in the 14th Alabama.

2. Mickleberry P. Ferrell became captain of Company F, 14th Alabama Regiment, on June 27, 1861, and was promoted to the rank of major on July 27, 1861. On December 2, 1862, he resigned from the army owing to chronic diarrhea.

3. Oliver T. Fears.

4. Susan M. Higginbothem was the older sister of Private John T. Higginbothem.

5. John L. Branch (1835–1920), a lieutenant in Company D, 21st Georgia, finally succeeded in resigning on February 4, 1862. On June 21, 1862, he enlisted as a private in Company A, 1st Georgia Cavalry. He was later appointed surgeon of the 1st Georgia Cavalry and served through the war.

6. Stephen A. Borders was captain of Company D, 21st Georgia Regiment. He resigned November 13, 1861, owing to disability and became captain of Company H, 10th Georgia State Guard Regiment.

Camp near Manassas
Feb 4th 1862

Dear Susie

I sent you a letter about two days ago by Sergt Henry Rowland and in order to keep up a continued current of news will write today and forward by mail. I do not know that I have anything new or interesting to write, but a few lines will be more agreable than none at all. I know this from my own feelings as I am quite anxious to hear from you and sincerely hope you have not waited for a letter from me before you wrote. I never wanted to hear from you so bad in my life. Write and let me know if Mr Boykin got Aleck Sample or not.[1]

I never can be satisfied away from you. With the love and society of you and our boy my cup of hapiness is filled. Long, long have I strugled to conciel the agony of feeling that I endure by being absent from you. In vain have I endeavored to assume an air of indiference to smother those outburst of sorrow that continually rise. But I am not my own master and confess my weakness to you only now.

It snowed here all day yesterday. I think it will average five inches, if not more. It is much colder here than I have known it at home in several winters, though the boys do not apear to care for it very much. I see some of the most hardy passing about without coats. We have no regular duty to do except guarding a few posts; such as the comissary wagonyard etc. The detail is not more than two men from a company. However the boys have to cut and bring their wood about three hundred yards. This, cooking, and roll call about three times daily is all. As for myself I have had some little dodging about to do as the captain has been here but two days. He probably would have remained longer if Lieut W. had have not gone to Richmond and it had not been necessary that we should finish our own quarters and those of the company. Thare is such a pressure for the teams that we must devote our attention to it personally or we will not get our dues. Immagine yourself in a tent frosen perfectly stiff. I can not say that we suffer any with cold. A good tent with fly and chimney is far preferable to a poor cabin. We would have a fine opportunity to improve ourselves by reading and study if it was not that bores and loafers did not predominate. I would be glad if the boys were supplied with a good number of books and papers, for the time imployed in persuing them would neither be lost, passed in idle talk or devilment. An interesting book is as much proof against the devil as a patent sermon. It was demonstrated a few Sundies ago that the men take more interest in an extempore cock fight than our Chaplain's warnings. The way of it was this. Shortly after preaching two cocks met and pitched into each other fiercer than two prise fighters; and a greater crowd collected than was at preaching. Among them were captains, lieutenants, privates, negroes, dogs and I would not be surprised if some of our old brokendown team horses did not catch the mania for this good catholic recreation. You may have the above nonsense for the trouble of reading it.

My cough has returned with more frequency, but less violence. A good many of our boys are troubled with coughs and diarhea. The latter I have no doubt is caused by imprudence. Some of them do not cook more than once a day and then eat enough to kill a horse. As a natural consequence, for the next forty eight hours they are unable to do duty. The fell destroyer death has again visited our ranks and we mourn the loss [of] John Betterton who died of nervous fever at Culpepper Courthouse on February 1st. He was a good boy and universaly beloved by both oficers and men. Write me a good long letter when you recieve this. I am geting so that I can hardly spell the most simple word. Kiss the boy for me. Name him Susie! Robert, Bartow, Edgar, or after myself if you choose. I would have sent you my ambrotipe if it had not been a cloudy day when I was in Richmond.[2] I hope I will get a chance to go again before spring.

Your boy

Ugie

1. James A. Sample (born 1828) was recruited as an overseer by John T. Boykin Sr. Sample enlisted in the Ben Hill Infantry on September 16, 1862.

2. Long exposure time and bright natural light were required for the ambrotype process. Some enterprising photographers traveled with tents equipped with a special skylight.

Camp near Manassas

Feb 7th 1862

Dear Susie

I would not write untill tomorrow but I have just been making out some muster rolls and have pen, ink, etc. convenient, so I write. You are more indebted to circumstances than inclination for this letter. For I have not more than two or three things to communicate. Captain Boykin was attacted with colora morbus[1] last night. However he is much better today, in fact doing well. I think he will be able for duty tomorrow, at least I hope so. I think it will be at least ten days before we get into our quarters. The teams are so poor and the roads so bad that it is almost impossible to get our timber halled.

It is necessary for one of us to come home recruiting soon, and as Waller and Henderson are absent and Capt Boykin wants to come after a while (which I would prefer) I think it will be me.[2] However if the captain does not improve of course he will come. We may come soon or probably a month hence. Let that be as it will. I do not want you to let any one know this for I might not be so fortunate as to get the apointment. Positively you must not let any one know this except Lizzie. You know my dear, how unpleasant it would be for me to be disapointed in this matter, especially if it became public.

This is all I have to write tonight. This is not a long letter, but I know you will pardon the briefness on account of the news. At least I would, and of course do.

Your boy

Ugie

1. Symptoms of cholera morbus, such as diarrhea and vomiting, mimicked those of the virulent epidemic cholera. Also known as cholera infantum, it was a common killer of children but was less often fatal for adults.

2. Allen's compiled service record reveals that he was detached on recruiting service beginning February 10, 1862.

4

ALONG THE RAPPAHANNOCK

I have been under fire of the anemy.

URING his month back in Troup County, Lieutenant Allen recruited twenty-seven new men for the Ben Hill Infantry. The recruits were welcome additions to the ranks; death had claimed several of the company's original volunteers, others had been discharged, and still others had been detached on special duties. Allen expressed contempt for many men in the latter group, including those who managed to find jobs as teamsters or hospital stewards.

Conditions in northern Virginia changed dramatically during Allen's absence. Confederate army commander Joseph E. Johnston pulled his forces back to the Rappahannock River in early March 1862, fearing that the Federals would bypass his defenses and march on Richmond from Fredericksburg or some point farther down the Potomac. General Richard S. Ewell's division, which included the 21st Georgia, helped cover the Confederate retreat from the old lines around Manassas.

Johnston initially concentrated much of his army south of the Rappahannock River in the vicinity of Orange Court House and Gordonsville. By early April 1862, with an enormous Federal army massing at the tip of the peninsula between the James and York rivers, Johnston began shifting his troops to meet the new threat to Richmond. Ewell's division was left behind with orders to guard the crossings of the Rappahannock.

On March 28, 1862, when Ewell learned of Johnston's impending move to Richmond, he ordered the destruction of the Orange and Alexandria Railroad trestle over the Rappahannock. Ugie Allen was among the detachment from the 21st Georgia that helped army engineers destroy the span. Approaching Union forces made the work hazardous, but the Confederates succeeded in burning the bridge and detonating explosives that toppled the arches spanning the massive stone abutments. The Ben Hill Infantry came under fire for the first time when Federal artillery fired shells across the river at southern soldiers watching the conflagration.

Wilmington N.C.
March 17th 1862

Dear Susie
We arived here about three hours ago and will not leave untill 2 PM today. We overtook two N.C. Regiments going to Newbern and failed to make connection or we should have got to Richmond tonight. I can not say when we will get thare. It is rumored here that the Federals have shelled Newbern, and also a boat filled with ladies. I think they are capable of doing anything mean. I have been looking about for the trunk that Boykin and Baily Reid lost, but have not found it. So far all of our baggage is safe; ten boxes and a trunk. The boys depend on me a great deal, many of them having never traveled. I am lucky in knowing the route and all the little minutia. I learn that our [army] has fallen back shure enough. I anticipate some trouble finding the Regement. I saw Dr. Blair[1] yesterday. He says that Col Mercer has gone back. Sam Fears did not meet me at LaGrange.[2] I expect he could not cross the creek. If he does not overtake me I will send him transportation as soon as I am able. Berry is all right and so are all the boys. Remarkable good humor pervades the whole crowd. Two more joined before I got to town. I saw Joe Green and will make arrangements to suit him when I get to the regement. I saw Dr. Low in Atlanta.[3] I do not know what his business was. I do not think Uncle W and Mr Boykin got home that night from town. Mr Greenwood is with us; he is going to see Johnny in Richmond.[4] I did not have time to go to see my cousin in Augusta nor get you those dresses. I will see what arrangement I can make in Richmond. Accept my love dear Susie and kiss my boy.
Ugie

1. Possibly Hugh Allen Blair, surgeon of the 32nd Georgia Regiment.

2. Samuel Ballard Fears (January 4, 1833–October 14, 1903) was the son of Samuel Baker and Mary Ballard Fears of Chambers County, Alabama. He disappointed Allen by enlisting in Company I, 47th Alabama Regiment, instead of the 21st Georgia.

3. Augustus W. Lowe practiced medicine in Antioch.

4. John T. Greenwood (born 1842), the son of Thomas Bristow and Ann Bass Greenwood, was a lieutenant in Company D, 14th Alabama Regiment.

Gordonville Va
March 21st 1862

Dear Susie

I arrived here this morning being detained two days in Richmond. I have had
no time to write since I left Wilmington and only a minute now. I am quite
busy drawing armes and rations for my men. I drew bounty and accoutre-
ments in Richmond. I also drew tents cooking utensils etc. They will not let
me carry anything but such as the men can toat on their backs any farther.
They may send me away in one hour or wait two days. If I remain you will
hear from me in a longer letter. We are all well, took some rain and came near
freezing last night. Our Regement is covering the retreat. Evrything they had
in the world but what they could toat is destroyed; burnt. I think my trunk is
safe but do not know. Blankets gone I know. To tell evrything in a few words,
the boys have their arms and what they had on when the retreat commenced
no tents only a few cooking utensils. We will leave all of our bagage here.
Thare is a gard here to take care of it. Cicero Whatley of our company is one.
Goodbye my dear Susie. Do not be uneasy if you do not hear from me in two
weeks. I will have no facility for writing. In haste.
your husband,
Ugie

P.S. I sent three hundred and ten dollars to you by old man Greenwood. I owe
Mr Boykin 240.
U

P.P.S. No danger of a fight soon.

Camp Near Rappahannock River
March 25th 1862

Dear Susie

I am in camps at last after nine days of troublesome suspence. I find the boys
all well except a few. Vatchel Whatley is in a very bad condition. So is Captain
Boykin. Boykin can not live much longer in camps. He has sent up his resigna-

tion with a certificate signed by the regemental and brigade surgeons. I have no doubt but that it will be accepted at an early day. He will go to the hospitle amediately if he can get conveyance, and proceed home if it is accepted. Poor fellow, I am sorry for him. Camp life will weigh heavily on me when he goes. Nothing can repay his loss. The whole company regret his loss. They feel like they were about to loose a benefactor and their best friend. You can see this in evry countenance read it in their thousand and one anxious queries, "How pleasures bright, when they take their flight."

We are camped in [a] piece of woods and build quarters by placing straw and leaves on rails and poles as you have seen wagonmen do. Only one tent is saved from the wreck and the Colonel occupies that. We have enough straw to sleep on and do not suffer from cold. Many blankets were lost but we have enough. The men lost nearly all of their cooking utensils. We have only one skillet ourselves. My trunk is safe at Gordonville. I do not know how many blankets I have. I will look them up soon. Nothing was saved but trunks and such as the men could cary on ther backs. Many of the soldiers threw away their knap-sacks (ours did not) and evrything else. We will get new tents as soon as we get settled. Too much praise can not be bestowed upon Cicero Whatley and two men of Capt Glovers company[1] who were detailed to take care of the bagage. When the cars were about starting they toated evry trunk in the regement and threw them on and are now guarding them. Waller was not in the retreat; but feigned himself sick and got off to Richmond so I hear. The boys say that it rained nearly all the time. And I am afraid it will rain again soon. It is still very cold here. Though we have nothing to complain of only smoke and scarcity of cooking utencils. It is no use to complain of that for you know we can not help ourselves though I will add parenthetically that if I had anything fit to eat I would feel much better. When I first came into camps I had quite a voracious appetite. Now I can not eat or digest such as we can fix up. I expect to send in the country and get something to cook and cook in. I left all the butter etc in Gordonville only such as I could bring in two haversacks. We had about as pleasant a time coming as any one could expect. Good passenger coaches all the way to Richmond. Thare was so many of the boys the time did not seem to drag heavily upon them. As for myself I was always buisy. I have several good soldiers along. Some of my recruits are a little unwell with cold and diarhea. Some of my boys have their bounty and have not been examined by a surgeon and are endeavoring to take an advantage of me by pleading unfitness for service. If they do I will loose their bounty and transportation here and home. However I know they have

to be quite shrewd if they make anything. A soldier can be imployed more different ways than a great many anticipate. Do you know the number I got? I will let Joe Green go and if Fears comes I will have twenty nine. I will send an order for transportation to Fears by Boykin. We have had no mail since I came nor do I know when we will have one. I will send this letter by Boykin when he goes. And also a ring apiece for you and my boy. His is made of ivy root from the field of Manassas. I have nothing to polish it with but a pocket knife. I made you one also but broke it before it was quite finished. I will make another and send it the first chance. The one I send is two large for our little boy at present but it will not be long before it will do. I send you perfect beauty made by a Yankee prisner in Richmond and presented to Robt Hunt. He gave it to me and I give it to my dear. My knee does not get any better. I expect to be very closely confined by duty henceforth or at least untill the recruits are drilled and we get settled somewhere or somehow. I do not know what a day will bring forth. I can not penetrate with my sight the misty vail of futurity that hangs before me. Genl Johnson is very much discouraged. If this does not prove a brilliant movement he will be scorned by evry soldier in the army. I am not able to give an opinoion satisfactory to myself or anyone else just now. I regret very much that I am unable to purchase and carry a good map of this part of Va. Thare are several things that I could tell you if I was with you that would loose their savour by writing. My dear be in as good cheer as possible and write me a good long letter. I know you will do this. Direct them to me 21st Reg Ga Vols, 7th Brigade (Genl Trimble), Near Gordonville, Army (of the) Potomac. You know I am anxious to hear from you. Let me know where George is so that I can write to him. Give my respects to Billy and Mrs E. I hope to be able to inform you in my next that we are better situated and can have something conducive to comfort and health. I am more anxious to be with you and our boy than ever. I hope it will not be long before this inhumane war will end. Let me know evrything about home affairs when you write. Give my respects to your Pa.
Your husband
Ugie

1. Thomas Coke Glover (born 1826) was captain of Company A, 21st Georgia, from Campbell County, Georgia. He was elected major on July 27, 1862. Following Colonel Mercer's death on April 18, 1864, Glover was promoted to the rank of lieutenant colonel. He was killed at Winchester, Virginia, on September 19, 1864.

Camp near Rappahannock River
March 30th 1862

Dear Susie

I wrote you a letter and sent it by Boykin on the 27th. Since that time I have been under fire of the anemy. On the next day two Lieuts, fifty men and myself were detailed to guard the bridge over the river. Our regement went out late in the day to relieve another on picket. As soon as they got out they were driven back by what we supposed to be a large body of the anemy. They passed us at the bridge; the Yankees following as fast as they could. When they passed we set fire to and blew up the bridge just as they commenced shelling us. I first set fire to the bridge with my own hand, John Hick touched off the fuse. He was struck in three places by fragments of stone from the arch; though was not more seriously hurt than being knocked over into the mud. I regard the escape of him and the engineers as miraculus.[1] The bursting of bombs and the whizing roar of fragments of stone from the bridge was a scene calculated to strike teror into the brest of the bravest. I must confess that I was somewhat frightened. I presume not more than others. The Yanks fired at us several times with cannon balls after we had fallen back about a mile. All of their balls passed over us. I can concieve of nothing more terrific than the crashing noise of a ball passing through the air. We slept in place on our arms that night without but little covering. We stood in the same place the greater part of yesterday while it snowed on us smartly for several hours. It wound up the day with a sleet and we returned to our old camp cold tired and hungry. It rained last night and the greater part of today. All of my bagage is sent back. I am lucky in procuring this single sheet and envelope and will send my letter when I have a chance. My dear wife I do not want you to be despondent for I will write whenever I have an opportunity. It may be several days before I get my carpet sack if I ever get it. A man must not calculate on having anything here but what he has on. I am somewhat debilitated today though on duty, being a little bilious and taking some cold. I have not recieved any letter from you yet. You know I am quite anxious to hear from you and our boy. While standing on the field in the snow yesterday I was struck forcibly with the sad comparison with the same day two years ago. How different from our fond anticipations! What will two more years bring to pass. What will one, what a month. Goodbye my dear Susie. I am ever your dear boy,
Ugie

1. This incident, with some variations, is also recorded in an obituary of John T. Higginbothem in the *Confederate Veteran Magazine* of October 1915.

Camp near Rappahannoc River
April 3d 1862

Dear Susie

I wrote you a few lines March 30th and also wrote again yesterday but we had to flurry around a little thinking the Yanks were coming and I distroyed it. I write this and put it in the same envelope and will continue to write untill I have a chance to send it off. I think we are in the rear of the army and have no mail facilities. I have not recieved a letter from you yet. None of us have heard anything from home since I returned. I know you are very much distressed about me; and I judge the people generaly are quite anxious to know something of us. Boykin will or aught to satisfy the people concerning us and our situation; that is in respect to mail facilities. I have not been as well for several days as I would like to be. I caught cold the day we were out and I am troubled very much with the diarhea. I am on duty today and presume will continue so. My dear don't you want a daily paper. Many stirring events will transpire soon and of course you would like to be posted. Take the Confederacy[1] if you do not prefer another. Probably Billy E. will subscribe part. If he does it will answer the same purpose. Be shure and take the Cultivator and the Field & Fireside also if you want it.

1. The *Southern Confederacy* was a wartime newspaper published in Atlanta.

5

THE SHENANDOAH VALLEY
CAMPAIGN

We have demolished Banks army, shelled the anemy
on Maryland Heights and successfully withdrawn
to the mountains though flanked by three generals, each one
with a force almost equal to our own, and brought away
four thousand prisoners and two millions of captured property.

N his letter of June 12, 1862, Ugie Allen succinctly summarized Confederate General Thomas J. Jackson's Shenandoah Valley campaign. Intended primarily as a diversion to prevent Union reinforcements from reaching General George B. McClellan's army east of Richmond, the Valley campaign marked Stonewall Jackson as a brilliant strategist and mitigated criticism of his idiosyncrasies and subsequent failures.

Richard Ewell's division, including the 21st Georgia Regiment of General Isaac R. Trimble's brigade, entered the Shenandoah Valley for the first time on April 30, 1862. Ewell was under orders to move through Swift Run Gap to Conrad's Store and hold in check a Union force commanded by General Nathaniel Banks. In the meantime, Jackson marched his Army of the Valley westward and on May 8 at McDowell, Virginia, defeated a Union division under General Robert Milroy.

Jackson then moved back into the Valley where he planned to combine his army with Ewell's force and attack Banks. The bulk of Ewell's division, including Trimble's brigade, united with Jackson's army on May 21, near Luray. The next day Jackson's force marched northward to descend on the Federal garrison at Front Royal.

On May 23, the vanguard of Ewell's division attacked and captured most of the small Union force at Front Royal. The following day, Confederate cavalry overtook and captured part of Nathaniel Banks's supply train as the northern general withdrew his force from Strasburg to Winchester. In the ensuing

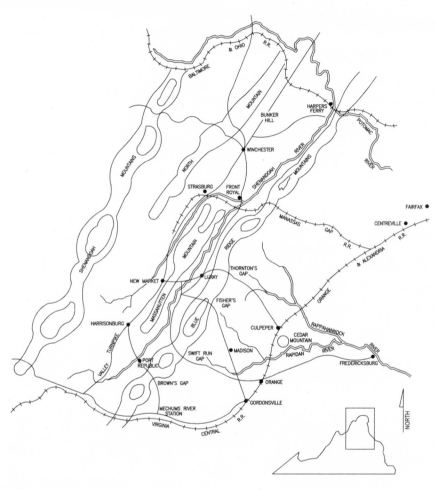

THE SHENANDOAH VALLEY

movement of Jackson's army to Winchester, Ewell's command, including Trimble's brigade, marched northward along the Front Royal Road.

Shortly after dawn on May 25, Trimble's skirmishers began driving Union pickets back through fog-shrouded fields toward Winchester. By 7:00 A.M., Trimble's men were within a mile of the town. Advancing in line of battle, the 21st Georgia soon came under Union artillery fire; one officer and several men were wounded. At the same time, the 21st North Carolina, Trimble's lead regiment, encountered a destructive rifle fire delivered by Union infantry regiments posted behind stone fences on either side of the Front Royal Road. Hoping to flank the Federals from their protected position, Colonel Mercer ordered the 21st Georgia to double-quick to the right of the North Carolinians. Mercer's movement helped clear the Federals from Trimble's front.

The decisive fighting at Winchester occurred west of the town. As the 21st Georgia watched from an eminence east of the city, General Richard Taylor's Louisiana brigade broke the Federal right flank in what many witnesses remembered as one of the most magnificent charges of the war.

Following its victory at Winchester, Jackson's Valley Army pursued Banks's retreating Federals to Harpers Ferry, but Jackson abandoned the chase when Federal forces to the south began closing on him. Between May 31 and June 7, Stonewall's "foot cavalry" marched eighty miles up the Valley, eluding Federal forces under Generals Robert Milroy, James Shields, and John C. Fremont. Heavy rains swelled the Shenandoah River to flood stage, and Jackson prevented a concentration of Federals by burning bridges as he retreated.

One of Jackson's primary concerns during his retreat was protecting a train of captured supplies, a double column of wagons seven miles long. Once he had guaranteed the safety of these supplies, he again turned his attention to offensive operations. His audacious plan called for leaving Ewell's division facing west to delay the forces of Fremont while the rest of the Valley Army moved southeast to attack Shields near the village of Port Republic. After defeating Shields, Jackson hoped to reunite his forces to deal with Fremont.

On the morning of June 8, Richard Ewell posted his four brigades along a ridge southeast of the community of Cross Keys. Ugie Allen wrote that his brigade held the Confederate center; in reality, Trimble's men were on Ewell's right. At midday on June 8, Fremont attacked Trimble's position. The men of the 21st Georgia, concealed behind a rail fence along a tree line, held their fire until the enemy had advanced to within approximately fifty steps of the southern position. At that point, the Georgians delivered several volleys of buck and ball into the startled ranks of the 8th New York Infantry Regiment. Trimble's subsequent counterattack pushed the shattered New York unit and other Federal regiments back some distance. As Federal officers attempted to reform their battle lines, the 16th Mississippi and 21st Georgia charged their front while General Trimble led the 15th Alabama in a flanking attack. The ensuing "short and sharp struggle" resulted in another Federal retreat. After dusk, Trimble sought permission from Ewell to attack the Federals again, but Ewell declined, arguing that his subordinate had "done well enough for one day." The 21st Georgia's casualties at Cross Keys had numbered four men killed, twenty-one wounded, and one missing.

Isaac Trimble's men left their lines at Cross Keys on the morning of June 9, marching slowly toward Port Republic. By 10:00 A.M., the brigade had passed over the North River Bridge. By burning the bridge behind them, Trimble's soldiers effectively blocked further pursuit by Fremont. After a brief stay at Brown's Gap in the Blue Ridge Mountains, Jackson marched his army back into the Valley to the vicinity of Weyer's Cave, where the men established camps and took a well-deserved rest.

Stonewall's victories in the Valley in 1862 raised the morale of southerners discouraged by bad news on other fronts, and Jackson's men looked upon their leader with newfound awe. James Cooper Nisbet, one of Ugie Allen's fellow officers in the 21st Georgia, voiced undoubtedly universal sentiments when he wrote to a friend at the close of the campaign, "Without tents and often with short rations, we cheerfully move wherever our glorious leader orders." Jackson, he added, "like old Frederick the Great, fights to win, and will win or die."

Bivouac near Brandy Station Va
Apr 18th 1862

My dear Susie
I recieved your letter of the 7th this morning certainly this is not the first you have written, if it was recieved first. I recieved a letter from Boykin also. I am in no enviable state of mind now and do not know how much I shall write. I would like for you to tell Mr Boykin if he pleased I want him to give Jim a very severe whipping. Not a little one, but whip him from head to foot; not less than two or three hundred. And tell Jim that I am the one that is having it done. If he is not whiped you might as well set them all free. It will be an

accomodation to me for some one to do it. It is my positive order that he does not go to his wifes house any more.[1]

Who recommended you to get potatoes from old man Lee?[2] Bob?[3] It looks just like some of his work. I expect he is going thare evry chance he gets. I sent Mr Boykin $310 and gave him my note for $220 and borrowed twenty from him in town. I also gave him a warehouse receipt to sell that bale of cotton. I requested him to pay Prophett for my ambrotipe and if necessary to advance money for anything that you needed and pay himself etc etc. He must be paid for his sheep for I must have them.

No election has come off yet.[4] I do not flatter myself with the prospect. If I am defeated I shall endeavor to leave them 'alone in their glory.' I will use evry means I possibly can to do this. Recollect this is confidential. Pray do not let it gain publicity. I can not see what is Boykins object in saying that I was as near heaven as I wanted to be; only to anoy you. You aught not to let such things trouble you. Thare is not a man living whose family and home is any dearer to him than mine is to me although my manifestations may not be as profuse. My whole life has been a yearning for a home and some one to love. The regular army has never entered my head. I am tiered of playing the soldier and my mind is ever turning to the time when I shall be free and can enjoy that quiet happiness which none but he who has endured hardships of a soldiers life can appreciate. Our company nor our regement did not run ten or even five miles. The picket line was not but four miles beyond the river. Our regement drew off in good order in quick and double quick time and formed a line of battle three times flanked by the cavelry. Our regement was opposed by about ten thousand Yanks ten pieces of artilery and a quantity of cavelry. I have told you other details in a previous letter. Tell Boykin that Arrington jumped on the cars and went to Orange C. H. He is now in the guard house for it by order of Col Mercer. We left our camp this morning with orders to come here and await farther orders. We are now cooking two days rations and will leave here soon for parts unknown. Some think we will go to Yorktown, others to join Jackson[5] in the valley about forty miles above here. Thare are rumors of a fight at Yorktown, you will hear of it before this reaches you. We hired a negro cook the day that Boykin left. I will give you information if anything occurs in the company worth notice. I have my eyes open. It is now raining and I will have to close. I will write when ever I have an opportunity. Tell Boykin that Terry says for him to send his pistol to his mother's. You must write often and long letters. I write twice a week recently. I sent you a ring in a letter. I am very sorry that my ring was not large enough. I know he is a sweet little thing. Kiss him for his absent father. We are about to leave for the valley.

Goodbye dear wife.

Ugie

1. Jim (born 1826) was valued at $2,500, according to Allen's estate records. For several years before Ugie Allen reached adulthood, Jim and the other slaves had been "hired out" or rented to work on neighboring plantations. If Jim was whipped, the punishment failed to prevent him from slipping away to visit his wife Selah. She gave birth to their fourth child in 1864.

2. Noah Lee (born 1780) was the patriarch of a prominent Antioch family.

3. Bob was another of Allen's slaves.

4. In April 1862, the Confederate Congress conscripted all males between eighteen and thirty-five. Among other provisions of the Conscription Act, preexisting military units were required to reenlist for the duration of the war and to hold new elections for officers. Some companies attempted to take advantage of the election to rid themselves of officers who were strict disciplinarians. General Trimble ordered one company into line and informed the recalcitrant soldiers that they would stand at attention until they elected the officers he preferred.

5. In the spring of 1862, General Thomas Jonathan "Stonewall" Jackson (1824–63) commanded a small Confederate army in the Shenandoah Valley.

Camp Near Rappadan River
April 24th 1862

My Dear Wife
When I last wrote you we were at Brandy Station. I was under the impression that we were going to the Valley to reinforce Genl Jackson. We marched on the 19th to reinforce him and the order was countermanded and were ordered to proceed across the Rappadan. We turned back and marched untill about eleven o'ck at night and halted at Mitchels Station; having come twenty miles. This was doing remarkably well when you consider that twelve miles is a good days march for soldiers carrying their knapsacks, ec. Only fifteen of our company made the march. The two Garrets, Tom Wilkes and myself being among them. All the others fell out along the railroad and slept all night. I do not think that more than seventy of the regement came up. I never was more fatigued in my life but once. You recollect the day that I ploughed. The next day we came ten or twelve miles; the next we came eight arriving at Gordonsville about ten o'ck A.M. We stopped the second day with forty-five and the third with fifty-five of seventy-nine men. All that fell out were unable to take the march except two or three. Our regement was the only one that marched the whole distance; others were picked up by the trains. It rained very near the whole time. It commenced raining the night before we

reached Gordonsville and rained a cold steady rain until the night after. Day before yesterday morning; the day after we got thare we were ordered back here fifteen miles. Fortunately we were sent on the train or we never could have stood it. We were all near dead and spent yesterday in resting. I do not think thare was a man in the regement but what slept several hours. Some of the boys have ventured out today after milk butter etc. Take my map and you can follow us in our march and see where we are at now. We will probably stay here several days longer. I understand that ours and Genl Taylors[1] brigades recieved marching orders for some unknown point the day we left Gordonsville. We were hungry, halt, lame "weary, and heavy leaden" when we got to G. and "poled" into our boxes in a hurry. My butter was fine and so was the hams. We cooked one whole one besides our regular rations. I do not know the object of this move. I suppose we are compelled to make it to meet or counter some move of the Yankees. We are kept in profound ignorance of the intentions of our officers. We get no news from the other parts of our army or anywhere else. I have received one letter only from you which I answered on the eighteenth. This is the first chance I have had of writing since then. And write squating under a blanket stretched over a pole while it is snowing very hard and the largest flakes that I ever saw. Some of our boys rather jocosely compare them to a pound of wool. I requested Cicero Whatley who was about writing to Boykin when I was in Gordonsville to tell him to let you know where I was and what we were doing. Cicero is guarding our bagage thare. I have lost all my blankets except four and probably will loose two of them. I think I can make out with them and my overcoat if we do not have much more cold weather. The fact is we have nothing but what we carry ourselves. We have endured many hardships recently. Much more than I ever thought I would be able to. Nothing has kept me up but the determination that I would not give up. Our camp is just on the bank of the Rappadan and several of our boys are fishing. I find this is a great country for fish. If I had some hooks I think I would vary our diet of bacon and bread. This is the most beautiful country that it has ever been my fortune to see. Beautiful and neat white cotages surrounded by broad fields of grain and clover, in which feed heards of cattle and flocks of sheep fit to grace any fair in our state. These farms are prototypes of what I have often and still dream of making our own home. Then with this beautiful emblem of prosperity and the cheering smiles of my boy and own darling Susie, my cup of happiness will be filled.

Boykin's resignation has not been heard of. The department is much crowded with business and naturally slow to act in such cases. I am in command of the company now. Waller is on the sick list and made an effort to go to Richmond or was about making one when we left Gordonsville. If he was successful he will probably stay four or five days. His pretext was to buy shoes hats etc for the company, and judging the future by the past will bring up some red eye to regale his friends upon. Susie I have not time to write more as I find that I can send this now and might not have a chance to send it in several days. The man is waiting on me. Berry R and Johnny Brewer are both well.

Goodbye my dear.

Ugie

P.S. I will write again in a day or two and have my letter ready to send off.

1. During the Shenandoah Valley campaign, General Richard Taylor (1826–79) commanded a brigade of Louisiana troops.

Camp on the Rappadan River
Apr 25th 1862

My Dear Susie

I wrote you a letter yesterday and will write again as I did not quite finish and may not have a chance of writing in a day or two. Let me tell you; you must never grow uneasy about me if you do not receive letters regular; for I do not think our facilities will be good in some time. I will add that I have writen tolerably regular up to the time we left Rappahannock. We have had no mail since then and no one seems to care. (I mean our officers) whether we ever do again or not. Ask anything about it and they will say, "I dont now. I've quit writing myself; have not recieved a letter in a month." Did you recieve my letter with the ring in it? I am sorry that the one I sent the boy was too small. However I can cut the R off and give it to the next one. What do you think of it? You wrote me something about sending my watch. I do not see how you can well do without it. If I find that I must have it I will let you know and we will get a good family clock. I hope some of our boys will make haste and come back. Half of our company are off of duty and half of the remainder are on detached service. They detailed my last sergeant to go to Richmond or some where else with some prisners that our cavelry picked up yesterday. We have as many men on duty as any one else. If you do not send me a letter by those boys I will never get one. Send my hair greece and anything else that you can conveniently. Our boys laugh and say that thare are some lice in the company so old that they have B. H. I. [Ben Hill Infantry] on their backs. Others I. F. W. (in for the war). You need not make me many if any shirts untill I write for them, because I can do without for a while yet and might not be able to take care of them. I have a change of clothing in my carpet sack with the wagons and I hear that they are ordered somewhere from Gordonsville. I hear that our bagage is being sent away from thare too. A thousand wash women could not keep this regement clean, situated as we have been. Half of the time we draw hard bread (crackers) and are compelled to broil our meat on a stick, using our pants shoes and coattails for handkerchiefs towels dishrags etc. It is quite common to see a person wipe his knife on his boot and commence eating. Let me tell you I made up some dough yesterday and baked some fine biscuits. No soda or salt. I also made some fritters without anything but water and flour. I sent Mike Clinton out this morning after some sweat milk and light bread, and told him never come back untill he got it. It is now about nine o'ck and I anticipate a harty breakfast. Mike will get it if anybody can. I have broiled my meat and laid it out on a cracker, ready when he comes. I expect you think by my writing this as Boykin says that I am as near heaven as I want to be. If I am I am certainly content with long range for it is the prevailing opinion among the soldiers that we are near the antipode. Speaking of light bread; the citizens have the finest in this country that I ever saw. It is made by the same process that I told you of that Mrs. Thornberry[1] used.

Thare will be a battle near here soon I think. In fact I know it. If we are in to it which we will be; I sincerely hope that I will have command of the company. I do not want to trot along behind with nothing to do.[2] It is my opinion that this war will not last very long unless we are defeated in the several great battles that will soon be fought. I expect the Yanks have Savannah by this time. If we make any fight thare at all we should go into it with the determination never to give up those batteries.[3]

Give my love to your Pa, George, Lizie, Boykin, Mr & Mrs Boykin. Tell Uncle Wisdom that Cousin Robert is well etc. Write me a long letter about evrything how you are geting along etc. Tell me of the Negroes, stock, crop, chickens. How many young ones have you? Good bye my dear Susie. Kiss our dear little boy for me. Call him Robert; you know I like Edgar, Ugene also if I do not survive this war.
Your boy
Ugie

1. Allen had probably boarded at the Thornberry residence during his illness in November 1861.

2. Junior officers functioned as file-closers during combat. Posted behind the battle lines, they were responsible for preventing straggling and desertion.

3. Federal soldiers mounted an amphibious threat to the Georgia coast in the spring of 1862. Fort Pulaski, near Savannah, surrendered on April 11, 1862, after a twenty-four-hour bombardment. Allen refers to the heavy seacoast batteries, on Caustin's Bluff, which defended the city.

Bivouac Near Stannardsville Va
Apr 29th 1862

Dear Susie
Day before yesterday we were ordered from Rappadan came to Gordonsville on the train and marched out six miles towards this place. We are in Green County I think on the Rockingham turnpike twenty one miles west or northwest of Gordonsville and two of Stannardsville, just at the foot of the mountains. We marched fifteen miles yesterday, and I would have writen then but lay down to rest and slept untill about night. I recieved your second letter the day that I mailed my last on the 26th. This sheet of paper came in good time; but I had much rather it had been writen upon. You must write often and direct to Gordonsville as you have been doing untill I let you know otherwise. We may leave here in a few hours, to join Genl Jackson beyond the mountains, and fight a battle. I have not more than forty men with me now. Many of the boys are absent sick and may never expect to go into any hard service or battle if they can prevent it. All that I have with me are quite indignant at the course a few of our men have taken recently. You need not say anything about this as I am not personal in my remarks. I have about as many as any of the companies. I think I have at least twenty men absent who are as able to take this hard service as some I have along. Cousin R. Joe Rodgers, Ol F, Hick, Johnny B, and Tom Wilkes are here. Berry is sick. Has Billie Edmondson finished planting yet? I am perfectly willing and rather anxious for Boykin to sell Ethan; if he can get a good bargain. I faver cash or good notes &. Have you sold any cotton yet. Recollect what I told you in a previous letter. I faver selling. I understand that Dr C[1] is buying corn at the crib for the government. Sell evry grain of corn peas oats etc that you can possibly spare. We must have more land and cash goes much farther than notes such times as these. Save your salt! Make the negroes put popler poles and hickory ashes in the lot for the mules.[2] Uncle W promised me long since that he would look to my hands when they were down thare. I dislike to ask evrything of Mr. B. It is true I am sacrificing and enduring much for my country. But I expect no favors, only from a few and dislike to burden them. "Blessed are thay that expect little, for they shall not be disappointed." You need not fear that writing will be stoped by the war department. Shure enough I gave Mrs Vance[3] a barrell of corn and did not think to tell you. I am sorry to hear that she was not worthy of the charity. I have just had a fine wash in the

mountain brook that runs merily in a few yards of our quarters. Appropos the quarters aluded to is more immaginative than real; a knapsack thrown up beside a tree on which I sit and write this and at other times when not on the ground or standing. My dear I have not time to write more. I have some company writing that must be done. I write evry time I have a chance depend on that. Give my respects to all.

Goodbye my dear Susie.

Ugie

P.S. I think it better to write just a few lines than not at all.

1. Dr. Henry Hamilton Cary.

2. Gnawing the soft bark of poplar trees and licking hickory ashes provided potassium and other essential elements for the livestock.

3. Elizabeth Vance was the widow of William Vance, a member of the Ben Hill Infantry who died at Sudley Church Hospital on November 18, 1861. Susan's reason for considering her unworthy of charity is unknown.

Swift Run Gap,
Blue Ridge Mountains Va
May 3d 1862

Dear Susie

I mailed you a letter three days ago, writen the day previous. I have nothing of interest to write now more than we left our old camp on the 29th about noon and marched here about thirteen miles that evning. We are now about thirty three miles from Gordonville and twenty from Harrisburg[1] or some other burg beginning with H. It always rains when we march or go on picket. No tents though it rained the greater part of the night. I have got so that I do not care anymore for rain than anything else now if I can get under something to shelter my face. I am quite fortunate in one respect; although I spern the accusation of being sleepy headed. I can sleep under as many adverse circumstances as anyone I know. I have to set up at night to report roll call at tattoo, and get up at reville to report. I do not dread sitting up but geting up goes rather hard, as you know. But I am compelled to do it, and do, with better grace than ever before. I am always the last to go to bed (blanket if you prefer) in our company. A good social chat is pleasant after the bustle and noise of camp in the day. You spoke of going to Jones[2] in your last letter. Be shure and go. I would be glad if I were at liberty to go with you. I can not say that I will have an opportunity of coming home in a long time. The sumer campaign has opened and I need not expect it. I have not been entirely free from diarhea for several weeks untill recently. I am quite stout and expect that I weigh more than I ever have since I was sick. I could do much better if we could have anything to eat. We can not get anything but bacon and bread. No salt rice shugar coffee and sometimes no soap. If we ever get settled down you must send me a box. You must make me a quantity of pickles preserves jelly etc shugar or no shugar. You had better buy your suply of shugar. I am now making out pay rolls for the boys and can send you $150.00 very easily if I had a chance. Are not strawberries ripe? The trees have just commenced budding here. The mornings are rather cool yet; I have not pulled off my flannels. I wish I had written to you to send me a shirt or two by Lieut. Henderson but it is too late now. They have sent all of our baggage away from G.[3] and I do not know when I can get to my trunk. Susie I have not one thing of interest to write only that I am thinking of the box that I spoke of. I have not recieved but two letters from you yet. Your first and second. You must write very often. You have a much better chance than I do. Do not wait for letters from me. I will write again soon if I can. Tell me of our little boy. Can he walk? How is the flopeared militia. Tell them to go into service they shant be hurt. Good bye.

Ugie

1. Harrisonburg, Virginia.

2. Susan contemplated visiting relatives in Jones County, Georgia, where her parents had lived before settling in Chambers County, Alabama.

3. Gordonsville, Virginia.

Swift Run Gap
Blue Ridge Mountains Va
May 5th 1862

Dear Susie

I recieved a letter from you this morning dated Apr 23d. I had writen you one two days ago, and will write now for fear we will move soon and I can not write. We had an alarm this morning and went out about a mile and came back again. We are standing face to face with the anemy. I have told you in previous letters that I thought we would fight soon. My opinion has not changed. Most of your letter is answered in previous letters. From what you say I expect Ned Henderson is on his way and will be here soon. I wrote you not to send any shirts, but hope you will not recieve the letter before he starts for I will need them. You did well to buy stamps. I sent you a few some time ago and have none for myself. Billy must have been thinking of the conscript law.[1] The proper way for you to do is to make a deposit of several dollars in the post office at Antioch. Pitts is so punctilious about small matters I would like for you to pay him up what we owe, and I will take care that he goes to the devil before I ever patronize him again. This is a fixed fact. I care little for the well wishes of a man whose accomodation ceases with adversity. I have made evry effort and have and am still denying myself things that are absolutely necessary to my comfort in order that I could hold a reputation of being punctual in the payment of my debts. It would be a good idea for you to keep money on hand for any emergency that might arise. I have no way of sending you any. Boykin wrote that he was coming back as soon as he was able to duty. I would be glad if he gets able and does. He is quite fortunate in being absent now. I do not look for him soon. If he does not I will do my utmost to defeat W and possibly will if the tables do not turn against me. He is a wiley trickster, and I never flatter myself. One thing certain I had rather be Lt Allen than Capt Waller in this regement. I must answer your question relative to defeat in the negative. Not if I could prevent it. Ask Boykin about patches for the negroes.[2] If they all work well I will give them more than they can make with patches and let them devote their holidays to rest etc. Remind the boys of my oxen, eight dollars for them and five for *the beast*. What about my stock?

We are required to keep one days rations cooked all the while. Tell George that he does not know anything of service. I met up with my old friend Dick Coleman[3] the other day who is now in the 15th Ala reg. He served a year at Pensacola in the 1st Ala. He is the one that gave me that knife. He heard me talking in a large crowd where some soldiers were resting and recognized my voice before he saw me. An old Athens friend recognized me in Richmond the same way. I have thought frequently about the slick cap in the ambrotipe. I was so very buisy that I forgot it. I know our dear little boy looks sweet with his white teeth. I would be so glad if I could possibly see him and his mother. You tell me to write. I tell you the same. My facilities are very bad. I have writen evry chance, and will continue to do so. I have nothing of interest to write now. The last few days have passed without anything of importance. Good bye my dear Susie.

Ugie

1. William P. Edmondson enlisted in Company K, 56th Georgia Regiment, on May 12, 1862. He was discharged owing to disability in 1863.

2. Slaves were sometimes allocated individual plots of land on which to cultivate vegetables or occasionally even cotton for their personal use.

3. After being discharged from the 1st Alabama Regiment, twenty-four-year-old Richard R. Coleman enlisted on March 4, 1862, in the "Glenville Guards," Company H, 15th Alabama. He was mortally wounded on June 27, 1862, at the Battle of Gaines's Mill, Virginia, and died four days later.

Blue Ridge Mountains Va
May 9th 1862

My dear Susie
I wrote you several days ago. We moved back near Stanardville the next day. I kept my letter some time before I could mail it. It may be the same way with this but if I had finished it one hour ago it would now have been on its way. I tell you this so that you can acount for not geting letters regularly. Of course some times I can not write regularly and I write now more on your account than from a pressure of news. In fact thare is none. We went back to or near S. and then came back here yesterday. I [am] now siting a la Turk on the highest point over which the road passes of the blue Ridge. The idea is grand and the reality exceedingly pleasant. The day is beautiful. Well worthy of the queen of months. And far below me lies a beautiful green valey through which meanders the poetic Shenandoah reflecting back with silvery brightness the rays of the morning sun. Beyond this rise in magestic grandeur the Shenandoah mountains. And far away beyond these are the Alegahnies mearly perceptible through the blue aether.

I am looking for Lieuts Waller and Henderson today. I heard that Henderson was in Richmond. If he knew how many anxious harts were yearning for tidings from dear ones at home he would certainly come on. We are all quite anxious for some old citizen at home to pay us a visit sometime soon. The boys want some things and want to send others home and they can not be accomodated any other way. We are under stricter dicipline than we ever were before. The Col[1] is using his fine comb. Two officers have been courtmartialed (Lt Rucker and Capt Kinman)[2] for leaving ranks on the march and about thirty privates have been in the guard house and are now on heavy duty for the same offence. The guard marches in the rear of the regiment and catch evry stragler from ranks. Our boys have escaped very well so far. Did I tell you in my last that Tom Wilkes and Berry were at the hospitle. Both of them will come back soon. I would like for you to write me whether Boykin is coming back or not. I can not come to any conclusion from his letters to me and Bagby. You aught to get George to stay with you much of his time. I would like for you to tell me how the conscripts are geting along. I find that I must close.

1. Colonel John T. Mercer.

2. Jesse G. Rucker of Fulton County, Georgia, was junior 2nd lieutenant in Company C, and Wesley Kinman was captain of Company G, the "Dabney Rifles," from Gordon County, Georgia.

May 11th 1862

Dear Susie

I wrote the above several days ago and could not mail it. Lieut H. and the boys have just come and brought me your sweet long letter. I know you are the greatest little woman living. You misconstrue my meaning in reference to the potatoes. I mearly ment that Bob had probably spoke of his having a fine variety and they being scarce you had goten them. I know he is quite partial to that family and I am quite as anxious to prevent any intercourse even of a business character. This is the fourth letter that I have recieved from you. I did not know where we were going and when I could write and I got Cicero W. to let you know what had become of me through the Captin. You will recieve several letters writen soon after this; writen from the Rappadan. It looks like when I write you a letter that all the news is out of date before you get it. Let us hope though that things do not get any worse. It is true we have a gloomy prospect before us; but if we whip at Williamsburg and Corinth I do not think the war will last long.[1] If we do not; a long series of disasters and much suffering will follow. Sometimes I am quite as hopefull as ever I was. If the Southern people are true to themselves we never can be whiped. If we do not whip the Yankees we will be whiped by our own people not them. Boykin wrote that some people were already whiped. I know this is true. Evry man who could possibly leave home and was subject to military duty was whiped if he had the courage to acknowledge it before our recent reverses. Some of our boys declare that ten men dressed in Yankee uniform by mounting a stove pipe on a pair of bugy wheels could take LaGrange.

Boykin has recieved letters from me before this time. I recieved only three from him. If Billy E goes to the war and Mrs E to Black Wilkes[2] you will be left alone. I would regret it very much if she leaves you. You must persuade George to come and stay with you and not go into service again soon.[3] I will write him a letter about it. You say he is not like the same person. Why?

I do not care if Boykin does sell Ethan, if he can get a good cash price. I wrote to you to sell our cotton. I do not know what is best. If we whip the Yankees in the two next great battles and are recognized by France as it is rumored, cotton will go up, if not we would do well to take what we can. The boys could not bring me but one shirt. When they got to Gordonville they sent the boxes on to Charlottesville, thinking that our regemental bagage was thare. It is in Lynchburg. I do not know that I will ever get them. I intend to try to get off for a few days about the end of this month in order to go and get up some things of mine and the boys. I do not know whether I can or not, nor do I know where we will be. I do not know whether I will need my valiese or not. I have a change of clothing in Mike's carpet sack. I intend to and must provide some way of carying more things. The falt of all this inconvenience lies with our Regemental and Brigade officers. I think I will get my trunk and prefer charges against the quartermaster if he does not have it hawled: as I am entitled to eighty pounds of bagage.

Ned says that Boykin is coming back in several weeks. Thare are several things he must get for our mess when he comes or we can not live hardly. I do not look for him very soon. Lieut W is struting around Richmond with a captns bars on his collar. I write this for your and Boykins special benefit. We will leave tomorrow morning for Fishers Gap. Where it is I do not know. You write to me to buy something to eat in the country. I would if I could. Thare is nothing to buy in country town or anywhere else.

Ned has delivered Boykins message to the Col. It is all right. Tell him to recruit up his health untill he is as fat as I am and come back. The boys all say that I look better than they ever saw me. You need not fear but what I will take the best possible care of myself. This marching and open air agrees with me finely. However I fear that a reaction will take place caused by the heat of summer and heavy diet. The days are warm and the nights remarkably cold here. I frequently use my overcoat for a short while in the morning.

My dear you must not despond. Let us hope that we will soon be together again. Certainly the war will not last much longer. I am rejoiced to see from the tone of your letters that you would not have me to be one of those human drones who hang back and are content to prove their patriotism by talking. I can think of nothing but my Susie, boy, home and the termination of this war. I would give everything just to be with you. I know our boy is the dearest thing living. Does he try to talk. Learn him to say Pa. Accept my love dear wife and kiss my boy.

Ugie

Direct to Gordonville naming Regement and Brigade.

1. Federal general George B. McClellan had begun his move up the Virginia Peninsula toward Richmond. On May 3, 1862, Confederates evacuated Yorktown, falling back to a second line near Williamsburg. In the West, after the Confederate defeat at Shiloh, Tennessee, on April 6–7, General P. G. T. Beauregard concentrated his troops near Corinth, Mississippi.

2. James Blackstone Wilkes (January 18, 1835–August 29, 1891).

3. George Fuller's term of enlistment in the 7th Alabama Regiment expired in April 1862. He joined Company I, 47th Alabama, in October 1862.

Bivouac Near Winchester Va
May 26th 1862

My Dear Susie

I know you are very uneasy about me. I have writen three letters to you since
the 12th and have not had an opportunity of mailing them. Since that time we
have marched over two hundred miles fought two battles, gained two victories. I could have mailed a letter from Madison C.H. but was compelled to
have my shoes mended as I was almost barefooted. Several of our boys wrote
and I hope you heard from us. I will give you everything in detail. On the
12th three companies of us marched from Swift Run Gap to Fishers Gap and
reinforced the N.C. Regiment.[1] Get your map and follow me up. The road
from Gordonville to New Market passes through this gap. We then went to
the Columbian bridge on the Shendoah on this road. We then took the back
track and marched to Madison C.H. Here we were turned back the same road
and came to the bridge again. We then took down on the east side of the river
and passed through the town of Luray. The next day we came up with our regiment and attacted and drove the anemy out of Front Royal. (Let me tell you in
the beginning that our regiment has not fired a gun.) This was on the 23rd.
Thare was only one whole and part of three other regiments in Front Royal.
We completely supprised and routed them. We captured about five hundred or
probably a thousand (I saw at least three hundred) prisners and all their bagage.[2] Major Wheats battallion of Louisianans and our Maryland Regiment
and two batteries of artillery were all that were engaged in the rout.[3] The prisoners, baggage, and artillery (two pieces) we captured in the pursuit by our
cavelry. Our first Maryland grappled the Yankee first Maryland, killed several
and took their colours. I saw one of our Baltimore Artillery recognised and
shook hands with his brother among the prisoners. If I was with you I could
tell you a thousand things that would not be interesting in my letter. On the
24th Genl Jackson jumped abroad of the anemy at Strasburg and almost ruined
them. They fell back here while we flanked them by coming up from Front
Royal. Sharp firing was kept up all night before last. Yesterday morning about
sunup Genl Jackson attacted from the frunt and we on the flank and by ten o'ck
we had completely routed the Yanks again. I saw the hotest part of the battle
from a distance. It was a heavy fight. We have at least fifty wagons, several thousand prisners and a great many commisary stores. I do not know what our loss

is nor theirs.[4] You will see all the particulars before this gets to you. Our regiment lost one killed and ten or twenty wounded. All of our boys are safe. I am compelled to close as the mail leaves in a minute. I will write again soon.
Your dear boy,
Ugie

1. The 21st North Carolina Infantry.

2. The Union garrison at Front Royal consisted of the 1st Maryland (U.S.) Infantry Regiment, two companies of the 29th Pennsylvania Infantry Regiment, one section of Knapp's (Pennsylvania) Battery, and two companies of the 5th New York Cavalry Regiment. These units lost 32 men killed, 122 wounded, and 750 captured in the engagement on May 23, 1862.

3. The Confederate forces mentioned by Allen include the 1st Maryland (C.S.) Infantry Regiment, the 1st Louisiana Special Battalion under Major Chatham R. Wheat, and the Baltimore Light Artillery.

4. Banks's casualties for May 23–25, 1862, were 62 killed, 243 wounded, and 1,714 captured or missing; for the period May 23–31, 1862, Jackson reported 68 killed, 329 wounded, and 3 missing.

Camp Near Harrisburg Va
June 6th 1862

My dear Wife
I last wrote you on the day after the battle of Winchester. I wrote to Boykin the next day. Since that time I have not had one spare moment nor nothing to write on nor with. We have been and now are in one of the most active campaigns of the whole war. We have marched to Harpers Ferry and are now on the retreat, while the anemy are harassing our rear evry hour in the day and endeavering to cut us off below and above. Gen Milroy is in our rear, Shields is coming up the Shenandoah on the south side and Fremont is above us. It is rumored that we are cut off and will be compelled to surrender or cut our way out. The anemy are trying to retake the prisoners and property that we took at Winchester and other places.

If I ever have a spare moment I will give you the details of all of our movements. We move at all hours of day and night. Sometimes we halt, check the anemy and continue our march at night. I might almost say that we have been in line of battle two weeks. The anemy came upon our rear today and were driven back by Ashbys cavelry,[1] killing several and taking their colours, colonel, major, two captains and about forty men. The Yankees have picked up a great many straglers and sick men who were unable to be moved. They may have several of our men. As I do not know, I will not say any more.

I recieved your letter of the 18th mailed the 20th yesterday. I think thare

are one or two written previous that have not come up. I am sorry you heard that I was killed. Our boys at the hospitle heard that I was quite sick. Probably you have heard this also. I have not been off of duty since I left Rappahanock.

My dear wife, it pains my hart to think of your situation. Let me encourage you to resist with a stout hart these adverse circumstances. You have already done better than anyone else could, and indeed are the most noble woman living.

You want to know what I think of the future. It is still bright. A united South imbued with the love of liberty never can be subjugated. This unholy fratricidal war certainly can not last much longer. If the human race is too depraved to stop it, certainly let us hope that the omnipotent ruler of the universe will stretch forth his hand and say to the contenting elements, "peace, be still." I have not time to write. Goodbye my dear little woman,
Your boy,
Ugie

Susie

As I have something of a private nature to write to you I will write it on a different piece of paper to prevent its gaining publicity. Do not tell it to anyone not even our boy. I can not bear for you to be situated like you are. I intend to make an attempt to resign. What do you think of it? I think I will get Genls Trimble and Ewell to give me permission to go to Richmond and I will get them to approve it and carry it to the Adjutant General and ask him to accept it. I may fail and of course intend that no one of the company or at home shall know anything of it. I think this is the most provident plan as it is contrary to law for any to be accepted only on surgeons certificate and I have no reason to believe that I will be successful. This may be an unpopular act in me. I love my country as dear as anyone, but am unwilling to sacrifice domestic hapiness to good public opinion. Anyone that would do it is unworthy of either. Boykin is coming back and of course I feel less delicacy in doing this. Set down as soon as you get this letter and tell me candidly what you think of this. I wrote this on my canteen while we rest. I know if you knew how we are situated you would not think hard of such a short letter. Dont find falt with me; but pray that I may be spared to come back to you safe.
Your loving husband,
Ugie

1. Turner Ashby (born October 23, 1828) commanded the majority of the cavalry in Stonewall Jackson's Valley Army. Ashby was killed on June 6, 1862, while directing a rear-guard engagement near Harrisonburg, Virginia.

Camp Near Fort Republic Va
June 12th 1862

Dear Susie

I wrote you a letter about the 7th. Since that time we have had a terrible battle. We were camped on a bye-road running from Harrisburg to Fort Republic[1] where the only bridge was across the Shenandoah that had not been burned. Genl Shields had passed up the South bank of the river from about Manassas or somewhere else and cut off our retreat holding the bridge while Fremont and Milroy were pressing our rear. I have already wrote to you about our daily skirmishes with them in order to hold them back. Harrisburg is about seven miles from Fort Republic. We passed thare on the evning of the 5th. The next day we had a cavelry engagement and drove them back under cover of their infantry. I neglected to state in my previous letter that here we lost one of the most gallant cavelry officers the world has ever produced, and by far the best in the Confederate service; Col. Ashby. That night we camped about half way between H. and F. R. On the 7th we did nothing. On the 8th Gen. Jackson swept down on Shields like an avalance, secured the bridge and drove him back. While this was going on Fremont advanced on our rear, thinking of course that they would crush us between their overwhelming masses. Our division (Ewells) was instantly put in motion and were in position with skirmishers thrown forward before the anemy aproached. Our brigade was the centre. Gen Taylors on the left wing and Elzy[2] on the right. About 9 o'ck our batteries opened on parties of the anemy who were feeling for our position and driving in our skirmishers. In about an hour the musketry opened on our left and continued for a while. About twelve our own regemental skirmishers commenced firing and falling back to our position. We took our position behind a fence on top of a hill while the anemy aproached across a field. The anemy could not see us as they were under the hill. They formed in line of battle and came up. The hill was steap and we saw their colours suddenly rise above the leavel. When they rose to the hips as sudden as lightning the whole fence seemed converted into a volcano more terrible than Vasuvious.[3] Their whole line seems to fall to the ground, they reel & stager for a moment and rush back down the hill in all the confusion immaginable. They ran in evry direction. The command forward is given and our boys mount the fence like deer and follow down the hill shooting straglers and such as were not beyond range. Thare was a regiment lying

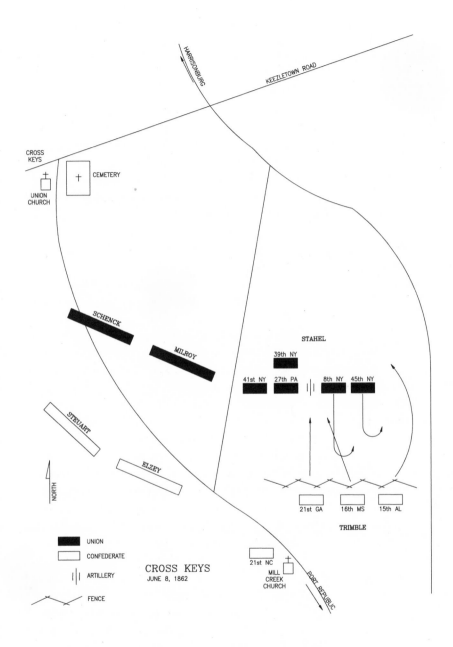

HARRISONBURG

KEEZLETOWN ROAD

CROSS
KEYS

CEMETERY

UNION
CHURCH

SCHENCK

MILROY

STAHEL

39th NY

41st NY   27th PA   8th NY   45th NY

STEUART

ELZEY

NORTH

21st GA   16th MS   15th AL

TRIMBLE

UNION

CONFEDERATE

ARTILLERY

CROSS KEYS
JUNE 8, 1862

21st NC

FENCE

MILL
CREEK
CHURCH

PORT REPUBLIC

behind the fence on the other side of the field waiting for us to come. The Colonel ordered us back. As we were going back they opened fire upon us though they did not do as much damage as a person under their fire would expect. Sam Pitts was shot through the leg and fell unable to get away. We took our old position and waited patiently the development of events. The Alabama regiment in a few minutes opened fire upon the flank of our antagonists. The anemy was shelling us from a battery across the field all this while, but hapily we were too far over the hill. The Ala. regiment was driving them back upon their battery when they threw forward another regiment from their rear. At this juncture we charged across the field at a sweeping pace in order that we might take their battery. But it was too far off (about five hundred yards) and they all, both infantry and artilery, made their escape before we got thare. We pressed forward after them, for about half a mile and had nearly passed (perhaps intentionally) a regiment in some woods while we were in a field. As quick as lightning by comand of our colonel we flew to the fence under a galling fire from their Enfield rifles. The Miss. regiment was on our right. Here the battle raged furiously for some time; they in the woods about eighty yards distant and we behind a fence. Our boys were all quite cool and when ever one showed himself a leaden messenger of death was sent after him. Here our regiment lost several men, among them our worthy sergent major.[4] Col Posey[5] of the Miss. [regiment] was also wounded. The fence was almost riddled with bullets.

I must particularly mention Johny Brewer and Billy Strong who were directly in frunt of me. They were sitting side by side in the corner, would load quickly and shoot alternately through the same crack, taking aim as deliberately as if they were shooting birds. Lt. Waller mentions Bagby, Higginbothem, and Cousin Robert who were at the head of the company as being remarkably cool and encouraged each other by pleasant words and laughing at each others jokes. None of our boys were excited. Our regiment did more execution than any regiment did. I think we killed about one hundred of the regiment that came up the hill on us. Their whole line was marked by a continuous pile of dead men and they were strewn promiscuously clear across the field to the woods. We killed their col and lt. col. and their colour bearer and captured their colours. I think the anemy lost four or five hundred killed and prisoners. We followed up the anemy and slept or lay upon our arms in line in about half mile of their camp. Our worthy fellow soldier David Porter[6] was mortally wounded by a ball from a bomb while engaged as a litter bearer and carying wounded from the field. The ball struck him and ranged either up or down, passing from his left brest near the collar bone out on the right hand side of the spine about the middle of the back; or visa versa. He has no feeling nor can not move himself below the wound. He thinks his back is broke. We have not seen him. This is what the ambulance driver tells me. Tom Tally, our other litter bearer, was shot through the canteen and grained on the hip while endeavouring to carry off Pitts. Genl. Jackson fought a very hard battle on the 9th just below Fort Republic and cut our way out. He took four pieces of artillery and about seven hundred prisoners. You will gain more general information about these fights from the papers than I will ever find out. Thus ends one of the most brilient campaigns recorded in modern history. We have demolished one army (Banks) shelled the anemy on Maryland Heights and successfully withdrawn to the mountains though flanked by three generals each one with a force almost equal to our own and brought away four thousand prisoners and two millions of captured property. This has been done in a little over twenty days and with a loss scarcely equal to the anemy's killed.

On Sunday previous to this we had an artilery engagement with Milroy at Strasburg, making three successive Sundays that we were engaged. Winchester, Strasburg and Fort Republic.

Who can paint the hardships and horors of war? What historian has ever fixed them indelibly on the minds of his readers? I answer none. The Revolution, the Crusades, the seige of Jerusalam by the Romans, or of Lucknow with all the imbelishments of the historian, are inadequate to make a correct impression on the human mind.

I write this letter by pieces as I am on a court martial today and of course all of my time is consumed, only a little in the morning and dinner. This is the first chance I have had of writing in a long time. To tell you the truth our bagage with the exception of blankets is hauled and if I had of had time and mail facilities I had nothing to write upon. Sometimes we do not see our bagage for a week. My clothes got wet at Winchester and have not been dry since, taking all the rains and I could not have a chance to dry them. They are almost roten, my papers all ruined. To give you an idea, some ground peas[7] that I had had sprouts two inches long. Now you see my dear you can form a faint idea how things are. If I had of finished this letter a few hours ago I could have sent it off but do not know when I will have a chance. You see that a private can sometimes be at his leisure when an officer is compelled to be at business. Lt. Waller is under arrest and being courtmartialed today. You must say nothing about this to anyone, not even to Boykin, for twenty gags could not keep his mouth shut. Let matters fully develop themselves.

The recruits came about two days ago. They brought me your dear long letter. I recieved the one you sent with Crouch's just a minute ago. Crouch is well and hearty. He is always buisy as the wagons break frequently on our marches and he is brigade wagon workman. He fairs better than anyone I know. He is with the wagons and always has a tent, and as much of the best that the brigade commisary afords as he wants. He is well liked by both the quartermaster and Gen Trimble. I heard him remark in his peculiar stile that the people at home found out that he was dead, and he believed he would let them find out that he was alive.

I am much troubled at your situation. You have not presented the subject to my mind for the first time. But my dear I did not know what remedy I had. I mentioned the subject to you in my last letter. Another recourse that I have is to apply to Gov Brown for an apointment in the State and by that means be able to be at home occasionaly. This idea suggest itself to me last night. Indeed we are in a deplorable situation. If you can not get some one to stay with you, break up! It is much easyer to say break up than where to go. In fact this is the only point that has ever troubled me. Anything to make you happy. We must have some one to stay thare and attend to the business. I aught to have done this when I was thare but poor delusive mortals, we always hope for better times and make no preparation for the future. Perhaps it would be prudent not to take any decisive steps for a while, even if you did not remain at home much during the time. I was in hopes that George would not go into service again. He has chosen the hardest though most exciting branch of the service. However thare are many soldiers in the war who do not know what service is; as much depends on where a person is sent to. Artilery is much the easyest branch though I believe a greater per cent is killed in battles. I speak from what I have seen in the Valley. Jesse can not well stand an active campaign, I dont think. Napoleon once truly remarked that it took three years to make an army. I am well as you could expect and as tough as whalebone and rawhide, though somewhat reduced in flesh. Recently I was young; now I am old phisacaly and in experience. I presume we will rest here for a few days and then will be away, away, like a meteor and fall upon the anemy at some exposed point—dealing such a blow as will remind him that the "Valley fox" Stonewall Jackson is again at his old pranks. I wish that I had time to give you a description of the phisic of this genious, the pride of the whole army and terror of his anemies.

I wish that I had time to write Boykin a letter today. You will read my letter writen to him concerning the Winchester battle. I think I will send you this in an envelope that some bold Yank did not want to be troubled with in their very slow retreat from that place. I could fill a small book with incidents connected with our campaign.

You seem to think that I have almost forgoten home. No! my dear no. As the mariner's compass ever turns to the pole star; so my hart ever turns to my home and loved ones far away in the low country where with whom I long to breathe out my life undisturbed by the wicked and tumultuous world without. Like the Christian soldier evry step that I take on the weary march and evry hour that passes over me, serves to remind me that if my life is spared by devine providence I am that much nearer home. Often do I think of poor Byron, as he sung: "O that the desert was my dweling place with one fond spirit for my minister, that I might all forget the human race and hating no one love but only her."[8] Goodbye and be asshured that I write when ever I can.

Your boy,

Ugie

P.S. The battle lasted until about night. I forgot to say that I only got one shirt. Just fits, many thanks. I have only two summer shirts and two pr socks, but do not trouble yourself about more.

1. Harrisonburg and Port Republic.

2. Arnold Elzey (1816–71) commanded a brigade in Richard Ewell's division.

3. Mount Vesuvius, an active volcano in western Italy, erupted in A.D. 79, destroying the cities of Pompeii and Herculaneum.

4. Benjamin P. Barton (born 1836 in South Carolina) listed his occupation as machinist when he enlisted as 3rd sergeant in the "Atlanta Volunteers" on June 26, 1861. The Volunteers were designated Company C when the 4th Battalion (21st Regiment) was organized on July 19, 1861, and Barton was appointed regimental sergeant major.

5. Colonel Carnot Posey (1818–63) commanded the 16th Mississippi Regiment in Trimble's brigade.

6. David A. Porter (born 1840) was sent from the field hospital to Charlottesville, Virginia, where he died from his wounds on June 13, 1862.

7. Peanuts.

8. From canto 4, stanza 177 of Byron's *Childe Harold's Pilgrimage,* 1812–18.

This charcoal reproduction, *ca.*1880, is believed to be
of a photograph taken *ca.* 1860 of Ujanirtus C. Allen.
Courtesy of Ann Strickland Petry

Susan Fuller Allen, the beloved "Susie" of Ugie Allen's letters
Courtesy of Troup County (Ga.) Archives

John Thomas Boykin Jr., the first captain of the Ben Hill Infantry, was Ugie Allen's brother-in-law and in many ways his brother.
Courtesy Troup County (Ga.) Archives

Private John W. Mathews was barely fifteen when he enlisted in the Ben Hill Infantry. Allen called him a "nice boy" but "high tempered" and once put him in the guardhouse for twelve days for disobedience.

Courtesy of Steve Mullinax

Private William Mobley was discharged in the summer of 1862 for disability caused by typhoid pneumonia. His relative Private Wiley Mobley had died of typhoid fever while in camp in September 1861, just two months after enlisting in the Ben Hill Infantry.
Courtesy of Troup County (Ga.) Archives/Thomas M. Mobley

Sudley Church, near Bull Run, served as a hospital for the many members of the 21st Georgia who fell ill in Virginia in the fall of 1861. Allen himself was hospitalized here that fall, suffering from "fever of a bilious type," probably typhus.

From Robert Underwood Johnson and Clarence Clough Buel, eds., Battles and Leaders of the Civil War *(4 vols.; New York, 1887–88)*

Allen's sketch of the Cedar Mountain battlefield from his August 11, 1862, letter to Susie
Courtesy of Randall Allen

Private Thomas Garrett, whom Allen mourned as one of "my best and bravest men," was killed in brutal fighting on August 28, 1862, at Groveton (Second Manassas). Of the 242 men of the 21st Georgia who went into action that day, only 69 were able to report for duty the next morning.
Courtesy of Lela W. Craft

Casualties from a Georgia regiment in the East Woods at Antietam (Sharpsburg), Maryland,
September 17, 1862. The artist may well have been depicting Allen's regiment,
who fought in these woods that day with heavy losses.
From Johnson and Buel, eds., Battles and Leaders

Confederates at Hamilton's Crossing, near Fredericksburg, December 13, 1862.
The 21st Georgia fought gallantly here in a Confederate victory.
From Johnson and Buel, eds., Battles and Leaders

Stonewall Jackson's troops assault the works of the Federal XI Corps,
Chancellorsville, May 2, 1863. It was in this attack that Ugie Allen received
the wound of which he died six days later.
From Johnson and Buel, eds., Battles and Leaders

Ujanirtus Allen's grave, Antioch Cemetery, Troup County, Georgia
Courtesy of Randall Allen

6

GAINES'S MILL AND RECOVERY AT RICHMOND

We rallied with a yell and double quick evry time.

S TONEWALL Jackson's Valley Army remained encamped in the vicinity of Weyer's Cave for a little more than two weeks following the battles of Cross Keys and Port Republic. On June 17, Trimble's brigade and the 21st Georgia crossed the Blue Ridge Mountains at Brown's Gap, marching nine miles toward Waynesboro on the Virginia Central Railroad. Unbeknownst to Jackson's men, their commander had instructions to march his troops to the aid of General Robert E. Lee's army, which was protecting Richmond from a Union army commanded by General George B. McClellan.

When the 21st Georgia reached Charlottesville, the footsore soldiers bivouacked on the campus of the University of Virginia. Hundreds of men, including Lieutenant Allen, had lagged behind on the march; they rested at a camp established for stragglers near Meacham River Station. After several days' recuperation, they took a train from Gordonsville to Ashland, where the soldiers from Trimble's brigade, formed into a company under Captain James C. Nisbet of the 21st, rejoined their various regiments.

Allen returned to the 21st Georgia just in time to participate in the second battle of the Seven Days' campaign at Gaines's Mill, on June 27, 1862. Around 2:00 P.M. on that day, while the sounds of fighting raged to the south, Trimble's men moved forward in line of battle, with the 21st Georgia thrown out in front of the brigade. While the men of the 21st waited in a field for orders to go in, their colonel, who "had been imbibing freely of the ardent," dismounted and fell asleep in a pine thicket. Upon seeing Colonel Mercer's condition, General Trimble placed him under arrest and ordered the lieutenant colonel of the 21st, Thomas Word Hooper, to take charge of the regiment.

Shortly after Mercer's arrest, his regiment joined the fight. Passing the de-

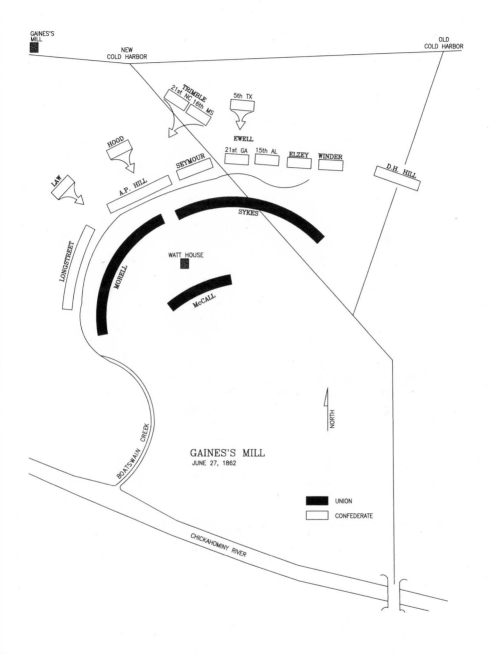

GAINES'S MILL

GAINES'S
MILL

NEW
COLD HARBOR

OLD
COLD HARBOR

TRIMBLE
21st NC 16th MS

5th TX

EWELL

21st GA   15th AL   ELZEY   WINDER

HOOD

SEYMOUR

D.H. HILL

LAW

A.P. HILL

SYKES

LONGSTREET

MORELL

WATT HOUSE

McCALL

NORTH

BOATSWAIN CREEK

GAINES'S MILL
JUNE 27, 1862

UNION

CONFEDERATE

CHICKAHOMINY RIVER

pleted ranks of Richard Taylor's Louisiana regiments, the Georgians entered a densely wooded swamp where they encountered a "furious discharge of musketry, shot and shell" from Union soldiers positioned behind log breastworks along a hillside. With dozens of men falling killed and wounded, the ranks of the 21st, along with those of the 15th Alabama regiment on their right, began to waver. "It was only with the greatest exertion," wrote the 21st's adjutant Thomas J. Verdery, "that the regiment could be rallied and induced to hold their position." Conspicuous among the officers attempting to steady the men was division commander Richard Ewell. According to Trimble, Ewell's "presence alone held the men in position for over an hour and a half under this terrific fire."

Succor for Trimble's hard-pressed regiments came late in the evening in the form of the 5th Texas Infantry. After firing volleys at the Federals for a few minutes, the Texans and the remnants of the Georgia and Alabama regiments charged through the swamp and broke the Federal line. Trimble's men helped capture six Federal cannon but at that point broke off their pursuit of the retreating Union force. By then, wrote Adjutant Verdery of the 21st, the men's ammunition was exhausted.

At Gaines's Mill, Robert E. Lee's nascent Army of Northern Virginia won a dramatic victory but at a terrible cost. Out of approximately 350 men carried into the battle, the 21st Georgia lost 20 men killed and 80 wounded. Among the wounded was Ugie Allen, who had been struck in the chest by a spent ball just before his regiment's final charge. Although the wound was not serious, Allen boarded for several weeks at a private home in Richmond before rejoining his regiment.

Near Beacheum Depot Va[1]
June 21st 1862

Dear Susie

I wrote you a letter a few days ago but could not mail it at the time, now it is out of my reach and I will write you a few lines and try to mail it here. We are again on the march and are within ten miles of Charlottesville. I have no idea where we are going. It is a secret movement to evrybody. All of the Yankees are going back towards Winchester and Frunt Royal. Probably they intend to cross the mountains and we are going to meet them. Some surmise that we are going to Richmond, some to Hanover Court House. I would write to Boykin but I expect he will have left home before this reaches you. If he has not thare are several things I would like for you to tell him. I would like for him to bring me a good pair of shoes No. 10. Be so kind as to send me some yeast cakes, and give me a few ideas about making the bread. Our boy[2] is sick and has been for some time. We mess to ourselves and do our own cooking. I can wade into a pan of flour with as much grace as eat the biscuits when cooked. I think I am growing rather proficient in the culinary art, though our boys wickedly persist in saying I am remarkably awkward. Anything that you can send or Boykin can bring will be a treasure to me. I got hold of a cup of rye coffee for the first time in two months, the other day and thought it the sweatest beverage that I ever drank.

You want to know what I think of the future. I do not know. Evrything is depending on Johnson at Richmond. My faith is sometimes shaken in his ability to defend it.[3] The war will take some turn before August passes. Whip them at Richmond and we will have peace. If we are whiped thare the war will be a long and protracted one. I find one thing from all the Yankee prisoners. Soldiers and evryone are tired of the war. They have no idea of subjugating us. Nothing but their national pride keeps their courage up.

Tell me my dear about what you have hinted to me in several letters; or at least our boy did in his. I am in much suspence and anxiety about you. I do not expect Boykin to remain here even if he comes. A good many of our boys have come in from the hospitles. Berry and Tom W.[4] are both here. Tom has not been nor is very well now. You need not give yourself much uneasyness about the conduct of certain persons that you wrote about some time ago. Go straight forward and pay no attention to it. Favor nothing nor any one that is not just and honorable, and court no one for their friendship. The intercourse between myself and those here is as always, of the most friendly and confidential nature. Let us always pursue the course that I have always recommended and those who are unwilling to affiliate with us are certainly too depraved for us to lose anything. I would write you a longer letter but write even this under difficulties. I write evry opportunity and as often as I can. I know you were very much distressed at recieving no letters from me after I left Swift Run Gap up to Winchester. I had no chance of mailing only once at Madison C. H. Then I was compelled to have my shoes mended. I wrote three and distroyed them. On the morning of the battle of W. I tore up one that I had been carrying several days. Write me often and a good long letter

evry time. You can write at any time almost. Do my dear; don't wait for letters from me to answer. Tell me much of yourself and our dear sweet boy. Tell
everything about home, your domestic arrangements etc. Good bye Susie.
Your Boy
Ugie

1. Allen spelled place-names, as well as common words, phonetically. His bivouac was near the depot at
Meacham's River, Virginia.

2. When Captain Boykin left the company, taking his servant, the remaining officers had hired a cook.

3. Allen was unaware that Robert E. Lee had assumed command of the army defending Richmond on
June 1, 1862, after Johnston was wounded at the Battle of Seven Pines.

4. Thomas B. Wilkes.

Camp Near Beachams River Va
June 22nd 1862

My Dear Susie
I wrote you a letter on the 20th dated 21st. I write again today fearing I may
not have another opportunity soon. The army has gone on somewhere, no
one knows where. I think it is about Gordonville now. Myself and several
hundred others from our brigade, like our broken down horses were left
behind to graze, and recruit up our exhausted frames; or clericaly speaking
energies. The fact is your humble servant was completely worn out; and was
compelled to stop. I dare not fall out on the march for fear of being arrested
and courtmartialed. I was afraid that I was taking the fever, but Dr. Capers[1]
left me with a pocket full of quinine, calomel, and opium which has eradi-
cated all symptoms of fever and I am doing very well. I am staying at a private
house which you know is a paradise compared with camp. I dreamed last
night of being at home with you and telling many things that occurred in our
recent campaign. Would to God it were reality instead of the vague musings
of a disturbed mind. I sometimes think that I have either made a good or lost
a poor constitution in the army. I understand that we will move forward
tomorrow and am somewhat impatient to be going, although we have not
rested but three days. I hear different rumors about our destination. Some say
Richmond. Some Fredericksburg, some that we will pass back into the valley
in rear of the anemy. I know one thing; our errand is an important one. I
must write something about our dear boy. How is he? How does the sweet little fellow look? How does he do? Does he try to talk or walk? My dear some
thief went into my carpet sack and stole your ambrotype. It is truly morti-

fying to see how depraved and perfectly unmindful of all sense of honor men become in an army. You must be shure and write often and very long letters. Tell Uncle Wisdom that Cousin Robert is well.

Good bye Susie,

Ugie

1. LeGrand G. Capers was appointed assistant surgeon when the 4th Battalion was organized on July 19, 1861. He transferred out of the 21st Regiment in November 1863 and at the end of the war was surgeon in Cutshaw's Artillery Battalion.

Hospitle Near Richmond Va
June 30th 1862

My Dear Susie
We had a great battle on the 27th inst. The fight commenced on the 26th and has not ceased yet. Our regiment is badly cut up, our company has sufered severely. I was badly bruised by a spent ball which struck me just below the junction of the left collar with the brest bone. Do not be uneasy for the ball did not enter, only bruised me, tearing my shirt and skin a little. My left arm, side and lung are very sore, though I walk about evrywhere. You know my powers of locomotion were always good. This happened on the 27th. I have not been with the regiment since nor can hear nothing definite from it. I will tell you all that I know of our boys. John Anderson was mortally wounded in the head and died yesterday evning. James and William Philips I fear will die. One shot through or about the brest, the other in the neck. I saw them when shot and thought they were dead, but hear that they are able to sit up. Tom Wilkes shot through the neck behind carying away part of the bone. He is here and doing well; walks & talks freely. He is siting beside me as I write, eating his breakfast and request that you tell Mrs. Wilkes how he is. He is compelled to hold his head erect and can not look down to write. Tell her also that he has not recieved a letter from her since Arch Tyree came. Tip Horsley is wounded with a ball and three buck shot in the muscle of the arm just below the shoulder joint. Joe Horsley has a flesh wound below the knee. No one else is badly hurt. Fears was struck on the arm by a bomb. Cousin Robert's knife was struck by a spent ball which gave him an inconvenient bruise in the groin. Clinton was grained on his ribs but is with the regiment. John Henderson had the skin knocked off between the eyes. George Williams was shot in the leg. I have not seen him. Israel Williams was also struck by a piece of the bomb on the leg. The two Horsley boys, Williams, Cousin Robert and

Fears are here. I expect the battle of the 27th was the greatest ever fought. We are still driving the anemy back. You will gain all the news from the papers. I do not know anything. Our regiment stood up and faced the anemy about an hour and a half. We were in some thick woods about eighty yards from them in the edge of it. We could not well see them and they knew our position precisely. We were driven back about ten or twenty steps several times, but rallied again without loosing even a fire. We rallied with a yell and double quick evry time. Our position was an important one. The Ala. Regiment was driven away from it just as we came up. Old Gen Ewell[1] was charging up and down the line all the while encouraging the men. I was very afraid they would kill him, though he was not hurt. His horse was killed. Maj. Hooper[2] who had command of our regiment is severely wounded in the arm. I know very well why we lose so many generals. They never send the men where they are afraid and do not go themselves. Old Stonewall never says go, but always come on boys! Our regiment was relieved by a Texas regiment. They then reformed and charged the anemy drove them across a large field and took a battery. This was about or near dark. I was shot just as the Texas regiment was coming up. Evrything is so confused I cant think straight. I will write again in a day or two. Direct your letters to Richmond, numbering the Reg. and brigade as before. I think I will get over my bruise in a few days. I have recieved no letter from you in about twenty days. Good bye my dear.
Your boy,
Ugie

1. Richard Stoddard Ewell (1817–72) commanded a division under Stonewall Jackson.

2. Thomas William Hooper (1840–86) had been appointed adjutant of the 4th Georgia Battalion on July 20, 1861; elected major on September 27, 1861; and promoted to lieutenant colonel on March 30, 1862. Hooper later became colonel of the 21st Regiment when Colonel Mercer was killed on April 18, 1864.

Richmond Va
July 2nd 1862

My Dear Susie
I wrote you a letter a few days ago from one of our field hospitles. I came here yesterday and accidently met Boykin. I am going back with him to the regiment tomorrow. I can use my arm tolerably well though my side is somewhat sore. I wrote you two letters from Beachams Station which you have recieved

before now. You speak of Boykin recieving his Winchester letter before you did yours. Both of them were mailed or sent off as soon as finished. I sent yours by mail and his by a Lieut who was going to Ga. Bill Jackson never brought any letters from the company; but from our hospitle boys and birds. He has not been to the company since he first went off. I have no doubt but what I write twice as often as any man with the company. Recollect that we do not cary more than fifty men with us and it is reasonable to suppose that two thirds of the letters recieved are not from the company. I sent you a letter the day before the Fort Republic fight. Did you recieve it? I know you are much distressed at not recieving letters; but my dear I do the best I can. I have not had a change of clothing in fifteen days because our things are in the wagons and we have not seen them. Probably it may be two weeks before I have a chance of writing again. No one but a soldier knows or can form any idea how we get along. Recollect that we are under Stonewall Jackson and grass never grows under his feet. We shell the anemy on Maryland Heights and in a few days defeat two proud and boastful armies at the lower end of the Valley. The thunder of his cannon scarcely dies away in the mountains before they again echo in the halls of our capital one hundred and fifty miles distant.

All of our wounded boys are doing well. For fear you will not get my other letter I will again [state] who are wounded. John Anderson died June 29th from a ball that entered the brain on the left side above the ear. Tom Wilkes and Wm Philips are both shot through the back of the neck near the head. Corpr Joe Horsley through the flesh part of the right leg below the knee, and Tip Horsley through the muscle of the arm just below the shoulder joint by a ball and three buck shot. Fears struck by a fragment of a bomb on the left arm. I A Williams struck on the leg. Cousin Robt. in the groin by a spent ball which struck his knife. Johns Henderson between the eyes. George Williams through the leg. Lt Waller grained on the lip and Mike Clinton on the side. A spent ball struck me just where the left collar bone and brest bone joins. It did not enter but tore the skin and inflicted a very inconvenient bruise. I thought that the bone was broke or fractured but I can now use my arm tolerably well. I am somewhat swolen and of a greenish yellow colour from below the nipple to my neck and shoulder. All of our boys except Joe H (and he crawls and slides) walk about anywhere they please. I am afraid they will try to do too much. Wisdom, Henderson and Fears wait upon the others all the while. W & H would go back to the regiment now if it were not for the others. Their wounds are kept wet all the while day and night and dressed when necessary. It is quite an arduous task. I have seen several die for the want of proper attention. The doctors do not stop day or night. I forgot to say that James Philips was shot through about two inches above the right nipple. The ball passed through a rib and part of his lung. This was all done on the evening of the 27th. I do not know where the regiment is or whether it has been engaged since or not. The wounded of our division of the army will be carried to Lynchburg and Charlottesville. You knew that Porter died from his wounds. Pitts is doing well and mending fast. I saw him at Charlottesville and he said that he would come to the regiment in four weeks. It will be at least ten before he can walk much as he can not move his leg now. John Higginbothem accidentally shot his left hand with a pistol a few days before the last fight. We miss him very much on such occasions.

I think it a very good idea that you broke up. Get Mr Hunt by all means.[1] I did not engage him because I did not think he ever would be able to attend to anything. I told him before we left Manassas that I had rather have him than any one else. By the way I owe him twelve dollars. Pay him amediately. I told Boykin to attend to it when he left; but he did not think of it. Boykin tells me many things about our boy. He says he is the greatest fellow living. I expect I will have to call him Stonewall yet. While I think of it direct your letters to Richmond just as you did to Gordonville. I am not proud of my grade; in fact had rather be an honor to it than for it to be an honor to me: but will hint that the title of Lieut. is a little more in vogue with us military fellows than simple Mr. Of course you know this is a joke. I did not expect my Boykin letter to be published. I have writen one to Willingham[2] about our compaign and the Fort Republic fight, but it is in my carpet sack and will be so old that I will not send it. But since it is published tell me what was thought of it. I see several very grave rhetorical errors in it. Towards the last all the sentences are too short and harsh to be pleasing or have an agreeable affect on the mind of the reader. Again thare is too frequent repetition of the same words showing a want of versatility by the writer. These are two falts that I have both in writing and speaking. Short sentences should always be guarded against in writing as much as long ones.

You are fortunate in having so much money to take care of. I am not much behind you for I drew four months pay today, whether I had any before or not it is best not to say. Money with soldiers is not as much of an object as a few other things. By the by; I was in hopes I would get something to eat here but am sadly disapointed although I pay $3.50 per day board. I think I will go out and get me a full suit of clothes out and out, take a shower bath, a cigar, shave and feel better generally. I feel as dry and am as dusty and hard featured as an

Egyptian mummy. My idea is to get enough money to pay at least the first payment on John Samples place[3] if I can buy it; and see clearly where the next is to come from. It is poor dependance to try to collect money on notes such times as these, or may be, "A bird in the hand is worth two in the bush," so get all the money from them that you can without gaining the reputation of a dun.

I must certainly write to Wilkerson. The fact is we have been so torn up since I came back here that I have no energy and less sense. Recollect that note that Broome[4] holds, and our last years accounts. Pay Hollie by all means. I think that cotton will jump up to twenty or twenty five cents as soon as our victory becomes generally known. If it does let it slide by all means. Recollect that Fortune is blind and no one knows when the tide may turn. A hundred dollars a bale for what cotton I have on hand, two hundred that I can send you with what you have will place me in a condition to look out for another home for you and that romping, saucy boy, without making any calculation on collecting. Sell all the corn that you can and put the money in your pocket. As soon as Boykin comes in I will have a long talk with him about that Sample place. I want it but you must not say anything about it only to Mr. Boykin. The fact is I must have more land. Besides it will look like beginning life anew to settle on that old place. However, if I can not do better some cabins must be put up amediately or before the year is out. Speaking in accordance with these war times, I will make a faint movement so as to decieve the anemy. Just imagine the war closed and we with a settlement down thare how pleasant it would be.

When I mentioned that Broome note I did not say pay it. My idea is to hold fast what I get to buy land and let those that I owe do as I have done untill I can see my way through. Wilders note learned me a lesson. I will not be caught in such another trap soon. I am very glad that Low brought that note.[5] I wanted it paid anyhow; besides it will be the means of bringing on a settlement between us. I think Boykin will come home in a few weeks. If he does not I will write to his father. I would have been glad to have done this before now but it is unnecessary to appologise. Also to your Pa and Jimmy. Why do you not mention them in your letters?

I hear that our regiment has not been engaged since last friday, but see from the morning papers report Jacksons division in the fight yesterday evning.[6] All of the wounded will be sent home as soon as they can travel without endangering their lives. I expect some of the citizens will come on here soon. They will probably find some dificulty in finding our boys. They must hunt for the wounded of Jackson and Ewells divisions. I have no doubt but what all will be sent to Lynchburg and Charlottesville as I said before. Johny Greenwood[7] died today. Egene Ware[8] was killed dead. Jim Strickland[9] is shot badly. The 14th Ala. is badly cut up. The 47th is here also. I told you in a previous letter that our little Maj. Hooper is wounded in the arm. Mercer got on a big bust just before the fight and is under arest. We had nobody to command us but stood the heaviest fire that ever mortal man saw or heard. Trees as large as my leg are actually cut down by musket balls. You would not think that an insect could have lived thare. I saw one of our regiment shot eight times. Recollect we were in some woods and the anemy at the edge of it. They had the best position for they knew where we were and we could scarcely ever see one of them the smoke was so thick. Our men did much greater execution than they did. Some of our companies lost many more than we, while others did not.

Like you I dislike to send blank paper. Give my respects to all. May He that rules the universe protect you and our dear boy and grant that I may return to you safely.

Your boy,

Ugie

P.S. Tell Mr. Mobly that Billy when last heard of was at Huganot Springs Hospitle very sick.

1. Susan moved into the Boykin household from the home she and Ugie had occupied at Houston. She employed Henry Hunt as overseer for the farm at Houston.

2. Charles H. C. Willingham (born 1829) was publisher of the LaGrange *Reporter.* Soldiers' letters were frequently published in their hometown newspapers. Unfortunately, few war-era issues of the weekly *Reporter* survive.

3. John W. Sample married Mary E. Formby on December 2, 1858. Their farm was part of the extensive Formby and Lee family holdings southeast of Houston. Sample joined Company K, 56th Georgia Regiment, on May 12, 1862. He was killed at Rocky Face Ridge, Georgia, on February 25, 1864. Dr. H. H. Cary purchased the Sample place from Mary in 1867.

4. John Rufus Broome (January 22, 1824–July 7, 1910) was a LaGrange merchant.

5. Isaac Lowe (born 1806) was an overseer for the Wilkerson family. Allen probably refers to the promissory note for $835.30 that he held against Jesse Wilkerson.

6. The Battle of Malvern Hill on July 1, 1862, was the last engagement of the Seven Days' campaign.

7. John Thomas Greenwood (born 1842) was 1st lieutenant of the "Yancey Greys," Company D, 14th Alabama Regiment. Greenwood was wounded on June 27, 1862, at Gaines's Mill.

7. Eugenius S. Ware (born 1833), junior 2nd lieutenant in the "LaGrange Light Guards," Company B, 4th Georgia Regiment, was killed at King's School House on June 25, 1862.

8. James Kinchen Strickland (April 7, 1834–April 22, 1882), son of Wilson and Teresa Pitman Strickland, was a private in the "LaGrange Light Guards." He was wounded at Malvern Hill on July 1, 1862.

Richmond Va
July 5th 1862

Dear Susie

I started to the regiment the other day and not being able to hold out, I came back. I found Wm Cooley and Reuben Akers here this morning wounded last Tuesday evning. A ball from a bomb passed through the muscle of Cooley's leg about half way between knee and ancle. Akers struck above the ancle by a fragment of a bomb. No bones broke. Our regiment was not engaged then but was under that terrible cannonade that you read of.[1] I understand that a cannon ball struck the ground just under Lt. Henderson and Corp. Tapley and threw them up in the air. I am glad to state that they were unhurt. Tell Uncle Wisdom that Cooley saw Cousin Frank a few days ago. I can learn nothing definite of the 14th or 47th Ala only that the 47th has not been engaged.

I know you want to hear something else besides this war news; but how can I help writing when it looks like my best friends are among the killed and wounded. And then I know if we do not totally demolish this army the war will be a long and protracted one. I will be in the field again in a few days. I know that twenty or thirty days relaxation would be of great benefit to me as well as thousands of others who were in our Harpers Ferry Campaign. But thare is no time for relaxation now. If we want peace now is the time to strike a blow that will make the tyrant and invader tremble. My policy is hope and fight for it. I put no confidence in the reports of foreign intervention and mediation and am truly sorry that our journals insert such trash. It has a demoralising afect on our army and people. Now mark what I tell you; if peace does not follow this battle we will meet with a succession of reverses which will well nigh prove our ruin.

Boykin speaks well of the negroes except Jim. He is a valuable negro and I have placed so much dependence in him that he is spoiled; besides going to see that wife of his is a great disadvantage. He will be ruined if I do not take some active and decided measure to stop him. I am truly glad to hear that Harve and Bob are so faithful. It seems quite reasonable that Martha could be spared now the crop is finished. Be shure and give her such a task as will keep her as diligently at work as if she was in the field. You know how easy it is for a person to loiter away time about a house. You are certainly thinking of winter clothes early. I have not got my spring ones yet. The same jeans coat and a pair of pants intended for the use of probably some defunct Yankee forms my outfit.

Too much care can not be taken of what few seed oats I have. Let the sheep be kept in as good order as possible so as to inshure a valuable flece and healthy increse. If the blocade is not raised very soon nor no prospect of it, you had better get a full supply of salt before thare is much demand for it.

I think you wrong me when you say in your letter "or just did not think enough of me to write." My dear you don't know what our situation was. I have not language to tell it. I had nothing to write with and even if I had probably could not have writen and know I had no mail. If you will show me a letter written by any member of Gen Jacksons army from the time we left Harpers Ferry until we passed Harisonburg I will make you queen of the greatest kingdom on earth (I sent you one at this time). We were in lines day and night besides it rained incesantly. The mud was from shoemouth to ancle deep much of the time. We frequently marched untill late in the night then rations were to be drawn and probably cooked by day in the morning and weary, weary, we would drop down to sleep without covering in a drenching rain and feel like death with all its horors would be a gracious relief. The scroll of the historian will be wet with tears when he records the sufferings of Jacksons men. Many a poor fellow has slept soundly while standing in lines and fell head long on the ground. At Strasburg I saw men sleep while in line of battle and our batteries and those of the anemy had been engaged and skirmishers had been sent out to reconoiter the position of the anemy. All I ask is for you to compare my and your situations and say who should write. I know you did not mean what you said but it is a stumbling block to me evrytime I read your dear sweet letter. I would give anything to see you and that saucy boy. I know he must be sweet. Let us hope that this horible war will soon close. Does he try to talk? Learn him to say Pa.

Good bye dear Susie

Ugie

1. On Tuesday, July 1, 1862, Confederates assaulted the Federal position at Malvern Hill. McClellan massed artillery which swept away piecemeal attacks by the divisions of Magruder, Huger, and D. H. Hill. The 21st Georgia was held in reserve for most of the day, supporting Courtney's Battery.

Richmond Va
July 7th 1862

Dear Susie
I wrote you a letter a few days ago; knowing your anxiety I write again today. I do not expect to recieve any letter from you untill I go to the regiment for you must recollect that I told you in a previous letter to direct yours to this

place precisely as you did to Gordonville. Of course they will all be sent to the regiment. If I was going to remain here longer than a day or two, I would write for you to come up. Nothing would please me better than to come home if circumstances would admit it. Many thanks for the socks which by the way are too large and handkerchief. I droped the latter on the dining room floor and some of the servants picked it up which was the last of it. I regret loosing it very much.

I met Dr. White[1] yesterday who informs me that he is sent here to look after our wounded boys. I fear that he will not be able to acomplish much. Only two—Akers and Wm Cooley—are here. I left the others out near the battlefield. They may possibly be thare now; but I have no doubt they are in Lynchburg & Charlottesville. Evryone will be furloughed as soon as they are able to travel; that is all who deserve them. This is my opinion; I may be mistaken. I saw Dr. Andrews[2] today. He saw Jesse in Wilmington with Sam Fears. He is sick and the Dr. thinks he will have a severe time of it. Fears is improving. Eight of McCoy's Company were killed. Among them Robt. Hunt.[3] I do not recollect the other names. Robt. Denham is unhurt and fighting like a tiger. Did I tell you about Jim Strickland. His right thumb fore and middle fingers are shot off. A ball entered his right fore arm above the rist and passed up some distance beyond the elbow. A buckshot struck his shoulder a spent ball struck him on the right brest, and a fragment of a bomb struck his haversack and hurt his hip and loins. He is doing remarkably well, and is in extra fine spirits. I have seen him twice and of course will visit him as long as he stays here.

I forgot to tell you to pay Pitts. I still insist that he is quite a poor specimen of humanity. Pay Perkins[4] by all means. Boykin tells me that money is no object with the people thare now. We do not know that the war is over by any means and times may become as hard as ever before the year is out. When Boykin comes I will send a great deal of word to you. My dear, I am afraid you are too parcimonious as regards yourself and my boy. I shall not like it if you are. Dont think of making wool dresses for him. Get worsted and flannel by all means. Certainly you can find some somewhere. Have you a nice hoop? Rather an impertinent question to ask—but—but—but; well, you know you aught to have.

I am truly sorry to hear that Mr Boykin is not in good health. Be shure and give him my best; and also Mrs B and Lizzie. I know they will excuse my not writing. Of course you always tell them the news if I am lucky enough to write any. I think this must be the hotest place in the Southern Confederacy. I have been trying to keep cool for three days and have not aproximated to it.

Most of the water used is from the James river no ice nothing to eat no nuthing but ten thousand drays passing along the paved streets making a noise equal to pandimonium. I always betray myself so that you find that I am sound on the eating question. That is the second and all important question with a soldier. "Where is your regiment at?" "Do you all get anything to eat down that way?" I do not know when I could get a box. I would like it very much if you and "Stonewall" could come with it. I know I have written enough of this trash. Before I commenced I thought I could write at least ten pages; but cant think of a thing now.

Good bye,

Ugie

P.S. I dont know where the regiment is, probably thirty miles from here.

1. Green Monroe White (October 15, 1820–May 20, 1892) practiced medicine in the White's Hill community of western Troup County.

2. When Allen wrote this letter, William H. Andrews was serving as a private in Company K, 13th Georgia Regiment. Andrews was later attached to the Confederate medical department in Richmond.

3. Captain D. H. McCoy's "Tom Watts' Greys" were Company C, 14th Alabama Regiment. Robert H. J. Hunt enlisted in the Greys on July 29, 1861. He was killed at Gaines's Mill on June 27, 1862.

4. Paul Perkins (born 1823) was an Antioch, Georgia, merchant.

Richmond Va
July 9th 1862

My Dear Susie
I wrote to you a day or two ago but I can not pass the evning more pleasantly than by writing again, if I can find anything to write. Uncle Wisdom got here yesterday. You know I was glad to see him. I do wish you had come along with him. If I had thought that I would have been off of duty this long I would have made application for a leave of absence and come home for a few days. It matters not how few [it] would have been [the] greatest conceivable gratification to me. I am not quite well yet but I am quite worn out with this town. In fact I do not think it is prudent for one accustomed to the open air and camps to stay here long. The whole air is filled [with] malaria from the thousands of sick wounded and unberied dead. It is a fact that some of the dead are still unberried. I was hurt worse than I supposed when I first wrote to you. Since the swelling has gone out I have become thoroughly convinced that the bone was fractured. Our wounded are still where I left them. I heard from them today. James Phillips wound will probably prove mortal.[1] Recol-

lect he was shot through the lung. All the others are doing finely. They recieve good attention from the surgeons and our boys who can wait upon them. Uncle W. wants to go out thare, but I do not know whether he will get a pass or not we will try this evning or tomorrow. Did you recieve a letter from me writen at the hospitle. You aught to have recieved it as soon as you did Boykins. I gave it to a man coming here who said he would mail it amediately. This is probably the last letter that I will write you from here. I hear that the regiment is in a few miles of here. Our forces are moving. Some surmise that Gen Jackson is going into the Valley again. Gen Ewell will get no credit for the fighting that his men have done, although thay have done a great deal. This is because Jackson ranks him by seniority of commission and we are looked upon as Jacksons forces. Many very intelligent men do not know that Ewell was even with Gen Jackson in "the Valley." Susie I declare I will have to send blank paper this time. I don't think of anything only you and that great boy, and the probabilities and possibilities of this war ever ending. I am anxious to know what the next two months will bring forth. Uncle W has just come by on his way out to the hospitle where our boys are. I gave him two hundred dollars to give to you not knowing whether I could see him again or not.

Good bye my dear,

Ugie

1. James H. Phillips died July 13, 1862, from wounds he received at the Battle of Gaines's Mill on June 27, 1862.

Richmond Va
July 12th 1862

Dear Susie

Here I am in this place yet. It certainly must be a sweet place. I shall not decieve you any more about going to the regiment. I had no idea that I would be off of duty more than a week, but have been decieved. I am not well of my wound yet, and believe that I will feel it for some time. You see, the ball struck me plumb and with such force as would have entered almost any other part of the body. The regiment is out about two miles from here taking a good rest. You know the poor fellows need it. You need not be supprised if you hear of "Old Stonewall" somewhere else pretty soon. I hear he says his men are perfectly worn out and must have some rest. If you want to keep troops healthy you must keep them moving, that is give them such exercise as will not tax their phisical strength. Man is like all other animals naturally indolent and never labors unless prompted by necessity or averice. Place a number of men in camps without any incentive to exercise only the mere love of it and they will soon become deseased from inaction. My dear I shuder to think of the deplorable state society will [be] in when the war ends even if it was to end now. It will be burdened with thousands of indolent, reckless, immoral men each one of them exercising a powerful and balefull influence. Not being able to evert the depravity of others I have always strived to learn a profitable lesson from their example. Appropos, we have the best and bravest set of boys in the army. It is true we have some exceptions to this; but the contrast only shows them more despicable and the others more honorable.

Were you ever so anxious for this war to end? It seems that I would give the world if I had it in my power for an honorable peace. Certainly it will come sometime or other. I thought when we whiped them here that our work would be finished and shure enough it would if Lincoln was not the despot that he is and keep the common people ignorant of the true state of affairs. My only hope for a speedy cessation of hostilities is that broken reed foreign intervention. The people are led to believe the most outrageous lies concerning the sentiment and condition of the Southern people. If they knew the truth all of Lincoln's grand army could not save his head from the halter or his hart from the dager of the assisin. From what I can learn thare are many soldiers in his army who look upon this war in total disgust. They have been decieved by falshoods and misrepresentations and only learn the true state of affairs when it is two late. He rules his soldiers with the iron rod of tyrany and they dare not speak. A few more such unparalelled victories as we have recently gained will greatly change the sentement of the Northern people.

I am boarding at a very pleasant place in the pretiest and most fashionable part of the city. I wrote you a letter last year giving a description of capitol square and other things worthy of note. With the exception of the drays and hacks evrything is more quiet here than ever before. The provost (pronounced provo) guard walk the streets day and night and arrest evrybody who do not have papers or some showing from the proper authority. I understand that yesterday they surrounded the Exchange hotel and arrested one hundred and thirteen officers and soldiers, a good squad of them were carried to the provost marshall for trial, their papers not being suficient to excuse them.

I have noticed two fashions here among the ladies. One is going without hoops, or wearing very small ones. I have not noticed but very few ladies on the streets without them but it is quite common at home. Another is the mortal long trail to their dresses. They wear them from four to eight inches, which gives them a remarkably slouchy appearence in my estimation. To a soldier they suggest a knife for their curtailment or a leather string to tie them up. I have also noticed that very near all the ladies where we have been dress in black as an expression for the condition of the country. The idea of not wearing hoops may be very well and in keeping with evrything else, but somehow or other they suggest faded flowers rather forcibly to my mind. Now tell me what fashion prevails where you live. I expect it is rather like it is among us poor fellows anything conducive to comfort or convenient. I know you are much pleasanter situated now than when by yourself, be contented and happy. Boykin says he does not think that Ethan will ever be as hardheaded again. I will never sell him at a sacrifice. He is a good horse and I and evrybody else know it. You all have certainly had a very bad year for farming. Mr Reid[1] said he only had about twenty five acres in cotton and the grass came near eating that up. He asked me what to tell you. Among other things I told him to say that I had glory enough. This thing of playing the soldier does very well to read and talk about but the reality is quite different.

Uncle Wisdom has not come back. I look for him tomorrow. Our boys will pass through here on their way to the hospitle. Probably some of them may come home soon. I have not heard from Phillips since I last wrote to you. Write to me how long it was after you recieved Boykins untill you recieved my letter. Jim Strickland is not doing very well. They have telegraphed the second time for his father to come. I heard yesterday that his father was at LaGrange about starting and some one told him that he was not badly wounded. This is a pity. I gave you a true statement of his wounds in my other letter. The eracipalas broke out on his arm yesterday. He also has chills. I saw him yesterday and of course will go again today. I think of nothing else at present. Give my respects to Mr. B. Mrs. B. and Lizzie. I never hear anything from her no more than if thare was not such a person she never sends any word. Tell her I feel slighted. Kiss the children for me. Write to me about that jolly boy.
Good bye Susie,
Ugie

P.S. I begin to look for letters from you. Direct as I told you.
Ugie

1. Wiley Reid (born 1814) was a farmer and mechanic, according to census records. His son James was a private in the Ben Hill Infantry.

7

CEDAR MOUNTAIN

The anemy is prowling about on the other side of the Rapidan.
I do not know their force or what are their intentions. However if
"Old Stonewall Jack" gets a chance at them he will make them quake.

LIEUTENANT Allen left Richmond by train on July 14, 1862, rejoining his regiment in Gordonsville the next night. The 21st Georgia, along with the balance of Richard Ewell's division and another division under Charles S. Winder, had been sent to Gordonsville under Stonewall Jackson to protect the vital Virginia Central Railroad from the newly created Union Army of Virginia. During the first week of August 1862, Jackson learned that a Union corps under General Nathaniel Banks was at Culpeper. On August 7, Jackson ordered his divisions to move northward, hoping to attack Banks's isolated corps before it joined with other Union forces.

Advancing sluggishly in the stifling ninety-five-degree heat, Jackson's divisions encountered Banks's Union force eight miles south of Culpeper on August 9. In the ensuing battle, Trimble's and Arnold Elzey's brigades anchored the Confederate right flank from the slopes of Cedar or Slaughter Mountain. Detailed to haul artillery pieces up the steep, rocky western face of the mountain, Allen and the men of the 21st dragged the guns into position around the parsonage of the Reverend Philip Slaughter. Slaughter's yard offered a splendid position for artillery and an equally fine vantage point from which the Georgians watched the fighting.

The Georgians' role as observers ended late in the afternoon on August 9, when General Trimble ordered his regiments to charge down the mountain and advance against the Federal artillery position along the Mitchell Station Road. Upon reaching the road and swinging northward, Trimble found his advance blocked by two obstacles—friendly artillery fire and a large mill pond to his right front. After a twenty-minute delay, the friendly fire had been silenced and Trimble's regiments, advancing en echelon, had negotiated the mill pond. Unfortunately, the halt had allowed Trimble's quarry, a Union battery, time to limber up and move away in the approaching darkness. Despite this disappointment, Trimble's men secured several prizes, including a number of abandoned cannon, caisons, limbers, ambulances, and wounded infantrymen. Because their positions throughout the battle had been relatively concealed from the view of the enemy, the regiments in Trimble's brigade suffered very light casualties; the 21st Georgia counted only four men wounded and none killed in the engagement.

The retreat of Banks's corps toward Culpeper on the night of August 9 left the Confederates in possession of the Cedar Mountain battlefield. While Jackson's men spent August 10 burying the dead and salvaging equipment from the field, Stonewall received reports from the Confederate cavalry of the arrival at Culpeper of Federal reinforcements. Deterred from further offensive action by this information, Jackson withdrew his command across the Rapidan on the night of August 11.

Gordonville Va
July 16th 1862

Dear Susie

I wrote a letter from Richmond last Saturday and sent it Sunday. I left thare on Monday evning and arrived here last night. I would have been glad to have writen another letter and sent it by Uncle W. or Boykin for I know you will feel disapointed. But the regiment were thare and gone before I heard of the move and I had to hurry to get ready before the next train left. I knew very well that if the regiment got up here on a campaign that I would be troubled to find it; besides I was very tired of that place. Uncle W. and Boykin will bring our wounded boys with them and will be at home before this reaches you. I never was so anxious to see you in my life. I can get nothing satisfactory out of Boykin or Uncle W. Their inveriable answer to my questions are: "finely," "well as could be expected," etc. This will be the case when they get home, and you will find them very unsatisfactory. What did you do with all your things when you left home? What of your pottery? Have you made any cordial or wine this summer? Dewberries are just getting ripe here. I think I will go out today and get some; as the boys say they are very fine. I do not know what will be the result of our coming here. I hear that thare is a small force of the anemy out about Rappidan river. If we do not keep a force about here they will take possession of the railroad and Charlottesville.

We have all just been marched down to a mill pond about a mile from here and had a very nice bath. I have no doubt but what it will be of great sanitary benefit as well as a luxury. I heard this morning that Gen. Trimble was going to send into the country and buy as many vegitables for us as he could. Our regiment and in fact our whole division has been reported by the surgeons to headquarters as unfit for duty. We have forty men for duty in the company now. Notwithstanding our campaign in the Valley we cary about as many men as any company from the county except Jones'[1] who has been in Savannah. I wrote to you in a previous letter about buying the Sample place. I would like for you to consult Mr. Boykin about it for me. What is it worth? What can it be bought at. What he thinks of the idea ets. You know I would like to have Uncle W's place but he says nothing about selling. And in fact I do not think he has any idea of it at present. Of course I would not insist. The only objection I have to the Sample place is the location. I had much rather be on
[incomplete]

1. Waters Burras Jones was captain of Company B, 60th Georgia Regiment, the "Fannin Guards."

Picket Guard On Rappidan Va
July 19th 1862

Dear Susie
I mailed you a letter the first writen since I left Richmond, day before yesterday. We celebrated the annaversiry of leaving home yesterday by marching out here through a drenching rain thirteen miles. It has rained four days in succession and will rain again today. I slept last night on a rail pile, night before that on a barn door, previous to that time used the ground. I have not seen my blankets since I was at Beachams River. Many of the boys threw away their blankets when they heard they were coming back here. I am not complaining at our hardships mearly telling you as I promised to do evrything as it occurs. I know that I tell many things that look incredulous. We dont

expect people to believe half that we tell. I told Uncle W. about our fight on the 27th and told him that I never would feel satisfied unless he went and saw the ground. He did so and says he does not expect people to believe anything like the real facts about it. I do not believe that thare was less than five bushels of lead passed across the length of our regiment. We only had seven companies and twelve men of two others.[1]

I forgot to tell you that I slept sound and with the exception of my wound am very well and as saucy as a fox.

Humbly beging your pardon I will take my text on lice this time. Why not? I am shure I am quite as familiar with this as any other subject. I never caught but very few off of me, but I must admit that I have been very fortunate. Thare is not a man in the regiment but what have had them. The fact is thare are men in our company that are actualy being eat up by them. They are sucking their very life's blood out of them. These nasty scamps scatter them whereever they lay down, sit or walk: and we are compelled to use the utmost precaution to keep free from them. The boys laughed at Boykin a great deal when he found himself full after being in camps only one day. Well may Lizzie make him darn his shirt this time.

By the way when ever you send me any clothes be careful to make them with round seams, or some other kind so that these vermin can not hide. If I can get my trunk I will not need any clothes unless it be a pair of drawers or two and a few pair of socks. I think it would be a good idea to line my pants—those I sent you. John Hick is a great fellow, rather fight than eat. He took a good cry because he was not with us when he heard we had been in a battle. Ol F. is at home on a furlough. He will be promoted for gallant conduct during the battle. He could not well use his gun after he was wounded; and when our colour bearer was shot he seized the colours and carried them through the fight. Him Cousin Robert, Thos Britton and Bagby were the coolest men that I saw in the fight. Old Company F out fights creation. I hope that I will soon get home to tell you evrything. I had better quit. I have a mind to not send this shabby letter.

Good bye Susie

Ugie

P.S. The Yankees are in frunt of us and we expect an attact hourly. I send the little boy a present in this. It come from the Yankees.

1. In May 1862, Captain John R. Hart's Company E was transferred to the cavalry, leaving the 21st Regiment with only nine companies until late 1864, when Captain Edward Smith's company became the new Company E.

Gordonville Va
Sunday Eve July 20th 1862

Dear Susie
We have just returned from picket on the Rapidan. I was sadly disapointed in
not recieving a letter from you. I must confess that I never was so extreamly
miserable in all my life. I can't concieve what can be the matter. The word miserable is wholly inadequate to express my feelings. I don't know what to think
say or do. Some of the boys recieved letters mailed at Antioch on the 12th.
Certainly at least three of mine reached you before this time. This is the
eighth that I have writen since I was wounded and in all of them I have asked
you to write to me. Your letters are all that I ever have to give me any happiness or cheer me on; poor lone wanderer that I am, cast piteously too and fro
on the rough billows of fortune. We start again tomorrow at 5 A.M. for some
unknown point. I cant tell when you will ever hear from me again.
Good bye
Ugie

Camp Near Sumerset Va
July 27th 1862

Dear Susie
I recieved your letters of the 10th and 16th writen from Boykins and home
yesterday. This is the first that I heard from you since Boykin came. I will not
attempt to tell my feelings. I told you this in my last Gordonville letter writen
about the 20th. I have not writen since. I could not write. I tried to write several times but was compelled to quit. And then what rendered circumstances
more agrevating I had a terrible dream. You know that I care but little about
dreams, still it caused me much misserable apprehension. Let me tell you. I,
like a bad boy got into a fit of passion once, and thought that I would not
write to anyone untill I recieved a letter—quit writing altogether; but soon
got ashamed of myself and in less than ten minutes sit down and wrote you a
long letter. The fact is I don't see how some people get along never write,
never receive any letters.

The greater part of your letter requiring an answer, is already answered in previous letters and in one written to Mr Boykin a few days since. I am very glad indeed that you sent Uncle W. How could I be otherwise. When we met didn't I hug him and didn't he hug me and with tears in his eyes say "thank God that you are no worse than you are," and it was echoed from the bottom of my hart. The boys were all glad to see him. Our wounded boys owe him a debt of gratitude. The boys frequently compare him to a man who was sent here to attend our wounded and didn't. My wound has not got well yet. I use my left arm very little and am unable to raise conveniently the weight of a musket. It was a hard blow and I do not expect to recover from the affect in some time. The anemy is prowling about on the other side of the Rappidan. I do not know their force or what are their intentions. However if "Old Stone-wall Jack" get a fair chance at them he will make them quake. O my dear, I wish you could just see him. See him before or after a battle as he passes the boys. They will run two hundred yards to see him and yell like wildcats. He invariably, when they cheer him, uncovers his head and dashes along at a rapid pace glancing his proud eagle eye from side to side. Then you aught to see him riding along when we are on the march, always calm and thoughtful with neat standing collar and old gray cap drawn down on his braud forehead. Him and Gen Ewell came around the other day and spent some time looking at us drill. I can not help from believing that our regiment will be mentioned in Gen Ewell's official report. I think it aught to. With only seven companies we faught for three hours drove back and whiped (they were already whiped before the Texans came up. All they needed was for someone to start them.) three regiments of the anemy. We did not know what we were doing untill next morning.[1]

We had an alarm yesterday and marched out near Gordonville and remained untill night. I do not know what will turn up. It is not necessary for me to tell you how anxious I am for this war to end. The late foreign news is somewhat encouraging, but alas! we must not rely on that. The Yankee nation are already whiped, but will never stop until some one tells them; or they have a good pretext for so doing. You nead not fear negroes. If they do not behave themselves they are emphaticaly great fools. I can take this company and two pieces of artillery and whip evry negro in ten miles of you, or in Troup. Let the whites dismiss their fears, do their duty and make the negroes do the same. Our company is selected out of this regiment to drill in the artillery drill so that we can man a captured battery or our own in cases of emergency. I have only drilled two lessons and we can man a gun now. If I have an opportunity I intend to drill them well. I wrote to you about shoes because we can not always get them for love or money. I paid ten dollars for a rough brogue in Richmond. We may have a better chance in a month or two. I will need a pair of boots for winter. I do not know whether I shall have Hollie to make them or not. I shall want the regular army boot. I do not know what we will do for blankets this winter. You must tell those that have friends in the company that the poor boys can not do well without blankets this winter. I have only two. You must send me yours when I want them. I frequently live in a very primitive maner. If the weather is dry pick out a soft and if wet a hard place on the ground pull my cap over my face put my head on a root or chunk and go to sleep. I frequently dine off of a piece of bread and an onion. An onion is a great relish and the soldiers are universily fond of them. The boys pay as high as ten cents apiece for them sometimes; though they have been given in our regular rations several times recently. We get the nicest beef that you ever saw. I am geting to be a great beef eater. Myself and Lt. Henderson dined today off of bread (leather hoe cake), irish potatoes, syrup and onion. Cared nothing for meat. We have great dificulty geting anything cooked on account of the scarcity of utensils. Harper cooks for us now. I have an idea of having Lee or Bill here. However the army is a bad place for a young negroe and besides the season would not suit very well.[2] We will soon have cold nights and very warm days. After the battles of Cross Keys and Fort Republic we did not have anyone to cook for us until recently. We sometimes have a berry or cherry pie. An officer in a company especially if in command always has his hands full. Besides regular duties thare are a thousand and one extras. Some people do not like the idea of an officers getting so much pay. I pity their ignorance and set them down as malcontents and grumblers. If an officer does his duty his pay is well urned. If he does not he is a nuisence and injury to the service and aught to be kicked out. The pay of an orderly Sergeant in the army is too little. Especially such a one as Bagby. I do not say too much when I say he is the best in the regiment. In fact that I ever saw.

Kiss the dear boy for me. I would give a thousand to gather him up and kiss him as he frisks and frolics about. He will soon try to talk, now. I expect he had been eating too much fruit when you wrote to me. I do not recollect what it was I sent to you. I think it was a scrap from a paper. I sent the boy a gold dollar from Gordonville. I would send you some receipts for blackberry wine cordial jellies etc, but the season will be too far advanced when you get them. Look in Lizzie's Goodeys Lady's book and you will probably find them. It does me good to think of such things if I can not get them unlike Capt Battle[3] who threatened to shoot me yesterday for giving him a bill of fare for a good home dinner at this season. Vegitables milk and peaches etc etc etc. I send you considerable space whether thare is news or not.

Good bye Susie

Your boy Ugie

1. In his report dated August 4, 1862, Major General Ewell stated that he could not "speak too highly of the conduct" of his command, including the 21st Georgia.

2. In 1862, Lee was sixteen and Bill was fourteen.

3. Henry T. Battle succeeded Stephen A. Borders as captain of Company D, the "Cedartown Guards," on November 18, 1861.

Near Sumerset Va

July 28th 1862

Dear Boykin

I write you a few lines in haste. Thos Henderson is discharged and carried the paper on which the surgeon's certificate is pasted with Glover's and Gen Trimble's approval home with him. Go and see him amediately and forward it back to me in order that it may be sent to the Adjt & Inspector Gen'l. I mean the paper having the approval of the commanders. It is in duplicate and has surgeons certificate pasted to it. He also has the "soldiers discharge" which he must retain. Now again, I have recieved no official notice of Bill Jackson's discharge. Go and see if he has one. I am compelled to keep him on the rolls and mark "absent without leave." I can not take any mans word. Official information must be had. He has writen for a final statement of what is due him, but if no official notice is recieved or he can not show his papers; he must not be so fast.

Yours in haste,

U. Allen 2nd Lt, Com'd'g Co. F, 21st Ga Reg

P.S. We have fifty men for duty. Give my respects to all the boys.

Bivouac Near Gordonville Va

July 30th 1862

Dear Susie

It was my intention to write to you yesterday but we were woke up night before last at midnight and set to cooking and left our old camp at sun up. We are about four miles from Gordonsville on the road that runs to Richmond. We may probably be going thare or to Fredericksburg or to Bever Dam Station on the railroad. As they do not look like making an early start this morning I thought it best to write a few lines for fear I will not have a chance soon. Possibly this will not be mailed in several days. I do not think my last letter was sent off from the regiment in two days after it was writen. We may stay here several days no one knows. Do you see I have got a new pencil? The health of the company is very good at present. We have more men now than have had since we started into the valley. I have only two well non commission officers, Corps Wisdom and Clinton. Bagby is sick and Sam Rowland acting Sergt Major. Mike and Cousin Robert are kept very buisy.

Capt. Glover is promoted major and Maj Hooper Lt Colonel. Col M is still in Richmond. Did I tell you that he was under arrest for geting drunk on the eve of the fight. Thare are some things about this man that I do abominate, still I have much confidence in him as an officer. Some of the men are very much displeased with him; while others say "give me Mercer drunk in preference to anyone else sober when we fight." I can place very little confidence in a man who is habitualy a drunkard. We are going to move. I have not time to write much more, neither have I much to write. Who can write anything more than mere generalities when evrything is in a figit. I think we will meneveur around yet untill we get into a fight up to our hatbands. I would be glad if it was not necessary for us to fight any more. Four battles and two skirmishes aught to satisfy most any one. As I told Mr Reid to tell you, I have glory enough. However we are geting tolerably well used to it if it is possible for a person to do so. It is possible to a great degree. You must have some one else to attend to the negroes. I would not stay thare alone. I am quite anxious to come home but know I cannot. No one can get a furlough now. If I could now I could not this winter. Let us hope the war will not last untill winter. If England does not propose mediation nor recognise us now, I am perfectly willing if the north will let us alone to join in with some power and whip her untill the lion can not even growl or wag his tail. I said I was willing, I mean I would be glad to see it done, but narry time do you catch me in it. The platform that I stand on now is quite simple: Peace, Old Stonewall and little Stonewall. I heard that Jesse was discharged. If he is you know it before now. I am convinced that he would not be able to do much in several months if ever. You must write often.

Your boy

Ugie

Camp near Sumerset Va
August 3rd 1862

Dear Susie

Although I am expecting a letter from you this morning I will write you a
few lines for fear I will not have another chance soon. For the last four days I
have been almost run to death or I would have writen sooner. They are
straightning out evrything in the army and we are crowded making reports of
diferent things connected with the company, making requisitions and besides
other things the pay rolls were to be fixed up and money drawn for the boys.
We have had about three months work to do since we have been up here. I
had just finished paying off the last man as the drum beat yesterday for us to
fall in and come back to this (our old) camp. I have not drawn nor never
intend to draw for a man that is not with the company. You know it is not prudent to have controll of other peoples money. I run no risk and it will wake
up these hospital birds. Some men stay off just as long as they have or you will
send them money. When ever a fellow begins to write for money you may
look for him to come to the company if he does not get it. Tell Boykin to
find out where Dock Parker is and let me know it. He has been away from the
company about five or six months. My dear it is no use for me to try to write.
I have been stoped and had to attend to other business four times since I commenced this. I have to attend to evrything myself. Tommy Pitts returned to
the company yesterday. Arch Tyree was taken suddenly sick and I am afraid he
will have a very bad time of it. The boys are loading their stomachs with the
greenest sourest apples imaginable. I am afraid we will have a great deal of
sickness this fall. It is my opinion we will have a great battle here soon, probably before this reaches you. The anemy are being reinforced. So are we. Long-
streets[1] and Hills[2] divisions are here, all of them picked troops. We may strike
out for Washington City for what I know. You and the boy are having a fine
time eating watermelons I hope. Somehow or other I never think about such
things now unless they are associated with other things. Boykin did not bring
my coat and pants home. I do not know whether to tell you to make me some
for winter or not. I know very well I must have some. Those that I got in
Richmond are geting worse for ware or dirt now. I sent you an envelope in
my last letter, so that you can enclose one in it. I like that style of backing better than the one we are using. You had better increase your deposit in the

office. We have no stamps nor can get any. I am quite well, with the exception of a cough. Whether it was caused by my wound or exposure I do not know. I would not send this poor thing if I thought I could do better soon. If things become quiet I will write again soon, especially if I recieve one from you. Nothing has a greater power to soothe my mind when evrything is in confusion than your letters.

Your boy

Ugie

P.S. Write to me about the boy.

1. James Longstreet (1821–1904) did not command a division at this time, as Allen states, but the right wing of Lee's Army of Northern Virginia.

2. Ambrose Powell Hill (1825–65) commanded the "Light Division" under Stonewall Jackson.

Camp Near Sumerset Va
August 4th 1862

My Dear Susie

I promised you yesterday that I would write soon if I got a letter from you yesterday evening. I did not recieve any but being at leisure just now I will follow the golden rule "do as you would be done by." I do not promise anything new or interesting. I heard that Jesse was discharged, did I tell you about it? What in the world kept Uncle W and Boykin so long? A little more and the boys time would expire before they got home. However this is not very material only that it deprived them of some comforts that they should have had. Write to me what they say about the fight and fighting generaly. Let me know how they are all getting along also. The people will not believe how the "bloody 21st" fought. By the way, did I ever tell you how we came by that name. It was given by Major Wheats battalion. When we first came into service evrybody was afraid of these fellows. While we were in winter quarters our boys found out that one tiger could not whip more than one comon man and turned in to whiping them whenever they became troublesome. They actualy made them afraid to pass by our regiment. And they gave us that name.[1] I have sent for my trunk. It is at Gordonsville now. You may know that I am elated at my prospect now. I only have one pair of socks. All others are gone the way of evrything in this regiment, lost and stoled. Did I tell you about loosing some clothes I bought in Richmond. I found two fellows wearing my shirts and requested them to wash and bring them up as they were taken through mistake.

The boys [are] all pretty quiet just now. Some are asleep, some siting quietly looking for lice. Johnny Brewer is buisy cooking. Berry Rowland singing. John Hick jolly as ever thrashing some fellow with a switch. Lt Henderson is sick. Arch Tyree was sent to the hospital this morning; he has a severe attact of the pleuracy. Some of the sick boys that were left behind the other day have not got up yet. I am very uneasy about them. The man that has health in an army aught shurly to be thankful. I recieved the Reporter of the 25th June yesterday. I did not know untill then that Ed Hill was dead.[2] I heard that Jim Strickland was dead. Is it so? Give me all the news when you answer this. I want at least ten, and would be glad of sixteen. Now it is no use talking I must have a long one. Tell Boykin that Glover is now our Major & Hooper our Lt Colonel. If Col M is dismissed from service, Capt Hamilton[3] will be promoted. Several promotions have been made to fill up vacancies caused by deth and resignation recently. I think if we do not fight here or in Tenn soon the fighting for this year is done. The north aught not to be allowed time to raise another grand army. I want to see our army advancing on Kentucky, not sit quietly at Chattanooga and wait for the Yanks to come down thare. It is a pity that we are not able to make this an agressive war. How are the crops? I am almost afraid to ask the question. How is evrything generaly? How is that great boy? I would give a thousand dollars to see him. Can he run about? You may think that these are simple questions, but they will be of interest to me. Good bye My dear.

Your boy

Ugie

1. Companies recruited from Louisiana's large immigrant population, with their gaudy Zouave uniforms and drills conducted in Gaelic or French, bewildered many upcountry southerners. The "Tiger" nickname was initially used by only one company of Major Chatham R. Wheat's 1st Louisiana Battalion, but it came into general use as the Louisianians gained a reputation for hard fighting both on and off the battlefield. James Cooper Nisbet in *Four Years on the Firing Line* and Richard Taylor in *Destruction and Reconstruction* recount similar encounters between the Louisianians and the 21st Georgia.

2. Edward Young Hill, Jr. (born March 31, 1833), son of Judge E. Y. and Arabella Dawson Hill of La-Grange and captain of the 9th Alabama Regiment, was killed at Gaines's Mill on June 27, 1862.

3. Algernon Sidney Hamilton (born 1833) was captain of the "Floyd Sharpshooters," Company B, 21st Georgia Regiment. When it became apparent that Colonel Mercer would not be removed from command, Hamilton was among the officers of the 21st who sought a transfer. He left the 21st Georgia on May 28, 1863.

Camp Near Sumerset Va
August 5th 1862

Dear Susie

I did not recieve a letter from you yesterday either. I think certainly I will get one this evning. I am becoming very uneasy, lest something is the matter. How can I be otherwise when I am so far away and can not hear from you. I have my trunk now; it makes me feel like I had met an old friend. I will do well if I do not loose it. If I do I will not be in any worse fix than I was in before. I can take care of anything you send me now. My dear have your own and the boys ambrotipe taken and send it to me by some of the boys. Will you? It makes me feel very sad when I think of you and our dear boy. I have long since ceased to endeavour to penetrate the dim vista of futurity with my short sight, and feel that I am only a waif on the uncertain sea of fortune; unable to evert my doom be it either good or bad. I have just recieved a letter from Mr Pitts relative to Dr Whites not visiting the company. The whole company are justly enraged at his pitiful littleness. I think he will endeavour to excuse himself by "ringing in" Lt W. and myself. I soon saw that he was not very anxious to see them and was very cautious not to comit myself to him in any maner. What Lt W. did I do not know. Uncle W and myself talked it all over before White left. I do not know what is his pretext for not going, but we both thought that it would be that he could not go to see or find them. I therefore urged him (Uncle Wisdom) to do what he intended and did do—go and look for them. I write this for you and no one else. Not wishing to give any opinion or make any statement of circumstances unless I am informed that my surmise is correct and am compelled to do so in self defence. I will answer Mr Pitts letter today or tomorrow or as soon as circumstances will admit. Hoping that you are well and I will get a letter from you this evning I am Your dear boy,
Ugie

❧

Camp Near Sumerset Va
August 7th 1862

Dear Boykin

I recieved your kind letter of August 1st last night. We had been out on the other side of the Rappidan, foraging, and did not get back untill about 11 ock. Although I was quite weary, I could not lay down untill I had made a fire and read it; hoping that I would recieve a word from Susie and her letter of the 16th July is the last. You ask for news. I have none. I have writen evrything of interest to Susie and told her to tell you. Uncle W said in his last letter to Cousin Robert that Susie recieved two letters from me in which I said we were expecting a battle hourly. I do not know that we are. The anemy are over on the other side of the river about Madison and Orange. We have just recieved orders to be ready to march at 3:30 P.M. This looks like the whole division was about to move. This maybe the last letter that I can write in several days. It is certainly the hotest weather that I ever felt. Worse than Richmond last summer with the exception of the flies. You may look out for much sickness if it continues. The nights are clear and beautiful. We were serenaded last night about 2 ock by the N.C. band[1] which has been absent for some time. You must be shure and attend to that company business that I wrote about. You knew that Glover was promoted did you not. Lt Waller I understand says that he is Capt of Co F but no one knows that it is so. His case has never been acted upon by our Major Genl. At least if it has nothing has been heard from it. Neither has he been promoted. He has been in R[2] ever since I left. Several inquiries have been sent down to the regiment, to know whether he was.[3] A great many of the boys have come in from the hospital recently. Dr. Capers is sick and Dr. Witt resigned.[4] Of course a few will not stay long. Some of our best boys are unwell and I am afraid if we go on a campaign we will miss them.

I would be glad if I could get some one to stay with the negroes all the while, but can think of no one to recommend at present. Be shure and write me how evrything is geting along and the prospect for a good crop. Answer my letter amediately giving all the news. Give my love to your father, mother and Lizzie.

Your friend

Allen

P. S. I inclose a few lines to Susie. Tell Uncle W. that Cousin R will not have time to write before we march, but will write the first chance.

1. An anonymous composition, the *Twenty-First North Carolina Regiment Quickstep* survives as testament to the North Carolina band's proficiency.

2. Richmond.

3. Friction between Allen and Waller intensified after Captain Boykin resigned on May 31, 1862. Waller petitioned General Trimble for an appointment to fill the vacancy, but Major Glover recommended Allen for the position, based on his performance commanding the company during Boykin's and Waller's frequent absences. Waller presented his case to Secretary of War George Wythe Randolph in a letter dated August 13,

1862. Allen, with the rank of 2nd lieutenant, continued to command the company in Waller's absence. The controversy dragged on until January 1863, when Allen was promoted to the rank of captain to date from May 31, 1862. Threatened with court-martial for being absent without leave, Waller resigned from the 21st Georgia on February 12, 1863.

4. William Francis DeWitt had been assigned to duty as assistant surgeon with the 21st Regiment on January 8, 1862. His resignation, on account of ill health, was not officially accepted until May 28, 1863. He later served on the medical examining board for conscripts at Albany, Georgia.

August 7th 1862

My dear:

I inclose you a few lines in a letter to Boykin, though it is the fourth in the last five days. We recieved orders to be ready to fall in with two days rations at 3:30 P.M. This may probably be the last chance that I will have in several days. Where we are going I do not know. I used to think that I would not care for a campaign if I could only write and recieve letters. But it seems that it will make no diference now as your letter of the 16th July was the last word that I have had from you. Tell me candidly my dear, why you treat me thus. Am I unworthy of you? Are you sick and will not let me know it? Have you no sympathy for the absent husband and father. No word of comfort, no balm of Gilead to heal my anxious bleeding heart. Boykin writes that my poor boy is sick but says nothing of you.

Good bye dear.

The forgoten one

On the Battlefield
Aug. 11th 1862

Dear Susie

We fought another battle day before yesterday the 9th on a creek called Ceder Run. Thank God! I have no casualties to tell you of this time. Only two men of the regiment are wounded and they slightly. We drove them from the field and still occupy it; while the anemy are burying their dead. I have been siting and watching them all the morning. I can also see their encampments some distance off. You can gather all the incidents of the battle sooner than I can. Possibly you will read of the battle this evning or tomorrow. Our loss I expect will amount to several hundred theirs is much greater.[1] We took Brig Gen Prince prisoner.[2] I am sorry to say that Brig Gen'l Winder is killed.[3] I have seen no one but men belonging to our brigade and I can not find out anything of interest and will be compelled to confine myself to what I saw. We occupied most of the while the side of a mountain and I could see the whole field. However very little was done untill night or about sundown.

Let me give you a rough sketch of the field. I am afraid you will not understand it. All this is open country except what I have marked as woods and corn. Those goose track looking things are intended to represent the timber. I have marked the rout of our regiment by a doted line. I have also denoted the enemy's batteries by the letters Y. B. 1st, 2nd, & 3rd. I have also marked Capt Courtney's Battery[4] by the letters C. B. You see it on the side of the mountain near the house. The anemies centre was about their 1st & 2nd batteries while their third battery was their extreme left. You see then that we (our brigade) attacted their left and was our right. The principle part of the battle was fought around their first and second batteries and in the woods above them or on the oposite side of the Culpeper Road. Our brigade got into the woods on the side of the mountain and were conceiled from their batteries untill our battery was brought into position about 3 1/2 hours before sundown. Then we came down into the corn just in frunt of it. Here we were also conceiled by the corn untill about sundown when we advanced on battery No 3. Simultaneous with this move was the grand move on their centre, and a heavy fight ensued lasting about one hour and a quarter. Previous to this time we had some sharp skirmishes comencing about 12 ock. The anemy comenced shelling the side of the mountain and their frunt about 2 ock just as we came up. From the time Capt Courtney battery got in position untill night or untill we drove them away the artillery fight was the heviest I ever heard. Capt Courtney had the position on them, the distance being about twenty five hundred and three thousand yards, and you may take my word that he gave their batteries sore bones. We did not have a chance of firing but a few musket shots at battery No 3 before the anemy ran away with it. This was done just as their other batteries and infantry were driven off. They then placed some batteries on a hill beyond the small branch and concentrated a murderous fire for half an hour upon our forces who followed them up and remained in the woods beyond and about the first branch. This was about 11 or 12 oclock. We remained at the end of the doted line all night and came back here yesterday morning. Our regiment is at the house on the mountain.[5] The country before me is a leavel plane and I can see just as far as the eye can reach. The scenery is as beautiful as any I have met with since I left the mountains. Culpeper C. H. is only about eight miles distant. It is my candid opinion that the battle will be resumed. The anemy I think will make a desperate stand. They have an overwhelming force, though they are crushed in spirit. I gather this from their prisoners. Good bye my dear Susie. I dont know what chance I will have to send this to you. Kiss our dear little boy for me.

Your boy

Ugie

1. On August 11, the Federals requested a truce so they could bury their dead. Stonewall Jackson reported Confederate losses as 241 killed, 1,120 wounded, and 4 missing. Nathaniel Banks lost 314 killed, 1,445 wounded and 622 captured or missing.

2. Brigadier General Henry Prince (1811–1892) commanded a brigade in General Christopher Augur's division. Private John Booker of the 23rd Virginia and Private George Pile of the 37th Virginia are credited with capturing Prince as he lagged behind his retreating troops.

3. Charles Sidney Winder (born 1829) was appointed brigadier general on March 7, 1862, and given command of Stonewall Jackson's old brigade. When Jackson was again promoted, Winder succeeded him to command the division. A Federal artillery shell killed Winder as he directed the fire of southern cannon.

4. Major Alfred Ransom Courtney (1833–1914) commanded a battalion of five artillery batteries attached to Richard Ewell's division. The Courtney (Virginia) Artillery, which the 21st Georgia helped haul up Cedar Mountain, was commanded by eighteen-year-old Captain Joseph White Latimer.

5. The residence of Episcopal rector D. F. Slaughter was near the summit of Cedar Mountain. It is remarkable that Allen, a lover of books, fails to mention Reverend Slaughter's extensive library. Other Confederates reported that Yankee soldiers who occupied the house scattered hundreds of volumes about the grounds.

Camp Near Sumerset Va
August 13th 1862

Dear Susie

I recieved your kind letter of Aug. 3rd yesterday evning. We whiped our cousin who never was whiped before,[1] taking his word for it on the 9th and I wrote you a letter from "the battlefield" on the 11th. Night come the flag of truce and Yankees left the field carying their badly wounded and such other prisoners as we paroled with them. We took not less than five hundred prisoners, probably more. Our regiment took (captured) a good many. I itched all over to get one myself, and would have done so, but was in command of the company and had to stay with it. When we got up to that house where battery No 3 was, parties were sent out over the fields and around the house and brought them in. I saw a fellow come sliping along in about fifty yards of us and sent John Hick after him. John hailed him and he said he belonged to the 3rd Maine.[2] John told him very blandly "very well sir just walk this way." The Yank rather demured for he thought we were his friends; Crack, crack[3] went John's gun as he commanded him imphaticaly, "walk! walk!!" You aught to have seen blue coat coming in. All of our forces except our regiment was conceiled on the 11th. That night about dark we left (in fact our whole Division came) marched all night and arrived here yesterday evning. It was a long weary tramp for us as we were on picket the night before. You know our camp is about 5 1/2 miles from Gordonsville; the battlefield about six miles from Culpeper C. H. We came by Orange C. H. so you see the distance is about fifteen miles. I am quite stupid and nervous this morning on acount of this ripit and you will find this a very uninteresting epistle. You did not acknowledge the receipt and date of my letters and I am at a loss to know how many you recieved. I have writen twelve or more since I left Richmond. I expect you think I scold you too much about not writing to me; but certainly will apreciate it when I tell you that your letter of June 11th was the last. You told me then that you would write again in two or three days. I did not know how much wheat I made untill I recieved this letter. I expect it will not be as good for sowing as my old wheat. If I am so fortunate as to get home again, I certainly will want "biscuit and beef." Did I tell you how fond I was of it? The boys would surprise the natives if they were turned loose in old Troup now. I understand our wounded fellows make the cooks quake at meal time. Poor fellows I am so glad they got home. Have you ever seen any of them? I know ten thousand questions are propounded to them. You advise me to put on leather straps when I go into battle. I have no doubt but that strap prevented a very serious wound, but our idea is to get rid of straps and blankets on acount of the excessive heat. I am not well of my wound yet. A ball from one of the anemys batteries passed in a few inches of some of our boys the other day. The shurest plan when they have the range is to lie down. It makes a person feel rather curious to hear a shot or shell coming directly towards them. I always feel like they are coming in my face. I could tell you many interesting things if I could see you. It looks like I have not seen you in an age. O, that winter would come and put an end to active service. Then I might come and see my dear little woman and boy again. What would you not give if this terible war would end. How long will it last? Sometimes I think it will soon end, at others it seams that evrything is indicative of a protracted one.

Tell me about that saucy Stonewall; is he a jolly hurahing or say nothing kind of a felow. My dear does he give any indications of a strong, well balanced intellect? How long will it be before he begins to talk? I think Boykin is somewhat afraid of Ethan. I have writen to Mr. Boykin about land and will soon expect an answer from him.

I have a Yankee sword, canteen and haversack. I swaped canteens with a prisoner. Their things are of much better quality than ours and our soldiers are quite eager to get them. The truth is all of them have them. I picked up as fine sword as I ever saw at Cross Keys, but gave it up again to the government. The one I have now is not such a one as I would like to have but worth forty of my old one. I came by it honestly by swaping with a soldier. Tell Boykin that Thos Williams says send his pistol to his wife or mother. Lt. Waller returned yesterday. Nothing has been heard from his trial or anything else. Thare will be another battle here soon I predict. I do not know what our division came back for; posibly the whole army came. I think the anemies second position must have been a very strong one, or 'old Stonewall' would have give them another round. It must have been humiliating to that bragart Pope to be thus defeated, bury his dead under a flag of truce, and see his victorious anemies lounging around looking at him.

Just as I told you in the beginning this is a stupid letter. I am glad it is finished, for I am troubled with the headache and diarhea. Write very often my dear.

Good bye

Ugie

P.S. I notice you backed your letter to Left.—not Lieut. This is wrong. Boykin is guilty of the same eror. It is spelt Lieutenant and sometimes though not generally pronounced leftenant. I send an envelope in this already backed. I think it is a very nice way to back letters to me.

1. John Pope (1822–92) was promoted to major general on March 21, 1862, and was Lincoln's choice to command the Army of Virginia. Contrary to Allen's assessment, Pope claimed victory at Cedar Mountain, having thwarted Jackson's attempt to destroy Banks's corps. Confederates saw the battle as a victory, not only because they held the field but also because they blocked Pope's movement into central Virginia.

2. The 3rd Maine was not among the Federal regiments engaged at Cedar Mountain. The prisoner might have belonged to the 3rd Maryland Regiment of Prince's brigade or to the 10th Maine, which made a valiant but futile and costly stand against the Confederates late in the day.

3. John Higginbothem did not shoot at the prisoner. "Click, click" might be a more accurate description of the sound made by the double cocking of the hammer on Civil War–era rifles. It was the same mechanism that gave rise to the phrase "going off half cocked."

Camp Near Sumerset Va
August 15th 1862

Dear Susie

I wrote you two days ago, but will write again today if I have time. I know my dear it is my duty to write, besides nothing gives me more pleasure unless it is receiving one from you. I hope to be the happy recepient of a letter from my dear little girl this evening. By order of Gen'l Jackson we observed yesterday as a day of thanksgiving for our recent successes. Genl Jackson is a strict presbiterian. My dear he is one of the greatest men living. So brave so pleasant in his intercourse and kind to the soldiers. He is the idol of the soldiers. You never hear a word against him unless, by chance some weary fellow will say that he is marched too hard; but he will invariably add, "I reckon old Stonewall knows what is best, don't think he would march us so hard unless it was necessary." Gen'l Ewell is as brave as the bravest, but is one of these crabed dispeptic kind of fellows. The boys all praise him for his bravery, but you never hear them whiling away the hours around the camp fire with jokes and stories of him as they do of Jackson.

We recieved the Reporter of the 8th yesterday. I noticed a very unkind cut given our company in it. Willingham in noticing Capt Spear, said that he would cary letters from the friends to the four companies from Troup under Jackson's command: Long's, Jones,' Williams' and the Hogansville company.[1] Willingham knows as well as you or I that we are, and have been under Jackson since April or in fact the middle of March. He also knows that those other companies never joined him untill recently. The Ben Hill Infantry do not seek public notoriety, but are proud of the well earned reputation of Jackson's troops and do not care to divide it with those who have not shared their hardships and have nothing to recommend them but the praise of aristocratic friends and a dirty country sheet. This is not the first kind notice the Reporter has given us. The 4th Ala was handled rather rough the other day. Where is George? What is his company and regiment?

I think that cotton comforts or quilts would answer as good purpose considering circumstances as blankets for the negroes. The question is will your cow hair blankets pay for your trouble. I may be compelled to call on you for one myself. I intend to gather up as many as I can before winter comes. What do you think of my having one of the boys to cook for me? The fact is I have lived very hard for several months. If I had one he could get me many things in the country. We are not alowed to draw from the commisary only the same quality and quantity of rations that the men get. Besides if any discrimination is made it is more frequently than otherwise in faver of the men. The men sometimes have and frequently take opportunities to leave camp. Not so with an officer. He must always be at his post. When an officer is sick he pays his own board, buys his own medicine and frequently employs his physician, never gets a furlough and is looked on with suspicion if he is able to walk and does not go to duty. High private goes to the hospital, stays as long as he pleases gets fat and has a fine time generally. I think high private always has the advantage over brass collar. Never mind we will have peace pretty soon, let

us be victorious in a few more battles. Lt. H. says his father proposes to send him a negro. If he does and I am well pleased with him probably I will not write for one of the boys. You know the company is about to undergo a change and I am cautious not to take decisive steps. I wish you had let all of the negroes had the measels this spring. I was well amused at you in one of your letters. You made a terible fuss about the negroes catching the measels from you, and I believe threatened to flee into the forest. I did not know the meaning of any of it untill I saw Jesse in Richmond and he told me you had been very uneasy for fear you would take them from him. O my little woman you know I had a good laugh at your expense. Don't you get tired of my stupid nonsense? I expect I had better quit. Possibly if I did not trouble you so often I would get more letters. Never mind, I expect to get a quantity when they do commence coming. How is the little fox, Stonewall? He has not writen to me in sometime. This is childish is it not? Very well let it be so.
Your boy,
Ugie

Susie
Here is something for you and no one else. Let me tell you Lt. W. heard of that afair I told you of and has made an apeal to Gen Trimble and the Secretary of War. I can not say that this will change things or have any bearing either pro or con. I do not care one cent whether he is successful or not. I am totally indifferent. Unless I have things as I want them I do not care to have them at all and will feel free to do or endeavor to do what I mentioned in my Fort Republic letter. I have a large apple pie for diner so I believe I will pitch into it or visa versa pitch it into me. It reminds me of summer at home with you to prepare some nice sauce for my special palate. By the by, LaGrange is under martial law.[2] What does it mean? Thare is no use in Gods world for it. It is perfect nonsense in fact rediculous that the government should go to the expence of a provost martial and guard for every one horse town especially when they have neither soldiers or public property about it. Recollect that provost is pronounced provo, as you have one so near you.
Goodbye,
Ugie

1. Daniel Norwood Speer, a LaGrange lawyer, was assistant quartermaster of the 60th Georgia Regiment. James A. Long commanded "Evans' Guards," Company K, 13th Georgia; Captain Waters Burrus Jones's "Fannin Guards" were Company B, 60th Georgia and Lee A. J. Williams was captain of Company D, 35th Georgia. The "Meriwether Volunteers," Company B, 13th Georgia Regiment, commanded by Captain James McCauley was recruited from Troup and Meriwether counties near the village of Hogansville.

2. According to the August 8, 1862, edition of the LaGrange *Reporter*, General Braxton Bragg had placed the town under martial law.

8

SECOND MANASSAS

The company is ruined.

FOLLOWING the battle at Cedar Mountain, General John Pope, the Union commander of the Army of Virginia, ordered his troops into defensive positions north of the Rapidan River. Robert E. Lee, hoping to strike Pope's men before they received reinforcements from George McClellan's force below Richmond, concentrated much of the Confederate army in Gordonsville. Lee planned to attack Pope on August 18, trapping the Union general and his army between the Rapidan and Rappahannock rivers. Logistical problems forced a delay in Lee's plan, and Pope, realizing he faced a superior opponent, slipped across the Rappahannock on August 18. For the next week heavy rains, poor staff coordination, and uncharacteristically aggressive Federal cavalry frustrated Confederate attempts to force a crossing of the Rappahannock.

Ugie Allen was absent from the ranks of the 21st Georgia in late August. Continued suffering from his chest wound coupled with severe diarrhea had forced him to leave the company and go to Lynchburg on August 16. In Lynchburg, the enfeebled young officer registered at General Hospital No. 1 but then decided, as he had in Richmond, to stay in a private home. While Allen rested for two weeks in Lynchburg, the men of the Ben Hill Infantry endured their bloodiest experience of the war.

On August 22, the 21st Georgia engaged in a heavy skirmish with a Union brigade under General Henry Bohlen at Freeman's Ford near the confluence of the Hazel and Rappahannock rivers. Bohlen had detected a Confederate wagon train moving along the south side of the Rappahannock and, hoping to attack the seemingly vulnerable target, led his men across the river. Trimble's brigade, reinforced by two brigades from General John B. Hood's division, surprised the Union troops and drove them back across the river, inflicting heavy losses.

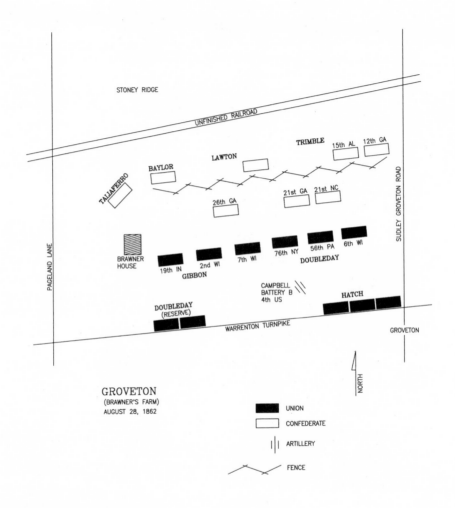

STONEY RIDGE

UNFINISHED RAILROAD

PAGELAND LANE

SUDLEY GROVETON ROAD

TALIAFERRO

BAYLOR

LAWTON

TRIMBLE

15th AL   12th GA

26th GA

21st GA   21st NC

BRAWNER
HOUSE

19th IN   2nd WI   7th WI   76th NY   56th PA   6th WI

GIBBON   DOUBLEDAY

CAMPBELL
BATTERY B
4th US

DOUBLEDAY
(RESERVE)

HATCH

WARRENTON TURNPIKE

GROVETON

NORTH

GROVETON
(BRAWNER'S FARM)
AUGUST 28, 1862

■ UNION

□ CONFEDERATE

||| ARTILLERY

⋀⋁ FENCE

Two days after the fight at Freeman's Ford, Robert E. Lee ordered Jackson's wing of the Confederate army on a long march around the right flank of Pope's army. Stonewall's "foot cavalry" marched fifty miles in two days and by the night of August 26 had severed Pope's supply line, the Orange and Alexandria Railroad, at Bristoe Station.

The same evening that Jackson's men captured Bristoe, General Trimble volunteered to take two of his regiments, the 21st Georgia and the 21st North Carolina, to capture the sizable Federal supply depot at Manassas Junction. Trimble's "two twenty-ones," as he admiringly called them, captured the junction after a brief engagement, seizing eight cannon, several hundred prisoners, and many tons of supplies. The affair resulted in light casualties for the 21st Georgia—four men killed and eleven wounded. Weeks later the normally subdued Stonewall Jackson termed the action "the most brilliant that has come under my observation during the present war."

His supply line severed, General Pope turned his attention to pursuing Jackson, hoping to destroy Stonewall's force before it could reunite with the rest of Lee's army. After leaving Manassas Junction, Jackson marched his men northward to a low ridge near the crossroads of Groveton, just north of and roughly parallel to the Warrenton Turnpike. For the 21st Georgia it was a homecoming of sorts—according to one officer, the regiment was "on the identical ground" where it had camped and drilled a year earlier.

About 6:00 P.M. on August 28, Jackson observed a Federal column marching across his front eastward along the Warrenton Turnpike toward Centreville. Jackson's simple order, "Bring out your men, gentlemen," set in motion the Confederate attack. Isaac Trimble later reported that his brigade had moved forward through open fields "in beautiful order in line of battle." After reaching a fence line close to the Federals, Trimble's men halted and began trading volleys of musketry with the enemy. Around dusk, Trimble gave orders to fix bayonets and charge. The men of the 21st Georgia, under the command of Major Hooper, leapt over the fence with "blood-curdling rebel yells," advancing to within thirty steps of the Union line. There, silhouetted on an open hillside and subjected to an intense enfilade fire, the Georgians fell by the score. Of 242 men taken into the action that evening by the 21st Georgia, only 69 could report for duty the next day.

Survivors of the 21st Georgia skirmished on the morning of August 29 but spent most of the day burying their dead and tending to their wounded. On the 30th, the regiment, numbering only forty men according to one member, lost three killed and five wounded as they participated in the victorious Confederate assaults that swept Pope's army from the Manassas battlefield. Under the command of Captain William M. Butt, the shattered remnants of the 21st joined in the pursuit of Pope and on September 1 fought at Chantilly, losing two men killed and eight wounded.

After the action at Chantilly, Lee's army continued northward toward the Potomac. At Fairfax Courthouse, Ugie Allen apparently rejoined his company, finding only eight men present for duty. During the Second Manassas campaign, the Ben Hill Infantry had lost seven men killed, two mortally wounded, and nineteen wounded. "The company is ruined," Allen lamented, "My best and bravest men are all killed."

Lynchburg Va
Sunday Aug. 17th 1862

My Dear Susie

I wrote you day before yesterday from camps. Yesterday the regiment marched with six days rations, two in their haversacks and four in the wagons. I had been unwell for several days with diarhea, and went about three miles with them and was sent back here. Evryone who was not able to march in lines was sent to the rear. I am very sorry that I could not go with the boys. I know they are going into a fight soon and I want to be thare. It would be some gratification to me to even in the rear, so that I could help take care of the boys if any were wounded. I am foolish enough to believe that the boys want me too. My dear I love those boys like they were my brothers and want to be with them. I hope I will be able to go back in a day or two. I have a diarhea caused by billiousness and indigestion; and the hot sun and water on a march uses me up. I understand that Maj. Henderson[1] boast that Lt. H. was the only officer of the company that went through the Richmond fight, that the "others faged and fell out." Now I am the last one to boast of my own or impute anothers courage, but such pityfull stuff as that frets me. Maj Henderson might as well dry up. Ned is my friend and a good clever fellow; but if his daddy ever says anything in your presence reflecting on other officers of the company, you may tell him that you understand from good authority, that his son was the only officer of the company in the Richmond fight who got behind a big pine and neglected his duty by staying thare. Now I want you to keep this to yourself, and say nothing about it, for perhaps I have been wrongly informed about what his father says, besides it is always best to let such things alone, but Maj. H. had better attend to his own business as far as I am concerned, for I certainly have the advantage of him. I hope I will be able for duty in a day of two, now I have some medical treatment and comforts. The truth is I have sufered. Direct your letters to the regiment as before. If I had more paper I would write more. I brought this from camp intending to write to you on the march. Did you see any sense in my diagram of the battle-field. Pope fell back the same night we did. I will tell you of it in my next letter.

Ugie

1. John M. Henderson (1805–90) had earned the rank of major in the Troup County militia during the Creek Indian disturbances of 1836.

Lynchburg Va
Aug. 18th 1862

My Dear Susie

I wrote my last letter on the 16th. Since that time nothing has occured worth notice; so I am left without anything of interest to write. I hear today that the army has fell back to Gordonsville again. Our cousin Pope crawfished so fast we could not catch him and were compelled to fall back to protect our rear from Burnsides.[1] Pope retreated from Culpeper the same night that we did. This is rather funny; but let me tell you all about it. Pope fell back from his second position to near Culpeper C. H. the night of the battle. The next day was so bad that we could not advance our trains and artillery. The next Pope detained us with his flag of truce in order that reinforcements under Burn-sides who is somewhere bellow might reach him. This was what we wanted and our [corps] under Longstreet were ordered to hasten on. Longstreet arrived at Gordonsville and would not advance for fear Burnsides would attact our rear. Why Burnsides did not advance I do not know. Night came but Longstreet did not. Neither did Burnsides. Jackson fearing that Pope was heavily reinforced and without any himself fell back. Pope thinking the same of Jackson fell back himself. Both retreated without the knowledge of the other.

I have not heard of Arch Tyree since he was sent from the regiment. I heard that Billy Cooley would leave home yesterday. He will probably come through here. I shall look for him when the train passes. My dear, it is no use talking. I must rely on you for such clothing as I may need. I can not buy a good shirt here for less than ten dollars, socks one dollar. I do not want anything of the kind just now. I regret that Boykin did not carry my old suit home. I can buy a tolerable pair of shoes here for twelve dollars. I can get such things (shoes) from the quartermaster if I can do no better. I think I am improving some. I told you I had no news. You must kiss that dear saucy boy for me. You must write me a long sweet letter about my little girl and boy. Nothing more today.

Good bye

Ugie

I will send a better looking letter next time. I believe I will hereafter write my name U. C. instead of U. What do you think of it?

1. Ambrose Everett Burnside (1824–81) commanded the newly created Federal IX Corps. Fear that the Confederates might attack his base near Fredericksburg kept Burnside from cooperating with Pope against Jackson.

Lynchburg Virginia
August 20th 1862

My Dear Susie

Lt. Waller proposes to go home for a few days tomorrow; to him you are indebted for this letter. Although my general health is improving I do not feel quite well today. You know I wrote to you some time since about a violent caugh. It is no better and I have serious fears lest it has taken hold of my lungs. These caughs are quite common in camp.

Passing along the street this morning my attention was arrested by an auctioneer selling some needles. I bought a few papers and send them to you. I do not know that you have any use for them now, possibly you may as they are very scarce. You must not interpret my sending them only as I do a favor for I think I heard you say when I was at home that you had but few. Susie I am half dead for a letter from you, and no hope of getting one untill I go to the regiment. Answer this amediately and direct to me at this place without stating Reg or Co and if I leave before it comes I will get a friend to forward it to me. I am worse than a boy looking for a letter from his sweethart.

Let me tell you all about it; for fear you think hard of me. Now Lt. W. has no furlough or leave of absence, but will endeavour to run the blockade. Now we do not want the people at home or the authorities to know anything about it. Now you know the secret; so keep mum. I am not quite bold enough to try this trick now. But am coming home this winter by fair or foul means. Lt. thinks his case a bad one anyhow I do not think I would be doing right to run off home now and would feel like a thief if caught. I dont blame Lt. a bit. I would have sliped off home long ago if I had of been in his situation. Let them arrest Allen for several months and he will see Susie and the baby certain. Wouldn't you? I can tell you whenever a fellow violates military law he is certainly geting into the wrong pew.

I have tolerable good fare; at least much better than camps. Two dollars a day. All kind of produce is remarkably high here. I go around to the market evry morning. Lynchburg is not as beautiful as Richmond. None of the Virginia cities rival ours, their southern sisters. The streets are generally very narrow besides many of the buildings are old and untastey in their design. Evrything is quiet about the army now. I thought thare would have been a battle before now. I am a poor prophit. I am expecting a fight at Chattanooga soon. Possibly you can hear the cannon when it takes place. Much depends on the state of the atmosphere. If we are defeated thare our own home may be desecrated by the anemy. But they will never succeed. May the Omnipotent Ruler of the universe revive the ranks and preserve the arms of our brave soldiers, to drive back this band of invaders, these murderers and robbers. Nothing more today. If I get very sick I will write to you. Good bye,
Your boy,
Ugie

P.S. Don't say a word to anyone about Lt. Waller coming home. The poor fellow has about [as much to] answer for as he can well shoulder without turning a whole community on him at once.

Lynchburg Va
August 22nd 1862

My Dear Susie
I sent you a letter by Lt Waller who left for home yesterday. Some of my friends say they think he went to the regiment instead of home but I think diferent. I am fortunate enough to have better paper than when I last wrote. I think a letter looses much of its interest when bloted and full of erors. Here let me apologise to you for the many carelessly written uncooth scratches that I have recently sent you; at the same time trying to make myself believe and you too that they were letters. You know my facilities for writing are fre-

quently very poor. Besides whenever I wish to write a good letter I am ashured to fail finding nothing to write. Now you need not take the hint and laugh at me, if this should prove a dull afair. If you do, let me warn you that I will not send you the next one.

Let me tell you now instead of waiting until I close I have no news, having heard of no births, deaths, marriages, desertions or promotions. Lynchburg is the same. On the street are the same raged soldiers (I saw one just now with the seat of his pants patched with a piece of black oilcloth eighteen inches in diameter.), the same fine horses, noisy drays and ladies prominading and shopping as when I last wrote. The same inocent little children are playing on the green & ward unconscious of the surrounding trouble and missery, God forbid that they should ever feel. Little children that I long to gather in my arms and kiss for the sake of my own dear boy and his mother. Yes, indeed; his mother; that mother whom I have ever loved. A love created when as children we engaged in childish sports, ripning with maturer years, consecrated at the marriage alter and sealed forever in the adamant of my lonely hart by the birth of my darling boy. How faithfully have I endeavoured and kept. You need not direct any more letters to me at Lynchburg as I would not probably be here. I will write again soon. Goodbye Susie

Your Boy,

Ugie

❧

Lynchburg Va
Aug 26th 1862

My Dear Susie

I write you my last letter from Lynchburg tonight. I start to the regiment at 6 AM tomorrow. I do not know precisely where I shall find it; possibly somewhere about Rappahanock River. You know the anemy is retreating and we are pursuing him closely. Do you take the "Confederacy" yet? I hope you find it interesting. No doubt you take much interest in following the movements of the army. Do you have a daily mail at Antioch? I saw old man Mobley a few days ago. He went on to Hugenott Springs. I have not seen him pass back. He could tell me nothing only that you were all well. He also told me that Boykin was out hunting a substitute. I do not know whether to laugh at or regret his ill luck. I believe I would be discharged again if I were him. But then, he might see quite a hard time. Mr. Mobley spoke very flatteringly of the boy. I anticipate a very pleasant time when I get to the regiment read-

ing letters from you and him. Yours of Aug 3d was my last so you know I am anxious to get one. I expect Billy Cooley has already passed here going back. Those Cooley boys are splendid soldiers; no discount there, certain. Who does not love a good soldier? Show me one and I will show you a man. By the by, are the people thinking of doing anything for the company this winter. I hope the boys will take care and send all the money home they can. They cant get clothing for it here; I think the government intends to clothe the soldiers hereafter. I hope it will. When I speak of the people assisting the company I do not mean gratuitously by any means. But the soldiers friends can procure clothing for them at much less cost than he can. I intend to investigate this matter as soon as I get back to the company, and take steps accordingly. It is something that I do not like to fool with, but there are a number of poor boys that someone must look to. I would feel more free to act if I knew all parties would be satisfied, and some other thing that I would like to know. I bought you a fan and will send it by express, made by a soldier from Columbus Ga. I think you will be well pleased with it. You must wrap the handle with ribon. It is made of one piece of wood. I must not excite your curiosity. I send it to LaGrange of course. I am afraid it will get ruined on the road. Susie I think it prudent to sell what cotton I have. What do you think? I say sell at 18 cents, or less if you cant get it. I am expecting an answer to a letter I wrote to Mr. Boykin. It would be something remarkable if we were to drive the anemy out of Virginia, wouldn't it not? I am quite anxious to get back to the company. Not that I love to fight so well by any means. Did you ever hear black Allen[1] tell his opinion of the bombs, "Bless God mars Berry Rowland, what is dem a making sich a fuss." "Lord only knows I dont like no sich." Such were some of his expressions while the anemy were shelling some of our forces about a half mile from us. I must close with the promising you another letter the first opportunity I have of writing. Good bye
Your Boy,
Ugie

1. Captain Boykin's servant.

Gordonsville Va
Aug 28th 1862

My Dear
I have recieved your letter of Aug 20th. The regiment is up about Warrington I hear. I will go out to the Rappidan on the train and walk from thare. Thare

will be no difficulty in finding it. Our boys have been in another skirmish.[1] Jeff Escoe is shot through the thigh. No other casualties that I know of. I will write when I can. Possibly it will be some time before you hear from me again.

Your boy

Ugie

1. Trimble's brigade repelled Brigadier General Henry Bohlen's Federals at Freeman's Ford on the Hazel River on August 22, 1862.

Fairfax C. H. Va

Sep 2nd 1862

Dear Susie

The company is ruined. I have only eight men for duty. My best and bravest men are all killed. On the night of the 28th we fought on the old battlefield of Manassas. Cousin Robert Wisdom, Rufus Bassett, William Formby, William Strong, Mount Bagby, Thomas Garrett, and Johnny Brewer all were killed dead on the field. Wisdom was carrying the colours in a charge. Joe Rodgers, George Glenn, Mike Clinton and Frederick Williams are severely wounded. James Vance, James Estes, Zachariah Estes, Franklin Goss, John Higginbothem, Marion Burke, Thomas Bagby, Sam Pitts, and Dick Reid are wounded. Many of the boys are broke down on the march. I will write other particulars as soon as I can. Tell the friends of the company to be patient untill I can write again. Harrison Ainsworth was also wounded. I write this on the march.

Ugie

Camp near Frederick Md.

Sep 6th 1862

Dear Susie

I will try to write; I do not know how much or what. We left our old lines near Fairfax on the 4th, came to Leesburg and crossed the Potomac yesterday and have stoped to prepare rations. I have very few incidents to tell you and will confine myself to our recent misfortunes. The "Ben Hill Infantry" mourns the loss of its best and bravest men. Robt Wisdom, Johnnie Brewer,

Billie Strong, William Thompson Formby, Rufus Bassett, Mount Bagby and Thomas Garrett. Such a set of patriots never went down to the grave together before. It is useless for me to attempt any ulegy: their memory is stamped indellibly on the minds of their comrades and if patriotism and all the adequates of a good soldier are virtues writen in letters that shall live with Eternity itself. Cousin Robert poor fellow, carried the colours on that eventful day. Evryone praises his gallant conduct. Column after column of the anemy was hurled against our lines and he stood like a statue and would wave them defiantly in their faces and encourage those around him. When the order was given to charge baonet he sprang proudly forward calling out "come ahead boys" and led the regiment. Just as the regiment reached a fence he was shot through from side to side the ball passing about the region of the diaphragm. He lived untill about ten ock the next day. He told the boys just before he died, "I shall not live very long tell my father and mother that I was killed bearing the colours of my regiment." He also made some other request which I will write to Uncle W. Billie Strong, brave boy, just at the moment the fatal ball struck him cried out, "give it to them boys *we will never give it up.*" I must tell you about our wounded and close. Joe Rodgers has lost his leg. George Glenn and Mike Clinton are severely wounded in the temple and cheek. Market through the arm. Fred Willliams arm and sholder. Sam Pitts arm and hip. Sam Wright in the side. James Estes knee, heel, and sholder. Henry Rowland thigh. John Higginbothem armpit. George Garrett chest and arm. Harrison Ainsworth leg. William Vance thigh and right hand. Dick Reid thigh. On the 1st Sep William Perry was wounded in the leg and George Williams the head. I have named all that are severely wounded and will add that they were all doing well a few days ago. None of them are considered dangerous. Rodgers, Glenn & Clinton are the most serious. The fight was on the old battlefield. Our boys fought in about a half mile of our old Pageland camp. They were burried decently and their graves marked. I have no more time today. I hope the boys who are only slightly wounded have writen often before now to their parents and friends of the company.
Goodbye
Ugie

P.S. Direct your letters to Gordonville, Va.

9

SHARPSBURG AND RESPITE
IN THE VALLEY

Thank God that I am spared to write you these few lines.

DESPITE the hardships his troops incurred in a month of almost constant marching and fighting, Robert E. Lee moved the Army of Northern Virginia into Maryland during the first week of September 1862. The 21st Georgia waded across the Potomac River at White's Ford on September 5. The Georgians, now in a brigade under Colonel James A. Walker, who replaced the convalescing Trimble, camped for several days near Frederick, Maryland.

On September 9, Lee divided his army, sending Jackson with six divisions to capture Harpers Ferry and thereby secure his supply lines to the Shenandoah Valley. General James Longstreet, with three Confederate divisions, advanced to the vicinity of Hagerstown, Maryland. Federal soldiers found a copy of Lee's Special Orders No. 191, detailing his plans for the Maryland campaign, in an abandoned Confederate camp at Frederick. Armed with the vital information, George B. McClellan, who was once again in command of the Federal army, placed his 87,000 men between the two wings of Lee's army, intending to defeat them in detail.

Jackson's command recrossed the Potomac on September 11 near Williamsport and by September 14 surrounded Harpers Ferry. Ewell's division, now under General Alexander Lawton, formed a line of battle along School House Ridge a short distance west of the besieged Federal garrison. According to Captain James C. Nisbet, Lawton's division had orders to charge the Federal works on the morning of September 15 and "was in motion when we saw the white flag go up."

By September 13, Lee recognized the threat to his divided army and ordered Longstreet to retreat. On September 14, while Jackson was successfully investing Harpers Ferry, Longstreet fought a delaying action against Federal forces at South Mountain, Maryland. At the news of Jackson's success, Lee, who was with Longstreet's command near the village of Sharpsburg, Maryland, decided to turn and fight. The scattered Confederate units, with an aggregate strength of less than 40,000, converged on Sharpsburg.

Shortly after the surrender of the Union garrison at Harpers Ferry, Lawton led two of his brigades, including Walker's, northward. They crossed the Potomac at Boteler's Ford on the morning of September 16. That evening the 21st Georgia, numbering probably no more than 150 men, took a position in the Confederate line of battle east of Sharpsburg.

At dawn on September 17, after a preliminary artillery bombardment, massed Union battle lines began marching southward through cornfields and pastures to attack the Confederate left flank. The 21st Georgia occupied the edge of a plowed field just south of the Smoketown Road on the Samuel Mumma farm. Major Thomas Glover, the commanding officer of the 21st, discovered a fence with a rock underpinning a short distance in front of his position and moved the regiment forward to take advantage of the additional cover. From there, the Georgians fired for some time at the enemy in their front.

When the Federals in front of Walker's position fell back, Major Glover informed Walker that in order to keep up an effective fire, the 21st Georgia needed to adjust its line again. By changing front forward on the left and swinging around into the Smoketown Road they could fire into the flank of Union troops assaulting Lawton's line.

While giving the order to advance, Major Glover received a serious wound through the body. Nisbet, the senior captain present, ordered the 21st to advance at the double quick in open order. Numerous men were hit making the movement, but the Georgians reached the road. Contrary to regulations, Nisbet, Allen, and the other officers shouldered muskets and joined their men, firing from behind the rail fence that bordered the Smoketown Road.

After an hour of intense fighting the Confederate line wavered. Allen noted that the 13th Georgia Regiment "ran like the hounds of h——l were after it." At that critical moment John B. Hood's division launched a ferocious counterattack that pushed the Federals northward through farmer D. R. Miller's cornfield. As Hood's men charged through Nisbet's position, the captain ordered his men into line on the left of the 4th Alabama Infantry. Pressing forward against the retreating foe, the 21st Georgia, 4th Alabama, and 5th Texas charged into a large grove known as the East Woods. Nisbet deployed his regiment in open order, instructing the men and officers "to take cover behind a tree or any kind of shelter they could find." The three small regiments held their position in the East Woods unchallenged for twenty minutes while on their left Hood's men vied for control of the cornfield.

About 8:00 A.M. Crawford's brigade of the Federal XII Corps advanced to reinforce the hard-pressed Federal I Corps. Led by the 10th Maine, the brigade marched in compact-column formation. The men of the 21st Georgia crept forward to the northern edge of the woods and fired into the mass of New Englanders. A Yankee officer recalled that they made "almost as good a target as a barn." Among the dead was the XII Corps's commander, Major General Joseph K. F. Mansfield.

At least five additional Federal regiments advanced toward the East Woods. When yet another Confederate division drove northward toward the cornfield, the 4th Alabama withdrew from the woods and was replaced by the 6th North Carolina. By 8:30 A.M. when the final Confederate counterattack faltered, the three regiments in the East Woods were forced to retreat. Ugie Allen's pride evidently prevented him from recounting the incident in his letters, but Captain Nisbet related in his memoirs that upon his command the men of the 21st Georgia ran for their lives to the safety of the second Confederate line near the Dunkard Church. From that position the survivors of the 21st Georgia, their ammunition nearly exhausted, retired to the town of Sharpsburg. In the bloodiest single day of fighting in the war, the 21st lost approximately seventy-six men killed and wounded.

Lee's exhausted Army of Northern Virginia recrossed the Potomac River on September 18. By September 27, Stonewall Jackson's command, including the 21st Georgia, had encamped near Bunker Hill, a small community northeast of Winchester. There the men spent the month of October resting and recuperating from the summer and fall campaign. As Ugie Allen's letters reflect, Jackson's soldiers delighted in wrecking sections of the Baltimore and Ohio and Manassas Gap railroad lines.

The respite along the banks of the Shenandoah was crucial for the Army of Northern Virginia. Returns showed only thirty thousand men present for duty immediately after Sharpsburg, but within a month that number had more than doubled and morale soared. General Lee organized the revitalized army into two corps under Longstreet and Jackson, making official the arrangement that had worked so successfully for him throughout the summer. General Jubal Early assumed command of Ewell's division and Colonel Robert F. Hoke of the 21st North Carolina was promoted to command Trimble's brigade.

After much cajoling from Washington, Union general McClellan began a southward movement through the Virginia Piedmont on October 26, 1862, intending to interpose his army between Lee and Richmond. Lee blocked McClellan's path by sending Longstreet's I Corps to the town of Culpeper on November 3. At the same time, Jackson persuaded Lee to allow him to remain in the Valley with the II Corps to continue the disruption of Federal supply lines and look for an opportunity to strike McClellan's flank or rear. By late November, Jackson's troops had started marching up the Valley to rejoin the rest of Lee's army at Fredericksburg.

Near Frederick Md.
Sep 8th 1862

My Dear Susie
Nothing of interest has transpired since I last wrote you. Your letters of Aug 7th & 17th were at the company when I arrived and I now acknowledge their receipt. Evrything is so torn up that I can not write. Lt. W. arrived here yesterday. I would have been glad of a letter by him but I know you had no chance to send one as he only stayed three days at home and did not come up about Antioch. I suppose you recieved mine, needles and all. He got through safe, but found the undertaking more hazardous than he anticipated. Gen'l. Bragg[1] I hear is the most strict diciplinarian in the army. What does George think of the cavelry service? If it was not for the cold winters here I would like for our little regiment to be transferred to the cavelry service. But it would be to severe in the winter. Did you recieve the fan? Let me know if you did. I have just recieved a letter from Dr. Cary with applications for an extension of furloughs for the Horsley boys. I must reply to it but it is hardly necessary. Nothing but an army surgeons certificate is regarded. The boys aught to know this. Besides thare is an order just issued from the war department requiring all soldiers at the expiration of furlough to report to their companies for duty or to a hospital for treatment. If we remain in Maryland you need not send me any more clothes. Evrything is as cheap as dirt here. If I had an opportunity I would send you all a box. Dont say anything about it but let me know what Mrs. B., Lizzie and yourself want and if I ever get a chance I will send you a small dry goods store. I may never be able to send you anything. Frederick is guarded and the doors of all business houses closed. Evrything of service will be pressed for the army. You probably want to know something about this

country and the sentiments of the people. I know very little. Hear a great deal. The land rivals the valley in fertility. The farms show more taste than a hundreth part of our Georgia gardens. Stately mansions and cotages unique and costly meet the view evrywhere. Fences barns and other outhouses unless built of stone or brick are invariably painted or whitewashed. The barns are frequently more costly than the dwellings. Several companies have been formed in Frederick in the last few days. The Southern people here are perfectly frantic with joy. The Unionists are quite frank and will tell you so in a minute. No blowing for hot and cold like some Virginians do. One farmer and a few of his neighbors have had conceiled for several months about eight hundred bbls[2] of flour waiting for Jackson and Ewell. Another gave Gen Jackson a horse well worth a thousand dollars.[3] You knew that Gen'ls Ewell and Trimble were wounded, the former lost his leg.[4] When I come home I will tell you how brave these men are and how we love them. Our and the N. C. regiment captured Manassas in the night. The anemy commenced playing on them with grape and cannister shot. Old Genl Trimble was along and said, "boys I want that battery. *Charge!!*" A wild hideous yell arose from the line and before the gunners could fire again our boys were on them with the baonet. The battery was composed of seven splendid pieces. The Gen'l charged with them and as soon as the noise was hushed some fellow cried out, "here General, here's your battery."[5] He spoke a few encouraging words to them and they were soon buisy capturing prisoners. We have twenty men with the company. I have no recent news from our wounded boys. You must direct your letters to Gordonsville, Va untill I tell you otherwise. I hope we will soon have a regular mail. Nothing more now.

Your boy,

Ugie

1. Braxton Bragg (1817–76) took command of what became the Army of Tennessee in late June 1862. He had a reputation as a stern disciplinarian.

2. Barrels.

3. When Jackson first attempted to mount the spirited mare, she reared, throwing him to the ground and injuring him.

4. At the height of the Battle of Groveton on August 28, General Ewell was shot in the left knee as he led the 12th Georgia Regiment. General Alexander Lawton succeeded Ewell as commander of the division. General Trimble was shot in the leg by a Yankee sharpshooter on the afternoon of August 29.

5. Trimble's men captured six pieces of the 11th New York Battery, commanded by Captain Albert A. von Puttkammer, and took approximately three hundred prisoners.

Near Martinsburg Va
Sep. 21st 1862

My Dear Susie
It has been a long while since I have had an opportunity of writing to you.
We have been on the march ever since I wrote from Frederick Md. At one
time I could have writen if I had paper, but do not know that I could have
mailed a letter. We marched from Frederick to Midletown and Williamsport
on the Patomoc, then to Martinsburg and Harpers Ferry which we captured
with about 12,000 prisoners and forty pieces of artilery with evrything else
precepary for the outfit of such an army. We then recrossed the Patomac at
Sheperdstown and fought a bloody battle at Boonsville Sep 17th.[1] This was a
terrible fight. I was in during the greater part of the day. Thank God that I am
spared to write you these few lines. I only carried in four muskets, two liter
bearers and one Sergeant Major, Sam Rowland. Three of my musket men
were painfully and one slightly wounded. Lonny Britton through the thigh,
Wm Skipper thigh, and James McCain brest. None of these wounds are serious. Two others were lightly wounded. Myself and Sam Rowland were the
only representatives of the B. H. I. when we went in the second time in the
evening. I have not time or paper to write one tenth of what I would like to
write. We occupied the greater part of the field. Remained the second day for
another attact. The anemy had been too roughly handled and endeavoured to
flank us by crossing the river above. We withdrew that night with evrything
bag and bagage to this side of the river. We were under fire yesterday and the
day previous.[2] Ol F. and Wm Cooley arrived on the nineteenth (19th). They
brought me the drawers and socks and more than all the ambrotipe and your
dear long letter. We have no mails and you can imagine the great pleasure it
gave me. I read it over again and again, like the hoosier speaking of a fight,
"they fout and they fout and they fout and they kept on fouting." Do not
expect an answer to all of it. Have Bogert & Forbes[3] to cut my coat by the
measure he took last winter. That was a little too small. I can get buttons for
it. One pair of pants will be enough. I will acept the boots, recollect the legs
large made of thick leather and come to the knee. Sole remarkably thick,
heels low. I want them for winter. I have my set shirts yet. I think I have
enough shirts. I admire the hat fashion that you speek of; my little girl must
have one by all means. Cut your hair; shingle it if you prefer. You know what
is my idea. Do not be afraid it will soon grow out better thicker and prettier
than ever before. Our boy has more hair than I expected. When will this war
ever end? I would give all that I possess in this world to see the country at

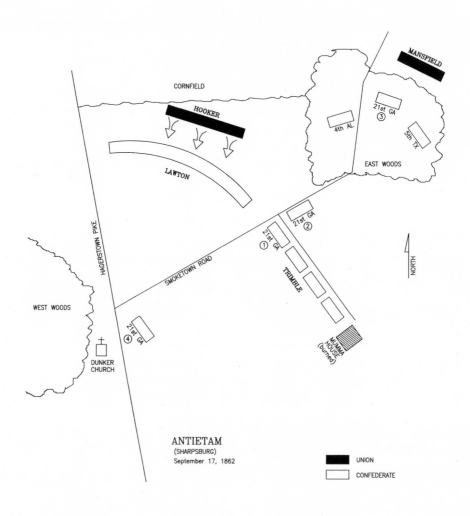

CORNFIELD

HOOKER

MANSFIELD

4th AL

21st GA
③

5th TX

EAST WOODS

LAWTON

HAGERSTOWN PIKE

21st GA
②

21st GA
①

TRIMBLE

NORTH

SMOKETOWN ROAD

WEST WOODS

21st GA
④

MUMMA
HOUSE
(burned)

DUNKER
CHURCH

ANTIETAM
(SHARPSBURG)
September 17, 1862

■ UNION
□ CONFEDERATE

peace and be at home with my dear wife and boy. We defeat them again and again but like the hordes of Goths and Vandals that laid waste to South Europe; still they come. O that winter would come and give us some respite. Our regiment has been under fire about twenty times and is not much larger than a company now. I have seen the twenty first Georgia as large as the seventh brigade. Our brigade repulsed successively three of the anemy and drove them near a mile and held our position near an hour. We were out of amunition and could only shoot what we gathered from dead men. The anemy reinforced before we did and we fell back. We did not have a round of ammunition. Even while we had none we remained to make a demonstration and thare held them back for a long time. Col Walker[4] commanding the brigade was wounded. So was Maj Glover of our reg. The latter severely and perhaps mortally. I have no more time. Give my respects to all. I congratulate Lizzie and Boykin. I send this in a Yankee envelope. Goodbye my dear. Your boy,
Ugie

1. The battle of September 17, 1862, is almost always referred to as Antietam or Sharpsburg. "Boonsville" is undoubtedly a reference to Boonsboro, Maryland.

2. On September 19 and 20, Lee's rear guard repulsed Federal pursuit in sharp skirmishing along the Potomac River near Shepherdstown, Virginia.

3. Peter Bogert (born 1805) and Gilbert Forbes (born 1806) migrated from New York in the 1830s and established a tailoring business in LaGrange.

4. James Alexander Walker (1832–1901) colonel of the 13th Virginia Regiment, was temporarily assigned to command General Trimble's brigade after Trimble was wounded at Second Manassas.

Near Martinsburg Va
Sep 23d 1862

My Dear Susie
I wrote to you two days ago will write now if I can think of anything interesting. Did you see any sense in my outline of the field at Ceder Run. I would have liked to have seen you when you got it. The anemy had the best position in the last fight[1] and made an artillery fight of it. He had some heavy batteries which controlled the right of the field. They were on the side of the mountain and we could do nothing with them. We drove in the left and held the centre while he held the right. Genl Lee says if evrybody else had fought like we did it would have been a great victory. He also says we had them whiped if our reinforcements had come time enough. The fact is our division and espe-

cially our brigade did the work quicker than Gen Lee expected.[2] We are now camped about five miles East of Martinsburg. This is our third days rest. I do not believe we will stay here much longer. I would like for us to get to some pleasant ground and rest for a while. I sometimes feel that if I was at home again I would never want to see or hear anybody. I am tired of so much noise and confusion. The boys tell me that Ethan looks very bad. Poor fellow, if he was not such a great sinner as to show his strength and spirit he would do better. We captured some of the finest teams at Harpers Ferry that I ever saw in my life. We Georgians do not know what fine horses are. If ever this war ends and I am able, I do not expect to own any common stock of any kind. From what I can learn the people are all doing much better than I expected. I regret that I had not sold all my cotton. By the by, you nor Mr. B have never acknowledged the receipt of two hundred dollars that I sent by Uncle W. I will answer Mr. Boykins letter as soon as I can conveniently. Indeed I do not know what to write. The anemy have captured our hospital at Middletown. No doubt they have such of our wounded as could not be moved. From what I hear they have Berry Rowland. He was not sick and only remained with Henry. No doubt they have Eb also. I have just received your letter of Aug 22nd. You can let Dr. Gunn[3] use my sadle for what I care. I don't care to sell it. You will find this a remarkably stupid epistle. But I hope it is better than none. So good bye.

Your boy,

Ugie

P.S. I send you a few stamps as I see you have none.

1. Sharpsburg (Antietam), Maryland, September 17, 1862.

2. Allen's assessment reflects a bit of self-delusion or perhaps hyperbole for the benefit of the homefolks. For a while Lee, and to a lesser extent Jackson, entertained thoughts of turning the Federal right flank, but reports of McClellan's massive reserves quashed the idea. Although the Confederates remained in position at Sharpsburg for another twenty-four hours, all indications are that the battle of September 17 was a struggle for survival on their part, with Lee shifting troops from one threatened portion of his line to another.

3. James M. Gunn (born 1829) was a Chambers County, Alabama, physician.

Camp in the Woods Va
Sep 26th 1862

Dear Susie

I cant tell you where we are at, only that we are "in the woods" have a pleasant camp and pleasant weather. We had quite a heavy frost this morning. I have seen it earlier in Georgia. We are moving about nearly evry day. I can not tell whether thare is anything of importance at hand or not. My opinion is that the first of November will close all very active service in this part of the Confederacy. I cant see what our soldiers will do unless we go into winter early. I look for the anemy to do much mischief on our coast this winter. Many of our boys are hoping that we will be ordered to Savanah this winter. I do not think it probable. For we are not a Georgia brigade, in fact have only two Georgia regiments (12th & 21st) in our division.[1] I forgot Lawton's, a Georgia brigade has been recently added to this division. I heard bad news a few days ago. Gen'l Trimble has lost his leg. I do not know this to be reliable and sincerely hope it is not so.[2] Take "Aunt Nancy" (as he is familiarly called) from us and we are not better than other men. This is somewhat like a certain Pharasee, is it not?

My dear, let me thank you for those clothes and add that they fit remarkably well. By the by make two brest pockets to my coat, one on each side. Mr. Boykin proposes to fix up the Betterton house for you if I can do no better for next year. How do you like the idea. If I am compelled to rent land to cultivate I think you could be tolerably comfortably situated here considering circumstances. I intend to see W. Formby as soon as I can. We are not allowed to go outside of the brigade lines. Never see our Troup County friends unless we meet them on the road and then we can only say, "how are you old fellows," and go on. These orders are caused by straglers and theives who commit all kinds of depridations on the farms. I understand that Genl Bragg is very much condemned for shooting such men. Bragg done perfectly right. Civilians can stay at home and prate as much as they please. Thare is not an honorable man in the Confederate army but says he did right. The common people do not know what an army is composed of. Thare are men here who can put the devil to shame in the conception and execution of wickedness. Genl Jackson has ordered the file closers to shoot on the spot any man who leaves ranks on the march. But has not surpressed it. I expect a good many executions will take place in this army soon. Our regiment has had a new uniform made. Kiss that dear saucy little fellow for his Pa. No news today. Good bye,
Ugie

P.S. Send your letters to Gordonville untill I tell you otherwise.

1. The 12th Georgia transferred from Early's brigade to Trimble's brigade on August 27, 1862, replacing the 16th Mississippi.

2. This rumor was not true, although Trimble's severe wound sparked speculation that he might have been shot by a type of exploding bullet.

Near Bunker Hill Va
Sep 28th 1862

My Dear Susie

We came to this place, half way between Martinsburg and Winchester yesterday. I do not know the object of this move. Whether it is intended to draw the anemy out or whether he is moving down about Manassas and we are falling back to be able to counteract such a movement. The soldiers are all worn out fighting and marching and need repose. We have recruited up our number considerably since the late battles; but could not make fight proportional to our numbers. Many of the men are unarmed as yet. But let the men know that it must be done and they will wake things up when the time comes. I earnestly hope that even if they do not make peace, that we will have no more fighting to do this season. I am heartily tired of their wholesale butchery and distruction, all about nothing. I think if Lincoln and his cabinet could see one battlefield, the mangled forms, blackened and distorted countanances of the dead; hear the piteous mouns of the wounded, see them reeling to and fro in their agony and dying in their own gore; their hearts would quake fearing the wrath of a just and avenging God, let us alone, and bring peace and quiet to the miserable millions of a once happy country. I fear you will never get my letters as I have no way to send them only when we can hear of some one going home. Today is Sunday and I have spent it very pleasantly. Slept very late this morning heard preaching and had quite a pleasant time talking of the past and prophesying for the future. The report of the Yanks capturing our wounded is contradicted. I hear that Lonny Britton is at Winchester and doing well. Let his mother know it. We have just heard from Genl Trimble. He sent a courier to us with the words, "Tell my lads that I am doing well and will soon be with them again." He always says "my boys," "my lads." Nothing more. So goodbye "my little Susie."

Your boy
Ugie

P.S. Trim my coat with blue if you can get it. Tell Mrs. R that Berry has returned to the company safe.

Near Bunker Hill Va
October 1st 1862

My Dear Susie

Who can write when they do not feel like it. The fact is I am becoming quite lazy for the last few days. Nothing to do but eat beef bread and drink coffee. We have had any quantity of the latter article ever since the capture of Manassas. Our commissary got three and a half barrels then and a sack or two at Harpers Ferry, so we have had as much as we could consume, or rather waste. It is rumored that the anemy are crossing the river at Sheperdstown. If this is true we will have another battle soon. I did hope that we were done for a while. Going into battle has always been a terrible thing with me. So it is with evry other man. I have been under fire fifteen diferent times. Still thare is that dreadful sadness lest having escaped so often I may at last sustain some injury. I do not live or fear for myself but for my own wife and boy. Thoughts of them are ever upermost in my mind. We had some men in the last fight just as thare is in all who acted disgracefully and fall out and will not go in the fight. You will see their names in the papers. It is justice to the brave men who do fight that the world should know these cowards. I only had seven men and three fell out. The other four went on like men. All were wounded. Fired with revenge when my poor boys were shot down I seized a gun (an Enfield rifle) and if I did not wake things up it is not because I did not try; and have time and an opportunity.

No vacancy in our company has been filled yet. An order came from the Sec of War for Lt. W. to be examined. They have been so long about it that I have lost all interest in it, and care but little about the matter. "Honor and fame from no condition rise. Act well your part, thare all the honor lies." I have done my duty I think, and might add some of other mens. We have had no mail since we have been here, nor do I see any prospect for any. We are pened up like a parcel of sheep, neither see nor hear anything to vary the monotony. We are living in a kind of chrysalis state; days come and go unnoted. We drill three times daily but no one takes any interest in it, men or officers. I have my load in the shape of a dosen conscripts recently arrived from Camp McDonnald[1] or camp something else. Nothing more today. Give my respects to Mr & Mrs B., Lizzie and B. and to all inquiring friends. Goodbye my dear. I hope that I will hear from you soon. Kiss the boy for his father. Ugie

Oct 3d, I mail this today.

1. Camp McDonald was Georgia's primary training camp for new recruits. Named for former governor Charles J. McDonald, it was located at Big Shanty in Cobb County.

Near Bunker Hill Va
October 4th 1862

Dear Susie
Here we are yet. This is all I have to say, for nothing has transpired worthy of
notice. This is wash day with the men—no drill—and I have made me a bed
in the shade and am acting big lazy on a grand scale. Too lazy to write, too
lazy to even think, too lazy to do anything but eat and scratch. By the by I
have on my dress suit for the first time since I left home. Don't feel natural in
the least. I am carried back to days of "auld lang sayne" when I went a cour-
tin. I have a good joke on myself about dress though I do not know that it is
any credit to me to tell it. My fatigue suit had become quite soiled and the gilt
bars coroded, and the other day while passing a sentinel he says "halt! halt!!
thare you fellow." Surprised, I asked what was the matter. "Go back over this
line; go back sir. Nobody is allowed to pass but commissioned officers." I
bawled out rather angrily "Well aint I a *commissioned* officer?" He scrutinised
me closely from head to foot and said apologeticaly, "You may be, but you
don't look much like one." This was a crusher to me and the next minute
found me hunting the wagons and my trunk.
  You spoke in your letter about Boykin or someone else coming to bring
clothes to the boys. They should not come untill we get somewhat stationary,
and get transportation for them to the regiment.
  Joe Rodgers and Wm Perry are dead. I know this to be so although I have
recieved no official notice of it. Perry was one of the best soldiers I ever saw.
He was wounded at Chantilly near Fairfax, Sep 1st. If I can find out anything
for his family I will let them know it. Nothing more today. Goodbye my dear.
Your boy,
Ugie

Near Bunker Hill Va
Oct 10th 1862

My dear Susie
I have answered your letter brought by Joe Horsley. But it is in my trunk and I
can not mail it. We are packed up bag & bagage to move at a minutes warn-

ing. I have a bit of news for *yourself.* Col. M. was placed in command of this brigade without ever being tried by a courtmartial, day before yesterday. Yesterday morning all the officers of this regiment called on Gen Early[1] com'dg this division making an inquiry why it was done. He told us that he would send to Gen Lee and make inquiry into it. We returned to duty untill this morning, then finding that Mercer had not been rearested and was still in command, we went to Maj Hooper and refused to serve while M. was in command. He placed us under arrest and the arrest has been confirmed by Gen Early. So you see the 21st Georgia has no commissioned officers for duty. We have a jolly crowd—twenty three. The sergeants have command of the companies. John T. Mercer is a perfect drunken cowardly sot, tyranical and unprincipled. He got beastly drunk before Richmond when we were in hearing of the anemies musketry on the 27th of June, fell from his horse and was blown by flies while in this condition. The charges against him are the most grave that could be brought against any man. We dont intend to let Mercer highfolutin and do just as he pleases when if we err a hairs bredth we are cursed like dogs or arrested and brought before a courtmartial. The consequences will be this: kept under arrest for some time, or reprimanded and fined, or dismissed from service. We all done this to show that we are men and intend to be respected as men. We dare not transgress the law. Neither shall our superiors.

Many thanks for your dear long letter by Corp Horsley. Many of your inquiries are answered in previous letters. I am in very good health, weigh one hundred and fifty eight pounds, two more than ever before. We all have remarkable good health. Tell Mrs. R that Berry is so fat that thare is no scales in the army sufficient to weight him. I estimate his weight at two tons being thirteen feet eleven inches in circumference. The report of Harry Ainsworth's death is untrue. The eracipalas has subsided and he is improving very fast. I know nothing of the other wounded boys. My trunk is here. I say sell our cotton for fifteen cents. I think it prudent. Go to Jones with your Pa, by all means and get one of the girls to come and stay with you. Thank Cousin Tudie in my behalf for her kind consideration of my welfare.[2]

We are having such an interesting time in our regiment today that I can think of nothing more. I have no more time. Goodbye my dear
Ugie

1. Jubal Anderson Early (1816–94) temporarily commanded Ewell's division after Ewell was wounded at Second Manassas.

2. "Cousin Tudie" was Susan A. Gunn (born 1839), the daughter of Thomas and Susan Gunn of Jones County, Georgia. Tudie was Susan Allen's cousin.

Near Bunker Hill Va
October 13th 1862

My Dear Susie

Nothing very interesting has transpired since I last wrote you concerning our burst up. Col M was arrested yesterday. I am rejoiced at this if for nothing else than the fullfilment of the old proverb misery loves company. Gen'l Trimble, hearing of his being in command wrote a letter to Genl Early and one also to Gen'l Jackson. These embraced about the same matter and were kindly shown to us by his courier. He said that he was surprised at hearing that M was in command and asked how it could be. He said he arrested M himself and that he feared that his reinstatement would have a pernicious influence on his brigade, and that if it had not been that we were moving so rapidly that he would have been courtmartialed before now; that one had been called and Mercer evaded it by feigning himself sick and that if he had of been courtmartialed he would not have commanded the seventh Brigade or any thing else as he was unworthy and that he was sattisfied that Mercer was a confirmed inebriate. So much for Aunt Nancy as we call the General. We are determined to see Mercer through this time. I stuck to him as long as thare was any reson in it; in fact was the last company officer to say aught against him. But the question is this; shall superior officers be guilty of offences that are not alowed in inferiors. So each one told Col Hooper boldly that he would not serve untill this matter was investigated by a courtmartial.

The report of Harry Ainsworth's death is false. The eracipolas has subsided and he is doing well. I know nothing of our other wounded boys. You atribute my safety to my absence during the battle of Manassas. Some of my friends have told me they were glad that I was not thare; Lieut H[1] has frequently. He demeaned himself with marked gallantry on that occasion. You tell me to escape in battle. How? Where? We do not see the leaden mesengers of death. In battle evryone avails himself of such protection as circumstances and nature present. In maneuvering large masses this is generalship; with individuals it is prudence and the first law of nature self protection. But to protect ones self to the neglect of duty is cowardice. In the battle of Cross Keys when the anemy opened a battery on our regiment the colonel commanded, "lie down men." (Half were already down.) Since that time the phrase has become a byword with the men when ever they hear an unusual noise. Thare is another phrase that some mischevious fellows use when they hear a shot or shell; "hide out children, your dad is coming home drunk." This is when no danger is brewing. The study of human nature about the time of a battle presents many strange and interesting features. I hope to come home and tell you many things.

The last few days have been rather chilly here. We are in a poor fix for winter. Quite a quantity of clothing has been sent to this brigade, but it is not very warm. Our regiment has had a suit of Columbus jeans[2] put up but it has not arrived yet. What the boys get from home will not be a burden to them. Unless the Yankees advance on us I do not think thare will be much more fighting this season in this department. I think we will fall back down the Valley to winter when it becomes cold enough. Thare is nothing here to winter on, besides we are to far from railroad transportation. I stop to read your letter of Oct 7th recieved this moment. I invariably write the first opportunity after a fight. I can not telegraph conveniently. I have no doubt but my letters reach you as early as any letters from the company. I think I have been the first to write after evry engagement. I understand we are to have an inspection tomorrow. Genls Jackson and Lee are expected to be around. The camp has been thoroughly policed, most of the officers have fixed up rather rough seats around their fires in frunt of their quarters and swept away the leaves nicely. This gives quite a nice and cheery appearance to the camp. Here we sit and chat and pass away the fleeting hours. No duty. "Old" Captin Kinnman[3] with his grey hair and beard is the patriarch of the flock. He talks as fine as a lady and very long. Yesterday he came around and sung out, "wouldn't it be so nice to have a cavelry company and Col Hooper for Captain if they dismissed us from service." Lt. Col. Hooper's heart is with us. By the by, suppose they shoot us; what do you think of that. We have a fine time doing nothing but eat bread and beef. We can make a Georgia cook ashamed of herself cooking beef. This is the fact; our boys excel in this. A soldier can live tolerably well and make himself comfortable where a civilian would starve and die. He is at home, with his canteen and haversack well stored. If night overtakes him he stops makes a cup of coffee and broils a bit of bacon, or perhaps he has an apple, a few beans, young pumpkin or rostinear; stews them in his cup and with the aid of a little peper and salt stored away as carefully as if it were gold; makes a good repast for a hungry man; rolls up in his blanket lord of all he surveys sleeps soundly and dreams of home. Did you ever see a picture called the soldiers dream? I have seen it somewhere, possibly in an old magazine. The artist had certainly seen life in camps and had a wife and baby.

You say that our boy is somewhat ill since he was sick and you whip the dear little fellow. Ma don't you know the little boy is not very well. Being ill when sick he is just like his father. Thare! I have commited myself. Wouldn't have liked for any one else to have said this, would I? You ask me if he does not look sweet. He does, little picture of mischevious innocence. He has such a sly saucy look. I think he will be a fast one when his Pa comes home and learns him all he knows. Then you will think he is sick all the time. Boykin says he has him under his special care. But finds fault with his excessive ugliness. This is only a ruse to excuse the looks of his own boy. My boys nose was not large enough; his too large.

You wish a piece of my hair. I wear it shingled all the while. So does evry soldier or at least evry decent man in camps.[4] I regret that I had it cut only a few days ago. I believe I will have a better head of hair than formally. Have you shingled yours? If you have not trim it around by all means, my little beauty. Do not shingle it if you are afraid of catching cold. As I told you in a previous letter you will soon have a fine head of hair by cutting it a few times. I would like very much to see you with your hair short—shingled. You know I have always insisted upon your cuting it; shurly you will know when it is the fashion. You are not going to set yourself up as an old woman, my dear before you are out of your teens, are you? I try to grow younger all the while and make a desparate effort to be good looking. Tell the lady that endeavoured to pass a compliment on you that she is mistaken. Such a thing would be an impossibility. Now shingle or at least trim your hair. And you did not get a hat. Shurly the milaners tremble when you go shoping. You came very near buying a hat. You say it cost three dollars. What if it does? Feel in your pockets and if you cant find that amount let me know it and I will try and make some arangements to send it to you. Take this as a joke as it is intended. But you aught to be laughed at. Sell Ethan by all means if you can get his value. I will try and get a nice horse that you can drive. I think of nothing more today. I am afraid it will be several days before I can send this off. You don't blame me for spreading words and letters when I have nothing to write, do you ? I have tried often to correct this eror. My words are none too far apart. I would write with a pen if I had a good one or any thing to write on. I approve the views you have taken of things in your last two letters. Kiss the dear little boy for me. Your boy,
Ugie

1. Edward M. "Ned" Henderson.

2. The Eagle Manufacturing Company of Columbus, Georgia, was one of the largest textile mills in the South. Jeans cloth was a fabric of interwoven cotton and wool threads.

3. Wesley Kinman (1806–69) was captain of Company G, 21st Georgia Regiment, the "Dabney Rifles," from Gordon County.

4. The short-cropped hairstyle became known after the war as a "Confederate crewcut."

Bunker Hill Va.
October 15th 1862

Dear Boykin

I received your letter several days ago. A few days ago all the officers in the regiment refused to serve under Col Mercer untill his case was investigated by a
courtmartial; we were arrested and are having a very interesting time about
now. I have tried to spend my time profitably reading and writing, but I have
been bored to death by loafers and fellows running in and out. I have been trying to write all day and have been bothered to death so that I am in no pleasant frame of mind now. I stop to read an order from Genl Early releasing us
from arrest. I feel under no special obligations to him. I want justice done the
regiment. If Mercer deserves command courtmartial him and clear him of
the charges. If he is unworthy of it why reinstate him.

We have never heard from the case that you spoke of in your letter, but
probably will soon. Bagby is writing to you now and says he is giving a sketch
of evrything that has passed since you saw us. You seem to be anxious to be in
a fight. I would have been pleased to have had you along in the Sharpsburg
afair. Our little band played such a conspicuous part thare. The whole regim-
nent had quite a hearty laugh over an issue of the "Reporter" Oct 3rd in
which it stated that Lieut Heard, Tobe Kidd, Shirley Sledge and some other
were shocked by a shell. Great pity that evry member of these pet companies
could not get a kind of honorary wound. If you could have seen the 13th
Georgia Reg runing like the hounds of h——l were after it while the 21st
stood like men and broke the anemy's line you would have thought that the
whole regiment was "shocked by a shell" and anticipated another shock.[1]

In reference to that matter that you spoke of it can not be done. I under-
stood that you have already writen to Col M about a position and that he had
promised one. If I were you and intended to go in sevice again I would prefer
the Commissary or Quartermasters departments, such as captain of a train or
something of the kind. Such a position is the easyest that I know of though it
requires a man of practical business qualifications. Black is Sergeant of a train
and I understand is highly esteemed in that position. I would not be much surprised if we made another trip into Maryland or Penn. Gen Steward, I understand has just returned from there having captured about seven hundred
prisoners and about a thousand fine horses.[2] I anticipate an end to this regimental disturbance in a few days. Somehow or other I can not but hope that

Col M will triumph as some men are acting from selfish motives not principle. The small pox are in D. H. Hills division. Tell Susie to vaxinate herself and the negroes and send me my scab also. Tell her it is in my little writing desk or among my cabinet of minerals folded carelessly in a paper. I regard this as a great national calamity and fear it will spread through the whole Confederacy.[3] Nothing more at present. I remain
Your Friend
Allen

My respects to your Pa, Ma & Lizzy

    1. Charles M. Heard, Devany A. Kidd, and Shirley N. Sledge were members of the "Evans Guards," Company K, 13th Georgia Regiment. Allen fails to point out that Lawton's brigade, including the 13th Georgia, bore the brunt of the initial Federal assault south of the "Miller Cornfield." The 13th Georgia lost 48 killed and 169 wounded compared to the 21st Georgia's 4 killed and 72 wounded. Allen's derision can be attributed to more than mere interregimental rivalry. In the spring of 1862, after strenuous duty in the mountains of western Virginia, the 13th was transferred to the Georgia coast, an assignment envied by other Georgia units. The 13th joined Stonewall Jackson's army in time to participate in the Seven Days' campaign, but their fellow Georgians still considered them "pets."

    2. In his "Chambersburg Raid" of October 9–12, 1862, General J. E. B. Stuart led a force of 1,800 cavalrymen on a 126-mile circuit around McClellan's army.

    3. Smallpox first appeared in the Army of Northern Virginia shortly after the Sharpsburg campaign, leading to speculation that the disease had been brought back from Maryland. Authorities ordered that vaccinations, accomplished by scratching the skin and applying a scab which contained the virus from a previous vaccination, be performed throughout the army. Soldiers so feared the disease that, if they could secure a scab, they rarely waited for a physician but vaccinated themselves with pocket knives or broken glass. Troup County also endured a smallpox scare when the disease struck the family of Eli McMillan in late December 1862. Local officials successfully quarantined the family.

Near Bunker Hill Va
October 24th 1862

My Dear Susie
I write you a few lines to let you know where we are and what has prevented me from writing. We have been working on one of "Old Stonewalls" railroad contracts; tearing up the Baltimore & Ohio road. As well as I can learn nearly the whole army has been employed. This is the seventh day since we left our old camp near this place, working four and taking a day to come and go about sixteen miles. It is my opinion that we distroyed about fifteen or twenty miles of the road, possibly more. The Baltimore and Ohio was no doubt the best road in the old Union, double tracks and macadamized. We tore up the iron and burnt it on the cross ties. It was the heaviest work I ever

saw done and we all worked the hardest. Set men to doing mischief and they dont complain of fatigue. Tearing up this road half starves Washington City and will prevent the anemy from wintering a large force in this part of the State. I write in haste as we are expecting to move evry minute; will write more if we remain here today. The small pox is raging here I understand. We have had one case in our brigade. You had better vaxcinate yourself and our little boy and also the negroes if thare is probility of its spreading through the country. No news only that we have recieved nothing from home recently. I write again soon.

Your boy

Ugie

Near Charlestown Va

Oct 27th 1862

My Dear Susie

I sent you a few lines and a promise on the 24th. The next day we marched at dawn and arrived at Charlestown at 9:30 P.M., commenced tearing up the Harpers Ferry & Winchester railroad, and worked all night and untill about noon yesterday. It rained all yesterday and last night. I have just recieved your letter of the 14th. I can only promise you a few lines now. My dear you ask me when will I come home. I can not say. I will be fortunate to get home at all. I shall make evry effort at an apropriate time. Evry officer in the regiment is wanting one (furlough). You had as well undertake to fly to the moon as get one now. I shall sing small untill I think I can push one through. Lt. W. left for the hospital a day or two ago. He will be home soon I predict. The court-martials sentance was suspension from command and pay for thirty days and reprimanded by the Major Genl commanding. Genl Jackson disapproved the sentance saying he considered his conduct very reprehensable and that the court did not treat the case with the gravity that it deserved. In other words, if you do not punish no more than this on such charges do not punish at all. W. labors very hard to get up the impression that Genl Jackson cleared him. Col Mercer is going about here. He will have his trial soon.

I was well amused at your trade. Do pray my dear dont buy any scrub stock. I want you to have a fine gentle horse. I am willing to pay three and if necessary four hundred dollers for such a one as I would like for you to have. Why my dear I would be ashamed to see my little girl clucking and whiping

along after an old broken down horse. It is all the result of training whether a horse is gentle or not, not age or condition. You aught to see these Virginia ladies riding their fine horses. Have one of the boys to drive you where ever you wish to go. I am glad to hear that some of our boys got home. Give them my respects and tell them to get thoroughly well before they come back as I have recieved no official notice of their being furloughed. I sincerely hope that Corp. Clinton will meet a hearty welcome whereever he goes. He is a good soldier and a brave man. I am very glad the Formby place will be sold so soon. I like it very much. I promise you a longer letter when I have a better chance to write. I write now more to relieve you of any anxiety than any thing else. Kiss the dear saucy boy for his Pa. Goodbye
Your boy
Ugie

October 30th 1862

My dear Susie
I have had very poor opportunities for writing for several weeks; we have been moving about so much and working on the railroads. I told you in my last about distroying the Harpers Ferry and Winchester road. We were on the march yesterday and the day before and traveled such circuituous roads that I am lost. Cant tell where we are only that we are about four miles from the Mountains and Shenandoah river, and I think about the same distance from a place called Berryville. Whether it is North South East or West I can't say. I know nothing that would interest you. We have just drawn a new suit of clothes for the men or for those that are present. I regret that so few of the company (about 30) are here. How do the friends of the company intend to send clothing to the boys. They must not send anything at the present for we are moving so much that the boys would be compelled to throw away what they did not wear. The quatermaster will furnish transportation for all things sent to the boys if any one should come along. The "Georgia Relief and Hospital Assocaition" is a good medium through which to send clothing to the soldiers.[1] You spoke of sending me a coat. Don't be too hasty about it at present. One thing we can not get; shoes. Many of the men are barefooted. Working on the railroad in the rain does not agree with me very well. We have a profusion of frost and some ice. I saw a small pond frosen over a few mornings since. You will find this a remarkable stupid letter. It accords very well with

my feelings; I am not very well today. I send you another scrip in this. Nothing more today.

Your boy

Ugie

1. The Georgia Relief and Hospital Association was a statewide organization formed in 1861 to provide medical attention and transportation for sick and wounded soldiers. The association also accepted private contributions of money, clothing, and medicine for needy Georgia soldiers.

Camp Near Berryville Va
Nov 1st 1862

My Dear Susie

My last was from this camp. I do not think we will remain here much longer. I do not know but believe that the army is about changing its position. Yesterday we were inspected and mustered for pay. Today the men are buisy washing and writing letters. All that are here have drawn an entire suit of clothes and look so neat and trim that you would not suspect us of being the Ragged Rebel Roadways Reedy Relief set that we were a few days ago. Now if the men could get shoes they would do very well for the present. I think it will at least be Christmas before we are stationary. I think I can do very well untill that time, with the exception of shoes. We are expecting a move evry minute and I have been in such a hurry to finish up all the muster rolls of the company that I have neglected writing for the last day or two. Another cause; I have been expecting a letter from you and knew I would want to answer it. I think some important movements are about to take place in the army though I have seen nothing very definite recently to authorise such an oppinion. We have recieved the Reporter of Oct 24th and regret to learn that Capt. Curtrights Company has suffered so much.[1] Still their loss was not as heavy as our losses in the recent battles. I have no news to tell you. Uncle W. wrote me relative to buying the rent corn on that place. I forgot to answer that part of his letter. If I can spare it I supose you might let him have it. You know whether I can or not. Tell me how much corn I have made, what wheat you have sowed and evrything interesting about the farm. No doubt you think I have forgotten the farm all together. You dont keep me well posted enough to make it interesting. You do all the managing yourself this year. Do you carry your rule in your pocket. So you read the Cultivator. I have forgoten whether I wrote for it or not. Hope I did. Has your Pa gone after your Cousin Tudie.

This is beautiful Indian sumer hear. More beautiful than our spring to me in this lattitude. It makes me want to come home very much. I envy Boykin the pleasure he has sporting on the river. These fellows may preach to me as much as they choose about thare being no pleasure at home. Tell me thare is no pleasure at home; no pleasure to be with those to whom we are united by the strongest ties that bind the human hart; and evry object brings to mind pleasant associations. It is all nonsense. True we may imagine ourselves heroes imortalising ourselves by deeds of valour on the bloody field, but this is only the dream of the enthusiast, fit only to be disapated by a simple night march or bomb.

Thare will be quite a rush among the soldiers to get home if we ever quit this fighting way we have got into. How does that great boy get along. Does he try to talk any. O that I could see him and his dear mother. Write me a good long letter my dear. Dont follow my example in this respect. Give my love to all. Goodbye my dear.

Your boy

Ugie

1. The "Troup Guards," Company E, 41st Georgia Regiment, lost ten men killed, including John C. Curtright, on October 8, 1862, at the Battle of Perryville, Kentucky.

Near Millwood Va
Nov 4th 1862

My Dear Susie

I write only a few lines, more to let you know where we are than to give news. Indeed I have not time to write much as I am expecting to leave evry minute. We have been hearing the cannons roar for several days and I predict lively times ere this reaches you.[1] We have just returned from picket at Berry's Ferry on the Shenandoah. I could distinctly hear the anemys drums over the mountain about Uperville. Bagby recieved Boykins letter of the 21st today. Yours of the 14th was my last. I hear of nothing of interest. We march in a few minutes. Good bye my dear Susie.

Your boy

Ugie

1. The artillery fire Allen heard probably came from a series of cavalry engagements fought in southern Loudoun County just east of the Blue Ridge Mountains.

Camp on Shenandoah River Va
Nov 7th 1862

My Dear Susie

I recieved your letter sent by Horsley last night. Be ashured that it gave me more than usual pleasure as your letter sent by Leahman[1] has not arived, and it was the only one since the 24th Oct. We are below Front Royal now. We move almost daily and I feel will move before I finish this. The anemy is somewhere near us. Today is the coldest day we have had this season. Some of the boys predict snow before night. You ask me relative to clothing. Most of your enquiries are answered in previous letters. I have a comfort. (My dear it is snowing now.) A good pair of gloves would be acceptable. If I can get a hat some blankets and shoes and boots I can do quite as well as last winter. I understand all the bed clothing sent to the rear last spring is distroyed. This being the case I have no blankets at all. I have a ruber cloth and two overcoats. I have good shoes now but was barefooted a few days ago. I anticipate quite a treat by way of something to eat and drink when our clothes are sent to us. Send me a good quantity of the latter and myself and Head Qrs will get on a bender and Allen will get a furlough. I am like the negro that studied mathematics—I am working head work now. The fact is my dear I fear we will not get many furloughs this winter. Several attempts have been made already but failed. Gen Jackson says no furloughs only on surgeons certificates and Capers[2] is a hard case. My idea is to say little and think much. I have an old Emory & Henry friend on Gen Earlys staff who commands this division.[3] Possibly this may be an advantage to me. We have moved camps since I wrote the above and have orders to march at a moments warning. O that I could have time to write one letter. Thare is always such an excitement and fuss, that a philosopher can not think on any one subject for a minute. It is now snowing very fast. Many of our soldiers will sufer this winter. I anticipate writing a letter to some of the citizens in answer to some inquiries today. I am glad to learn that I will make such a corn crop. Possibly it would be a good idea to sell all the surplus at home and not move it. I say sell all my cotton as soon as possible. I do not expect any recognition or raising of the blockade soon. Tell Boykin to kill ducks and catch fish and think of me. I wish I was thare to get wet all over in Chattahoochee.[4] I have just been comparing duck killing and killing and being killed by the Yankees. You say we would be the happiest persons living if the war would end. Yes, we would my dear, we would. We will all know how to appreciate peace and liberty when we gain it. "How blessings bright, when they take their flight." O that I could see our sweet boy. Kiss the dear little innocence for me and tell him to be nice. My dear you must excuse this short letter. I am anxious to write more if I could. You must think of our situation. Write often. I fear you can not read this with any satisfaction. Good bye.

Your Boy

Ugie

P.S. Give my love to all. I often think of the pleasure of a kind of family reunion on a winter night; with cheerful blazing fire on the hearth.

U

1. Albert Lehman (born in 1833 in the kingdom of Hanover) married Frances Posey Britton from Antioch. Lehman was a goldsmith and silversmith.

2. LeGrand G. Capers, assistant regimental surgeon of the 21st Georgia.

3. Samuel Hale Jr. from Rocky Mount, Virginia, was in the class ahead of Allen's at Emory and Henry. In November 1862, Hale was a major with the position of acting assistant adjutant general on the staff of General Jubal A. Early.

4. The Chattahoochee River flows through the northwestern portion of Troup County, Georgia.

Camp on Shenandoah
November 9th 1862

My Dear Susie

We recieved marching orders moved off but returned to our same camp to remain in I think not longer than today. Possibly a rumor that the anemy are falling back on the other side of the mountains is false, and was the cause of our not moving. I think your dress is beautiful. I think much finer and I know better wove than Mrs. Rowlands. The ladies cotton dresses reminds me of a substitute for shoes we are beginning to adopt in the army; moccasines made of raw hide. We have the hides and any one can soon make a pair. I think it would be a good idea for the farmers to adopt them. Be shure that the sheep are well taken care of and fed. I cant say that I need anything more than you propose to send me, and could do without the pants and vest for some time and if I was shure of coming home I would rather you would not send them. By the by send me some handkerchiefs—cotton, silk, osnaburg or bagging. I am using my last which is nothing more than the skirt of an ancient shirt. Send me some paper also if convenient; cap as well as letter, for I am using about the last I have and do not know what will be my facilities for get-ing more. We are now on the eve of a battle or long march. I can not tell which. At least I think so. You may think I speak of battles quite indiferently. No one dreads them more than myself. But if we must fight let us go at it hop-ing and praying and with a determination to do our best. We can not controll circumstances, neither does our own fate rest in our own hands.

My dear I would like that you would not drive that mule any more. Try and get you a good gentle horse. I expect that mule is loosing her spirit, if so trade her off. Possibly you can buy a horse from a drove. I have no doubt but that horses are scarce, but be shure that you get a good one and one that suits you. Do not be in two great a hurry, but make a permanent investment. I do not want poor trifling stock. Of course you will sell Ethan, but as I said before do not be in too great a hurry. I wish it was possible for me to bring you a horse. If the young sows are promising perhaps you had better kill the one I got off Garrett (the guinea). I want that Formby place (Aaron).[1] You must do as Mr. B thinks best about fixing up the Beddington house.

I do not think that my conduct relative to the Colonel will have any influ-ence in the matter you spoke of. You see it [was] a unanimus thing with all the officers. Mercer is out (I think he is) with the whole pack. But says he does not blame a number of officers who acted from principle. But threatens a few who he says acted from selfish motives. Thare will be no more official communications relative to that matter and I am expecting the grand finale soon. Goodbye my dear Susie,

Ugie

1. Aaron Formby (1775–1862) deeded most of his extensive land holdings to his children but retained one tract near Antioch which was sold as part of his estate settlement.

Camp on Shenandoah
November 14th 1862

Dear Susie

Although I expect a leter next mail I will write today as it is now the fifth since my last. The day that I wrote my last we went out on picket; or at least went down to a mill some half mile from camp stacked arms, lay down on the grass in the sun and wallowed for three days. Some said we were on picket, others that we were guarding the mill. Whether picket or mill guarding, we had an easy time. Three regiments of the brigade have been tearing up the Manassas Gap railroad; and we go out tomorow. It may be interesting to you

to know that we will ford the river. This will be quite a cool proceeding, though may be an advantage as I heard one dirty fellow say a few days ago he wished we would cross another river as his ablutions had not been copeous as would suit the taste of most men. His last foot washing was when we came out of Md. This is the exception not the rule. I wish you could see our boys now with their nice grey suit and healthy looks. We have remarkable good health in the army now. Sergt Bagby however, is somewhat sick today. You need not send me your blankets untill I write for them. I want no pants at present. Have you all anything good to eat these days? This question is suggested by my seeing three stout fellows beating one peice of dough on a stump. Let me tell you of the coon hunt. An unlucky coon weighing eighteen lbs stragled into the regiment and went up a tree. The boys armed themselves with sticks cut down the tree and had quite an exciting time which ended in the outflanking and capture of "old zip."[1] Of course this variation of camp monotony was very agreeable, and gave rise to many yarns (and possibly some lies) about coon hunts down in the Empire State. I am near the bottom of the page, besides have nothing of interest to write. Write very often. Goodbye
Your boy
Ugie

1. The 1834 tune "Old Zip Coon," attributed to Bob Farrell, was published in Elias Howe's *School for the Violin* in 1851.

Camp on Shenandoah
Nov 18th 1862

My Dear Susie
We came in from tearing up the railroad yesterday, moved camp this morning about three miles up the river and nearer Front Royal. I have a huge log fire in front of my tent, have just demolished a pound of pork, to say nothing of buiscuits and feel remarkably well, despite the rain which has been falling at intervals for two days. It always rains by contract of two four and twenty days in this climate. I have not recieved a letter since Horsley came. Now I am not grumbling, only tell you by way of news. I'm in the best humor possible. I know I have several on the road. I console myself like the philosophic Irishman who saw the steam dirt diger; "ah by faith, you can take away me trade, but niver me vote" if the mail does not bring me a letter I still have the glorious privilege of writing, or at least of sending my name and love to my dear little girl and boy. I am using a piece of paper and envelope stowed away for

this special purpose (trunk is in the wagon) about the time I prophesied about that long march or battle. I am a poor prophet, am I not; and you are glad of it in this instance. We must have that Formby land. I shall make evry effort to come home about the time it will be sold. You must try to sell evrything about the farm that can be spared. Possibly you can sell several hundred bushels of corn and some pork. Have you any potatoes for me to eat if I should be lucky enough to come home. How do you Georgians live, look and do? You may ask me the same questions. We live on beef and bread. I am quite hansome; we do "tolerably well, how do you do." Goodbye my dear, may heaven protect you and give you strength to triumph over the many trials that you are called to meet.
Your boy
Ugie

10

FREDERICKSBURG AND PORT ROYAL

He is Burnsides now, but if he will come out in good weather
he will be Burnt-all-over.

THE appearance of the Union Army of the Potomac in front of Fredericksburg in late November 1862 prompted concern in the Confederate high command. In an effort to keep Ambrose E. Burnside's enormous army north of the Rappahannock River, Robert E. Lee called for the prompt reunification of his two corps under Longstreet and Jackson.

Jackson's corps marched out of the Shenandoah Valley through Fisher's Gap in the Blue Ridge Mountains on November 25. The "foot cavalry" moved through Madison Courthouse on November 26 and, after a day of rest, continued eastward. Arriving in the environs of Fredericksburg on December 3, Jackson's men went into position to the right of Longstreet's corps, extending Lee's line southward along the Rappahannock River. Jackson sent Jubal A. Early's division, which included the 21st Georgia, to the vicinity of Skinker's Neck on the Rappahannock to guard a river crossing.

Burnside's troops began crossing the Rappahannock at several points on December 11, a process that continued throughout the following day. Realizing that the hour of battle was near and that a Federal attack in the vicinity of Fredericksburg was a certainty, Jackson ordered Early's division to leave Skinker's Neck. After a late afternoon departure on December 12, Early's troops marched fifteen miles to Hamilton's Crossing, arriving before midnight.

The 21st Georgia, as part of a brigade under the command of Colonel Robert F. Hoke, remained in reserve throughout the morning of December 13. Although in the rear, the Georgians were still under fire, and a massive Union artillery barrage caused numerous casualties in the regiment. As the sounds of musketry fire grew louder and nearer, General Early rode up to Colonel Hoke and ordered the brigade forward. Upon reaching the front, Hoke and his men found that the Confederate line had broken. A Union division under General George G. Meade, charging through a densely wooded area, had shattered a Confederate brigade defending a portion of Jackson's position on Prospect Hill.

With orders to restore the line, Hoke's and other fresh southern brigades charged and swept Meade's Pennsylvanians out of the trenches on the crest of Prospect Hill and back to the embankment of the Richmond, Fredericksburg, and Potomac Railroad. When the Federals rallied along the railroad embankment, Hoke's regiments charged "with a shout that made the welkin ring," according to a member of the 21st Georgia. Running over the Federal position, Hoke's men shot down and captured dozens of enemy soldiers.

After a brief halt at the railroad, Hoke's brigade continued ahead another four hundred yards, driving one of Meade's regiments from behind the cover of a fence. At that point Hoke ordered Lieutenant Colonel Hooper, the commander of the 21st, to take part of the brigade back to the railroad embankment "with orders to hold it to the last." The rest of Hoke's brigade retired back to the crest of Prospect Hill. "The boys were outraged at being ordered back," wrote one member of the 21st of the withdrawal, "as they say they had a position they could have held." Nonetheless the men conceded that "Gen. Jackson knows too well what to do."

Out of 340 men carried into the battle of Fredericksburg, the 21st Georgia suffered comparatively few casualties—only 3 men killed or mortally wounded and 23 wounded. Numerous officers, including Ugie Allen, sang the regiment's praises for its role in the fighting. Lieutenant Colonel Hooper told one of his soldiers that "men never behaved with more gallantry than did the 21st Georgia."

Ambrose Burnside's defeated army withdrew across the river on the night of December 15. The two armies spread out along the Rappahannock to watch each other and settle into winter quarters. General Early's division, including the 21st Georgia, went into camp near the town of Port Royal south of Fredericksburg. The Georgians' camp was spartan; Captain Thomas Hightower of the 21st wrote on January 1, 1863, that the men were "digging out pits in the ground and stretching our tents over them to make ourselves as comfortable as possible."

In mid-January 1863, in a move intended to boost esprit in the ranks, a reorganization occurred within several brigades of the Army of Northern Virginia. One of the consequences of this restructuring was the parting of Isaac Trimble's beloved "two twenty-ones." The 21st Georgia, along with the 12th Georgia from Trimble's old brigade, became part of a new brigade composed of four Georgia regiments commanded by General George Pierce Doles. The 21st North Carolina joined the brigade commanded by Colonel Hoke.

Near Madison C.H. Va.
Nov 26th 1862

My Dear Susie
We have been on the march for the last five days—averaging more than twenty miles a day. We have camped and will possibly remain here today. I am quite well though somewhat fatigued and only write to prevent any anxiety on your part. I can not say where we are going. Probably towards, Richmond or below. I think there is something pressing. You see the long march came although I had given it out. I can not give you a detailed account of our march. We came down the Valley to New Market crossed the Shenandoah Mts. and river then the blue ridge at Fishers gap, the same place that Col Kirkland[1] was at when we reinforced him last spring. We had a sprinkle of snow on the 23rd and this morning the mountains are white. I have no news to write you. Probably can tell you more in my next. Recollect that I may not have an opportunity of writing again soon. I do not know when I can mail this as we have had no mail on the march. Accept my love my dear.
Your boy
Ugie

P.S. Nov 27th We march at daylight tomorrow morning. I would have writen another letter but have been very busy for two days paying off the men.

2nd P.S. I send you some nice dress patterns. They are decidedly the prettyest things I ever saw.

1. Colonel William Whedbee Kirkland commanded the 21st North Carolina regiment until he received a severe wound at the battle of First Winchester on May 25, 1862.

Bivouac Near Fredericksburg Va
December 1st 1862

My Dear Susie

I write you a few lines this evning and will not add anything of importance untill I send off this sheet. We have been on the march ever since I last wrote you from Maddison C. H. We have had no mails nor any chance to mail letters. It is go, go, keep going with us, but the weather and roads are fine and we stand it remarkably well. We aproached to within six miles of Fredericksburg and are now I think about fifteen south of it. Our forces and those of the anemy are in sight of each other; the river between them. Wilkes was at Gordonsville while we were at Orange C. H. but has not caught up yet. I am exceedingly anxious for him to come, as Horsley brought the last news from my dear Susie. I did hope that I could come home the last of this or the first of next month, but do not think it probable. Therefore I must tell you something about the business which you can tell Mr. Boykin, provided he does not recieve a letter from me in a few days. I am sorry to learn, though not much surprised, that cotton is worth nothing. I must have that Formby place, though do not care that it is generally known for fear I am compelled to pay more than it is worth. It would be a good idea for you to give out that you are going to live at the Betterton place and cultivate some of Mr. B's land. See if you can not collect enough on notes to make the first payment, but no more. I understand money is quite plentifull, and had much rather have good notes than money; that is if I had no debts to pay. Retain Mr. Hunt to attend to the negroes if you possibly can. Evrything is so high here that a Lieutenant's pay does not much more support him decently. I am very much displeased with my bad fortune recently. I think great injustice has been done the company and myself. I have had all the labor and responsibility of the company (besides the mental anxiety. There is several thousand dollars Quartermasters accounts) since Boykin left about eight months [ago] while a ranking officer frolicks about and spends what should go to the quartermaster. I am anxious that the vacancies in the company should be filled.[1]

Near Port Royal Va.
Dec 5th 1862

My Dear

I wrote the above several days ago. Tom Wilkes came day before yesterday and brought me your dear long letter. He also brought my vest and handkerchief, for which accept my love. Holle had sold my boots. I know you are as much disappointed as I was. Tell Boykin to tell Holle that I think it rather hard that after patronising him as much as I have and am enduring the hardships of camp life and dangers of battle while he is at home with his family, and cant get a pair of boots to protect me from the mud and snow. Possibly I am too sensitive about such things; anyhow I would like for this war to end. You are quite anxious for me to come home, though not more so than I am to come. My dear I see no possible chance to come. We are in the midst of another campaign and I can not tell where or when it will end. It is the policy of the Yankee government to fight or horass us all winter and not go into winter quarters. Even if they do not endeavour to take Richmond they will make inroads on our coast. No furloughs are being granted now, neither is any furlough or leave of absence valid unless signed by Gen Lee himself. An officer and guard patroles every railroad train and enforces this order. You say I am as smart as Waller or Black. I don't think so. If I am I am not half such a ————. I am fully conscious of the necesity for my coming and shall do evrything in my power to do so. I see nothing to encourage a belief that I can come, and am frank to confess it. Possibly after Christmas cold weather will bring on a temporary suspension of hostilities. Thare was nothing definite passed between me and Billy Edmondson about cotton seed. He wanted them in the trade. I did not consent to this but remarked when he had given me his note that we would not quarrel about them. Let him have what you do not need, though do not consider that I am under any obligations to let him [have] more than enough to plant a small crop. He was to pay me cost, cash for the shop tools. That is the tools that I got from Wilder. I paid forty dollars. Harve knows what I got from Wilder. I paid three dollars for the benches. Of course if Mrs. E. wants anything else she must pay for it. Recollect your board bill. I would be glad to retain the shop tools as they are quite high now. Of course you will move them if he does not pay you cash for them.

You ask me if I was not surprised to hear of Carrie S. marrying again. No, not in the least; but sympathise with her father and Lt. Henderson who was much opposed to it. Neither would I be surprised if she left this husband for another at the expiration of the honeymoon.[2]

About your loom. I am well pleased with it and think evry one should have one in such times as these. I have sent you some scraps of cloth which you will say surpasses anything of home manufacture that you have ever seen. You do not have such fine material in Ga.

We heard heavy firing yesterday last night and today; it is down about the river somewhere. I do not feel much like there will be a general engagement here. It is rumored that the anemy is about four hundred thousand strong, but I do not believe it.[3]

You say Mr. H wants me to say something about Johnny Mathews, to satisfy his father, I expect. John has given me a blowing up at home recently. Johnny is a nice boy but somewhat high tempered. I ordered him to the guardhouse one night for disobedience of orders and insolense. He refused to go and said he would not go. I sent him and kept him in twelve days. I would have relieved him the fourth day but Col. Hoke[4] would not let me. If he had not been young and I had not respected his parents I would have courtmartialed him. However I am glad the affair terminated as it did. For he is a nice boy and I think more of him than any in the company. He was very much incensed against me at first but I think is becoming reconciled. It is a great undertaking to command a number of men. No one knows anything about it but those who have tried it. A man with a company has just as many children to look after and provide for and protect. And evry one is watching critically evry act and word of an officer for fear some injustice may be done him. I had rather be anything else than Captain of a company. Circumstances have placed me in command and I endeavour to do my duty and exercise it with justice and kindness but with firmness. It is a cold rainy day and I can scarcely use my pen. I think of nothing more just now and will close. Give my love to all. Kiss Bobbie for me.

Your boy

Ugie

P.S. You say Boykin proposes to attend to my business next year. This being the case you must use your own pleasure about employing Mr. Hunt. You will want some company. Where is Cousin Tudie?

1. Allen interrupted his letter at this point and resumed writing four days later.

2. Sophronia Caroline Henderson married Thomas J. Sample in July 1859. Sample, 4th Corporal of the Ben Hill Infantry, died at Richmond on December 18, 1861. In November 1862, Carrie married Martin V. McCutchen.

3. Burnside's army numbered 122,000 and Lee's 78,500.

4. Col. Robert Frederick Hoke (1837–1912) of the 21st North Carolina commanded Trimble's brigade for a brief time after Sharpsburg. In the reorganization of January 1863, the 21st North Carolina transferred to an all–North Carolina brigade under Hoke's command.

Near Fort Royal Va
Dec 7th 1862

Dear Sir, [John T. Boykin Sr.]
Col. Fannin[1] called on us yesterday; he starts back tomorrow. I will try to write you a few lines, though I consider it an attempt to do good under

adverse circumstances. For it is remarkable cold and my eyes are half out from the smoke. Day before yesterday we had a sharp snow which is still with us; evrything is frosen up. We pass our time reading "Old Abe's" message,[2] speculating on the place where the next great act in the drama of our war will be performed and trying to keep warm. I think we will soon go to Richmond or below. I have no idea that Burnsides will endeavour to approach Richmond by this route. He is Burnsides now, but if he will come out in good weather he will be Burnt-all-over. Mark what I tell you. The soldiers all say they will do it. I am very sorry to learn that the people at home have given up all hope of gaining our independance. On the contrary the soldiers are quite cheerful and in high spirits. It is true we see no prospects of an early peace; but it is equally true we see none of being whiped. All the soldiers who are the least disheartened caught it from home. In some respects our National prospects are gloomey, and I would like to say more; but I write by firelight and must pass on. What little I have said about my business recently has been to Susie, no doubt she has told you all. I have been putting off writing to you, always waiting for a better time. No doubt you know I would like for you to buy that Formby place for me. I am willing to pay as much and even more than it is worth for it. I would be more definite about the price but I do not know how lands are selling, only quite high. I hear thare are several persons wanting this place. I did hope that I could come home by sale day or soon after, but do not know that I will get a chance judging by some orders calling in all absent officers. Gen. Lee wants evry man at his post. Susie relys principally on you for advice relative to my afairs; and I hope you will feel no delicacy in recommending anything to my interest. Prices are high evrywhere in the Confederacy caused by a depreciation in our currency. Now is a good time to pay off old debts and contract no new one so that when the impending financial crisis comes we will not be crushed. I esteem good individual notes higher than Confederate. Not that I have any doubts about our success, but as worth more money. Give my respects to Mrs. B, Lizzie and Boykin. Very Resp't'ly

Your friend

Ujanirtus Allen

1. James Henry Fannin (1825–1909) of LaGrange, Georgia, was colonel of the 1st Georgia Reserve Regiment.

2. On December 1, 1862, Lincoln delivered his State of the Union address to the 37th Congress.

Near Port Royal Va
Dec 10th 1862

My Dear Susie
I will write you a few lines more on business than with a hope of eliciting anything interesting. This remarkable cold weather reminds me very forcibly that
I would like to have my coat. If I thought I could come home in a few weeks
I would not write for anything; for I could then get such things as I liked. I
am thinking of having Sergt Henry Rowland to bring evrything to the boys.
If I do you can send me whatever you choose. I am thinking that we will
soon be near Richmond. If we are I will let you know so that you can express
anything you wish. We are near the railroad now, but I learn that the authorities will not let anything come farther than Richmond. This is what makes
me believe we are going thare. My dear I almost believe that cotton is warmer
for socks than wool. Do not trouble yourself about wool. Tom Wilkes says
Mr Hunt said that I would scarcely have corn enough to do me. Tell the
negroes that they must use the utmost economy as I will not buy any.

Tell me in your next how much money you have on hand and how much
you need. Possibly I might send you as much as a hundred dollars Christmas,
but can not say. I have been out of money for some time untill recently, just
precisely a fix that I do not wish to be in again. It is quite cold here now.
Night before last I could not sleep in my tent, so about 2 o.ck. I crawled out,
gave a few civil yells, chunked up our large log fire, rolled up in my blanket
and slept sound though at the same time adding a comical coat of ashes and
smut to my physiognomy. Last night with the help of a few pine boughs I
slept well. Lawton's brigade of Georgians in our division have not tents at all.
Neither do they trouble themselves to fix up bunks of brush or do anything
else but grumble and wish themselves back at Savannah. We have only three
fly tents (tents half closed at the ends like this; /) to the company. I am sorry
for them. It is somewhat amusing to us to hear them pining about Savannah
and relate their many hardships. We always tell them we are used to such and
don't think hard of it. Nothing more. Write very often, my dear.
Your boy
Ugie

P.S. I would be glad if you could send me a pair of boots and also a pair of
shoes. I am thinking of having all my shoes made at home, and try and take
care of them.
Ugie

Battle Field—Fredericksburg Va
Evening—Dec 15th 1862

My Dear Susie

We were engaged all day on the 13th. Kind Providence has again protected
me and I have passed the ordeal unhurt. Or at least without any serious injury.
The casualties in the company are: Jesse Bennett wounded slightly in left side
by a shell and John Reynolds wounded slightly behind the right shoulder.
The casualties in the regiment are few, but among them I mention the death
of our esteemed adjutant Thos. J. Verdery.[1] The incidents of the fight are
more interesting than any we have yet been in. I have no time to give any
details. I want time to sketch the field when I write the details. Our brigade
made one of the most brilliant and daring charges ever recorded; eight hundred yards over a field as level as prarie, raked by grape from at least eight
heavy guns. I do not believe we were exceding ninety seconds in the charge.
We stopped in the railroad cut about half way for about thirty seconds. I do
not exagerate. We (our regiment) charged over several hundred Yanks like
they were so much chaff. They were perfectly terror stricken, and as we
passed over them ran perfectly frantic to our rear to escape death from their
own batteries.[2] I hear that Lawton's brigade fought splendidly and is redeem-
ing its character. I know of no casualties in our Troup Co. companies.[3] The
LaG. Lt. Gds. have not been in yet but are near the frunt today.[4] We were in
the frunt line untill this morning; are now in the rear line. I prefer that "pos-
ish" to this. In full view of the whole or greater part of the Yankee army. We
were in a ditch tolerably [safe] from their artillery, and exchanged shots during the whole day yesterday with their sharpshooters. We are waiting for the
anemy to advance. We will have a bloody time of it yet, I fear.

Tom and Berry request that you tell Mrs W and R that they are quite well.
Accept my love and kiss the dear little boy for his father.
Ugie

P.S. One hour later. I have just recieved your letter of Nov 23rd. Strange you
were so anxious and hopeful.

1. Thomas Jefferson Verdery (born June 16, 1828) enlisted as a 1st lieutenant in the "Cedartown Guards,"
Company D, 21st Georgia Regiment on June 27, 1861. He received an appointment to the rank of regimental adjutant on October 12, 1861. Verdery died on December 13, when an unexploded artillery shell struck
him.

2. Confederate officers reported that so many prisoners were taken that guards could not be spared for all
of them and some were ordered to the rear unescorted.

3. Lawton's brigade (commanded at Fredericksburg by Colonel Edmund N. Atkinson of the 26th Georgia) pursued the retreating Yankees all the way to the Federal artillery line and gained distinction by fighting
their way out of the situation. The ground over which they fought became known as the "Slaughter Pen."

The 13th Georgia Regiment, whose Company K was the "Evans Guards" from Troup County, became separated from Lawton's brigade early in the engagement and ended up fighting beside the 21st Georgia along the railroad.

4. The "LaGrange Light Guards" were Company B, 4th Georgia Regiment. Although the 4th Georgia came under artillery fire at Fredericksburg, losing one man killed and six wounded, the regiment never engaged the enemy.

[The first four pages of this letter are missing. It was written from Fredericksburg, Virginia, about December 17, 1862, and describes the battle fought there a few days earlier.]

some wounded and many unhurt. We paid no attention to them looking forward to the heavy columns in the field beyond the second ditch not yet in good range. We were not here exceeding half a minute before were ordered forward again. This was done as rapidly as we came to the cut and we gained the second ditch.[1] The grape came thick and fast from their guns about five hundred yards distant. Doler Cooley by my side was struck by a piece of wood from the fence. [We] were quite anxious to fire on a regiment on our left that was fighting some of Lawtons brigade.[2] They were some distance off; but possibly we might have thrown them in confusion. (It is too dark to follow lines) On account of the dificulty in transmiting orders we were ordered to be guided by the right. The right finding itself exposed to a flank movement of the anemy retreated.[3] Col Hooper ordered us to retreat to the railroad in order. When we rose it looked like the world was tearing in two behind us, and it kept tearing untill we gained the railroad. Their shots were rather high. Several men were killed. Here Johnny Reynolds was struck by a bomb fragment. Him and Bennett both are with us but unable for duty. The 21st NC and our regiment remained in the railroad; the 12th Ga and 15th Ala passed on. Our officers saw the importance of this point of the road in protecting our lines from their sharpshooters deployed us as skirmishers along it. Soon we recieved an order from Gen Early and Col Hoke to hold it at all hazards. Our rifles exchanged occasional shots with their skirmishers and we remained untill just before day the next morning when we were relieved. We came back to our line of battle along the first ditch[4] and remained a day and night. During the time the anemy's sharpshooters amused themselves by shooting at us. They were some eight hundred yds. off and did no harm. Our men would expose themselves and then dodge when ever their guns would fire. We enjoyed it too. We only returned a few shots, for it was against orders. We were also ordered to keep down to conceil our strength. Nine of Capt Longs[5] com-

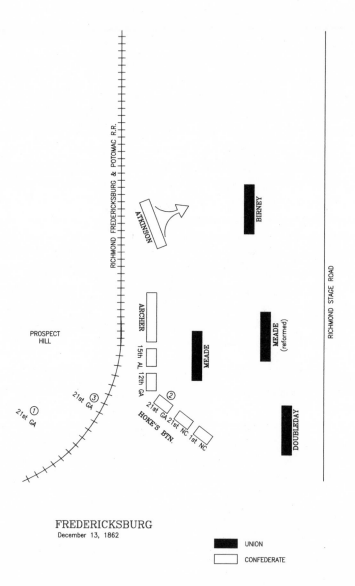

RICHMOND FREDERICKSBURG & POTOMAC R.R.

NORTH

RICHMOND STAGE ROAD

ATKINSON

BIRNEY

PROSPECT
HILL

ARCHER

15th AL

12th GA

MEADE

MEADE
(reformed)

21st GA ③

21st GA ①

② 21st GA

HOKE'S BTN.

21st NC

1st NC

DOUBLEDAY

FREDERICKSBURG
December 13, 1862

■ UNION
□ CONFEDERATE

pany were wounded and some wounded and one killed the evning previous
on this same ditch and fence by the anemys artillery while we were in the cut
perfectly secure. They also use their artillery on us here but fortunately with
no affect. This position was preferable to me I said in my last letter, because we
were better protected or at least as well as our suports and in case of a fight
would not be exposed to their artillery in coming up. Give me a position and I
had much rather open than reinforce in a fight. The anemy remained in about
3/4 to one mile of us all day. Late in the evning they sent in a flag of truce to
bury their dead. But violated it by comencing to cary off the wounded who
were our prisoners, and the truce ceased. Let me tell you this ground between
the ditches was covered with dead and wounded Yankees. Many of our and
their men mingled together and talked etc. When the truce ceased each party
double quicked back to their respective lines and the field was clear again. It is
reported (we have many camp reports) in camp but not credited that the Yankee soldiers mutinied and would not advance on us. Brig. Gen Jackson[6] (Federal) was killed; his aid was probably mortally wounded in the railroad. I paid
him much attention.[7] He gave me two of the finest blankets that I ever saw if I
would go upon the field after them. I got them and placed them under him to
keep him warm. He was sent back to our hospital and I do not supose I will
ever see him or them again. I spent much time that night in doing what I
could in assisting their wounded, for which I recieved their thanks and blessings. I can shoot them as deliberately and eagerly as ever I did any game; but I
can not pass a wounded man without doing what I can for him, if it is nothing
more than a sympathising word or look. Is not thare a line, "Lord that mercy I
to others show, that mercy show to me." It is always in my mind on such occasions. I captured a fine Sharp's rifle, spring trigers, shoots a thousand yards.[8] I
also got some rations and among them a nice quantity of coffee. This was
given to me by a wounded man who I gave water. I wish you were here to take
a cup with me, or rather I was with you. Many of our men robed the dead
while at the railroad that night. I did not do this but assisted the wounded.
However I robed a dead horse of a very fine bridle.

I forgot to tell you in previous letters to pay Jim Vance $40.00. I sent his
money to him but he did not get it. You say Boykin complains that I do not
write. I have answered all his letters punctually and am ahead of him. Tell B.
that Capt Thomas Settle[9] was killed. I believe they are some kin. Thinking of
nothing but war news and fearing what I have already writen will not prove interesting I will close. Goodbye my own dear Susie. Write to me often.
Your Boy
Ugie

1. The "cut" is the railroad ditch, but the "second ditch" is difficult to identify. Other contemporary accounts indicate that a series of ditches traversed the plain between the railroad and the Richmond Stage Road. Allen probably refers to a stone wall east of the railroad where most of Archer's and Hoke's men halted their pursuit of Meade's Yankees. The 21st North Carolina, 21st Georgia, and 1st North Carolina Battalion crossed the wall to flank the 9th Pennsylvania Reserves.

2. Lawton's (Atkinson's) men were pinned down in the "Slaughter Pen."

3. Colonel Hoke and General Early concluded that Federal general Abner Doubleday's division posed a significant threat to the Confederate right flank and ordered a withdrawal to the original line on Prospect Hill.

4. The first ditch, in this case, is probably a reference to the Confederate earthworks occupied during the initial phase of the battle by General James J. Archer's Brigade.

5. James A. Long commanded the "Evans Guards," Company K, 13th Georgia Regiment of Lawton's (Atkinson's) brigade.

6. Conrad Feger Jackson (born 1813), commander of the 3rd Brigade of Meade's division, was killed near the railroad cut as he led his brigade forward in the initial Federal assault. With Jackson down his brigade advanced no farther, remaining in the railroad ditch until being forced out by Hoke's brigade.

7. The only member of C. Feger Jackson's staff listed as being both wounded and captured at Fredericksburg was Lieutenant T. Brent Swearingen. He recovered from his wounds.

8. The weapon was likely carried by a member of the 13th Pennsylvania Reserves, the only Union regiment on the southern end of the Fredericksburg battlefield armed with Sharps rifles.

9. Thomas Battle Settle was captain of the "Monroe Crowders," Company D, 31st Georgia Regiment of Lawton's brigade.

Camp Near "The North Pole"
Dec 19th 1862

My Dear Susie

I recieved your welcome letter of Dec 7th yesterday. I know you would be very uneasy about not recieving a letter from me on the march but we had no chance to write untill we got to Maddison or mail untill we got to Orange C.H. Twas at Maddison that Tip Bowling saw me. I was hard at work on pay rols and he poked his head in my tent and said, "how are ye Lt." I thought he had come to report for duty and was so buisy that I only returned the salutation. The fact is he has been absent from the company ever since we came out of the Valley. Ten pages would not tell his history. He is now a deserter; and has ran home. Arch Tyree stoped at Gordonsville while returning from the hospital, had himself detailed for something and is reported absent without leave from the company. Henry Goss is with him. Anything to keep out of marching and fighting. You would be surprised to know how men disgrace themselves for this purpose. The very trees of "Old Troup" would weep over the degeneracy of her sons if the secret history of this and other companies

was writen. I will put about half of this company against the world for bravery and manliness; while thare is a number perfectly devoid of all principles
of pride and honor. If ever I come home I shall answer candidly evry inquiry
about the men. I shall take special pains to let the people know who are worthy of praise. Hospital birds and renegade teamsters shall not share the laurels
won by the B.H.I. on the battlefield. Tell Mrs. Brewer that I doubt whether
we will ever see that bagage again or not. I honor her as the mother of a brave
son, and will do what I can for her. I dreamed last night that I had got evrything and sent to her.

   We do not know where the anemy has gone. I heard canons firing this
morning. Possibly he will attempt to cross the river again below here under
cover of his gunboats. It was (Federal) Brig. Gen. Jackson's bridle that I got. I
could have got his saddle also but did not know that I could have taken care
of it. I took his blankets and put them under a wounded Yankee. I have his
ruber legins. If I had known these things were his I would have kept them as
trophies. If I can take care of it I intend that my "little girl" shall have his bridle. I know she will prize it very high because I fought for it. My dear I shall
come home if I can. It is very hard to get off. I have known several failures,
but no one to get furlough. I am somewhat stupid this morning, as I have a
cold. It is rather cold here now. You see I write from the arctic regions. Send
me at least two leaves instead of one. I always write as much as I can. Goodbye
for the present.
Your Boy
Ugie

Near Fort Royal Va[1]
Dec 23rd 1862

My dear Susie
I write you a few lines so as to keep up the currrent of correspondence. We
are siting in camps and never hear or see anything interesting. We sometimes
get a paper and mail. The last letter I wrote to you was on hand two days
before it went off.

   Christmas is coming but we do not realise the same pleasure in anticipating
it that we formally did. What a great theme for reflection that this festival that
was formally devoted entirely to pleasure should now be passed unnoticed.

Even the saboth here comes and goes and we never know it. Some of the boys are making great efforts to get hold of some whiskey and eggs but their efforts have been in vain. Whiskey sells at a dollar a drink in camp and none at that. A poor quality of ginger cakes fifty cents. Late last night I eat some and such dreams you never heard of before. I thought I was instructor in a female military school, was a member of congress, was an army sergeon, saw Lord Lyons[2] and last and most laughable, came home and my little girl became *enciente*. Of course you will not let any one see this. You understand me. I have just sent in a request for a leave of absence but I have no hope of geting one. All attempts for them as yet have failed. It will probably be two weeks or even three before I hear from it as it must go to Genl Lee. I sent up one for John Hick two weeks ago but it has not yet returned. The ball is still in his arm. If it does not come back untill March if approved I shall send him home. John is a great soldier. I have long since reduced Terry and promoted him. The commanding officer of a company now has the power to reduce to ranks and promote for meritorious conduct. This regime rids the service of a number of ignorant and trifling non-commissioned officers. Wm. McClain who was a division teamster left for home yesterday. I do not know how he got off only through the quartermaster. He did not let any of us know anything about it. I still adhear to what I told you about coming home if I can ever find it practical. Do not say a word about it not even to Lizzie. I presume you would tell her before anyone else. I have not been very well for the last few days but am on duty and better. Cold no doubt. Something like neuralgia in my sholders and limbs, while my knees and feet are swolen. Today is as pleasant as spring. I anticipate rain. We have the greatest fires you ever saw. We cut logs fourteen feet long and have a blase several feet high all night. We smoke as black as chimney skeeps. Fancy me with tags of soot hanging to my whiskers. We smoke also, each man is armed with a small sack of tobacco and a pipe. We use beef bladders and the sack around the hart dressed with flour with a little draw string (like your grandmothers pocket) at the mouth to carry our tobacco in. They are very nice. I know you would like to have one to keep little tricks in. One day while I was dressing one, one bystander said I would not ask my wife to sow a tape on one for me. Another said mine would not do it. I said nothing but thought if I were to ask "little Susie" to fix one for me she would take the greatest pleasure in doing it very nice wouldn't she? She is the best woman living.

Your boy

Ugie

1. Port Royal.

2. Richard Bickerton Pemell Lyons was the British minister in Washington, D.C.

Near Fort Royal Va
Dec 25th 1862

My Dear

Hoping that you will have a merry Christmas and claiming a Christmas gift, I bid you good morning.[1] This not being my day in course to write and news being scarce I will give you one or two incidents of the light order of the Fredericksburg fight. When we gained the railroad a wounded or scared Yank or possibly both whined out to Captin B[2] in a femenine tone, "is the rebels advancing?" He replied, "no they are already here. I'm one." "Well I didn't know it." Captin H[3] is one of the nicest men you ever saw full [of] dry wit and somewhat of an oddity in his way. No one paid any attention to the presence of these fellows as we had a number of others just beyond that required our attention. One fellow near Capt H was very noisy bawling, "Don't shoot me." "I'm a prisoner." "I surrender." H turned around to him and said contemptuously through his clinched teeth stamping his foot on the ground. "Kiss my ———."

A notorious character, Billy Patterson, alias "Blue Lightning" came in camps about 4 oclock this morning and has caused considerable excitement. His advent was the signal for a general onset and a terrible battle ensued between him and the men. The battle rages furiously and is still undecided. Billy is being cut to pieces but the field is strewn with his antagonists. I was in the early part of the engagement, but "skedaddled" unhurt under cover of reinforcements. (If you see anything wrong in this letter it's the pen, not me.)

We do not know where the Yankees have gone to. I hear artillery firing evry day. I think it is picket firing across the river. I expect we will go on picket in a day or two and muster and pay rolls are to be made out; possibly I can not write again in a few days. I think we will recieve one the next mail, as it has been near ten days since your last. Write me a long letter and tell me about "my little girl and boy."

Your Boy,

Ugie

1. "Christmas gift" was the traditional Christmas-morning greeting in many southern families. Guests who used the salutation upon entering a home were entitled to a special gift.

2. Captain Henry T. Battle, Company D, 21st Georgia Regiment.

3. Captain Algernon S. Hamilton, Company B, 21st Georgia Regiment.

Near Fort Royal Va.
Dec 28th 1862

My Dear Susie
I recieved your letter of the 16th last night. Your letter is more interesting than usual; and I would like that I had time to answer it as it deserves
before the mail goes out. If I do not answer it now it will be two days before
I can mail another. I dislike to be hurried when writing about anything of
serious import. Your new home naturally promps reflection about your welfare and the condition of my business. Truly it is not very flattering. You have
not the same pleasant cheerful home that was formally your own, but an
inconvenient uncomfortable place belonging to another.[1] If you can be
happy be so; your condition is quite humiliating to me. At first glance it
would seem that circumstances would offer some palliation and so they
would if men were men and selfishness avarice and rapine did not rule the
country. I have previously told you that if we are overwhelmed in this struggle it will not be by the baonets of our anemies. I have thought about the
proposition that you wrote me; but did not mention it to you. Recently it has
become a matter of serious consideration and I may adopt it. However I
would like to come home first. I intend to come home sooner or later. I will
investigate the matter soon. I hope that this as well as anything else that I may
write on this subject will remain confidential between us. Recollect this and
do not commit yourself to anyone; but write me anything that has the least
bearing on the subject. With me thare is a pressure here. I do not like the situation of affairs or my treatment by those high in authority. For almost a year
my labors have been almost superhuman. I have sacraficed evrything for my
country and welfare of the company. I am worn out phisically and my
patience is exhausted. Those who might help me are a disadvantage. The men
are anxious that they should have a corps of company officers. It gives a company more prominence in the regiment. Besides this I can say that they do
not attatch the same dignity to a subordinate officer as captain and I find I
have new difficulties to contend with daily. I frequently wish that I could be
away for several months so that some one else could try it. Besides I think I
could come back to duty in better spirits and take greater interest in it. I want
relaxation. My strength and patience is exhausted. I would not care so much
about it if it was my part to do all. W. has not done a months duty this year.
While he has both rank and pay. I repeat that him as well as H. is a disadvan-

tage to me.[2] No one must read this but you and then distroy it. Goodbye for
the present.
Your boy
Ugie

1. Susan and her eighteen-month-old son had moved into a tenant house on the Boykin plantation.
2. "W." refers to Lieutenant Leroy T. Waller and "H." is Lieutenant Edward M. Henderson. Henderson,
along with several other officers of the 21st Regiment, had signed a statement verifying that Waller had commanded the company and displayed good conduct during the Battle of Gaines's Mill (Cold Harbor). Allen
took the statement as an endorsement of Waller's claim to command.

Near Fort Royal Va
Dec 31st 1862

My Dear Susie
I will try to write a few lines but it is a bad chance tonight. I am judge
advocate in a regimental courtmartial now in session and of course am
much more than buisy all day. I have writen about twelve pages of cap today outside of business hours. Evrybody has been buisy putting up bunks and
flies for cold weather. We dug down on a hillside and have made a small chimney to one end of our fly. The back is made of brick and we propose to fasten
up the other end with cloths or blankets to keep out the cold. I think I will
fix up a small table to write on and if I do and am as comfortable as I anticipate I will write to you much oftener. By the by I think you have almost quit
the good old way of writing twice a week and govern yourself by my stru-
gling epistles. And I only get a letter evry ten or fifteen days. Write oftener
and risk the mails. I think they will be more regular now. That poor pittiful
furlough of mine has gone under. Let me tell you. Ned proposes that we procure a couple of femenine sex to keep us company in our new quarters. I
have given no definite answer yet not that I have any objection; but think prudent to consult you about it. Be shure and let me know your opinion about
it; as I am in suspence. The weather after being pleasant for some time has
turned off rather cold. I expect snow tonight. Nothing more tonight.
Goodbye.
Your Boy
Ugie

Camp near Port Republic Va
Jan 5th 1863

My Darling Susie

I sent you a few lines by Curren, Lt Henderson's boy a few days ago. I enclosed ($100.) one hundred dollars in the letter, and also sent you a captured bridle. Please acknowledge the receipt of them. Nothing of interest has transpired here since I last wrote you. The regimental courtmartial is still in session. We try from two to three cases a day. Company F is tolerably well represented in the court. All the charges are cowardly and unsoldierlike conduct. The specifications are that they laged behind to avoid the battle of Fredericksburg. I know that some one will write home about it, and for fear of mistakes I will say that Wince Harper was honorably acquited by the court. Wearing the flour barrel shirt and marking time on the head of a barrel for several hours a day for twenty days is common among the sentences. The court is tolerably severe. I told you I was judge advocate; which is about the same as prosecutor and clerk in civil cases, and send them to Hdquarters.

Tell Boykin that I have given a pair of boots he had in Ned's trunk to Bagby. I also have his sash and will retain it with his permission. Let me tell you. I heard this evening that brave old Gen Ewell married not long since.[1] Vance is here, he brought no letters. Pay his mother and take receipt for what is due him. I do not know that I can succeed but I will make an effort to get him an unlimited furlough. He can then draw pay as long as the war last. I do not wish to discharge any wounded men. Do not trouble Curren when he comes back with anything but a letter for me as Lt H has writen his father not to let him bring anything for anyone.

No officer can go to a private house or hospital now without a furlough from his Brig. Genl. The chances to get off are geting worse. Thare will be an officer sent to all the counties from which thare is a company in this regiment to procure shoes for the soldiers. I will invite him to call on you and Boykin. Nothing more today. What about the dear little boy?

Your boy
Ugie

1. The widow Lizinka Campbell Brown, whom Ewell courted for some time, had supervised the general's convalescence following his wounding at Groveton. Reverend Charles Minnegerode, rector of St. Paul's Church in Richmond, officiated at their wedding on May 24, 1863.

Camp near Port Royal Va
Jan 6th 1863

My Dear Susie
Our daily mail arrives at night and goes out early in the morning. I will get a
letter from you tonight. I know you think me quite a grumbler. How can I
help it when a letter evry ten or twelve day is my average. Yours of the 16th
Dec was my last. The falt must be in the superscription. Try this: Fredericksburg Va. (21st Ga Reg. Trimble's Brigade, Ewell's Division). Nothing gives me
more relief when I recieve no letters than writing to you. I must confess I envy
you my dear, if you experience the same pleasure at the reception of my letters
that I do of yours. I sometimes fear mine are more frequent than interesting.

For the want of something better I will tell you how I live and have spent
my time for the last few days. I rise at reville a little after day. This matter of
rising is harder than anything else. Bagby, Ned and myself quarter together.
Bagby being subject to nightmare and N. to diarhea I take the middle and am
as warm as a bug in a rug. Put on my hat and shoes at my head and coat which
is under it, and rush out to roll call, come back make a fire and by this time it
is light enough to write. I generally write out a case by eight or nine oclock,
wash, eat and hurry to court martial. Sometimes breakfast is not ready and I
walk into court picking my teeth just as if I had been to a feast. We try several
cases and always ajourn by three P.M. Nothing of this kind is concidered valid
unless done between eight and three. I then return and write untill too dark.
Then eat. Now, for what I eat. Bread and beef staked or, washed down by
spicewood tea. We have been drawing as much shugar as we wanted for the
last week. With dark the day is finished for us as we have no candles. About
this time the mail comes. We get the Richmond papers, chunk up the fire
and read the news. Then comes, whistling, whittling, visiting and receiving
visits. I feel lost without candles. Cant read or write without them at night
with any satisfaction. Let us look at it. I do not usualy retire before ten or
eleven. So you see about one fifth of my time is spent without any permanent
advantage. This brings to mind another reflection. I will soon be twenty four
years old. Where have the years gone, and what am I? The sadest reflection of
all is that three years ago, we set out on lifes journey hand in hand so happily
together and for half the time you have been left to buffet the tide of fortune
alone, while I am away amid the sufferings and dangers incident to camp life.
I do not murmer at the stern decree of fate; but still I cannot but wish it were
otherwise. Nothing more today. Tell me all about the dear little boy.
Your Boy
Ugie

P.S. Send me a pocket knife and [part] monie by all means.
U.

2nd P.S. The fact is we can get nothing here. It would take a thousand(?) to set me in good running order. Cant go to Richmond or anywhere else unless the regiment goes. If those clothes dont come soon I will be bare headed, bare-footed and bare backed. That is the fact.

Port Royal Va
Jan 7th 1863

My Dear Susie
I have just received your letter of Dec 30th and if I have time will answer it before dark. I would certainly have put on a very long face in this letter if yours had not come to hand. My dear I see no possible chance to come home soon unless I desert and not even then. I do not recollect ever seeing the man Burk that you spoke. I have never said anything to anyone but yourself about coming home. Tip Bowling will repent the day that he went home. Maj Glover knows all the facts and ordered me to advertise him as a deserter. Who is the loquacious new neighbor you spoke of? Tell B that it is not timidity but humanity that causes me or any soldier to assist or alleviate the sufferings of a dying anemy on the battlefield. He may think he would not assist one: but I know him too well. He could not resist when a poor dying mortal said; "for God's sake spread my blanket to keep me from freezing. I'm shot through the lungs or abdomen, or my thigh is torn to pieces." Or another with palid coun-tanance and sunken eyes mutters almost too inarticulate to be heard as he looks at your canteeen "one drop, just one drop." When necessary and any-thing is at stake I can pass among the wounded and dead as carelessly as if they were stones. Happily we are not always called upon for such exebitions of feel-ing. Our men will give a wounded yankee the last drop of water they have if none of our wounded are about and then strip his dead comrade. Take their shoes, caps, haversacks, canteens and especially their money.

I am quite anxious to recieve your answer to a letter wrote about Christ-mas. I have made no inquiries about it yet. If I act I shall do it promptly with-out communicating it to anyone here. You have an idea of my reasons for acting thus. I learn from your postscript why you do not write oftener than from 16th to the 30th. Its the little saucy, michevious boy that prevents you. Kiss him for me.
Ugie

Camp near Port Royal Va.
January 11th 1863

Dear Boykin

Capt. Hood[1] starts tomorrow to Georgia to procure shoes for the regement. He will go to evry county from which thare is a company or correspond with some one in the county if he finds his time, only twenty days, too limited for this. I have, or rather will, give him your name and also that of John G. Goss[2] knowing that you would give him all the assistance possible to furnish shoes to the barefooted of the company and regiment. The Government will pay six dollars per pair for shoes for the soldiers provided they are furnished under the supervision of the inferior court or other civil authority of a county. I would be glad if you could have several hundred or fifty or even a dozen pair provided so that the captain could get them. Don't let it be said that old Troup is a laggard in providing for her barefooted soldiers. The captain may wish these things sent to Atlanta. I cant say. He will write to you about it. Again; Capt. Hood will bring any shoes or clothing that any person may wish to send to any member of the company. Let evry article and package be distinctly marked with the owners name and these packed in a large box marked with the letter of the company. Please give publicity to this last, and tell the people I say the men are barefooted and want shoes. And they must have them. The boys send their money home to them and will be satisfied if they can only get shoes socks and hats. They can get a limited supply of other things from "Jeff Davis." We can not get shoes!!

Susie says you complain that I do not write. You have never answered my Bunker Hill letter. We are doing as well as usual. Several of the boys have been araigned before a court martial. These old foxes that have been skulking battle are at last cought. Our cousin Tip Bowling came in yesterday. I know Maj. Glover will prefer charges against him. Between me and you I am dissatisfied with the treatment the company and myself have recieved about our vacancy, and have an idea of resigning or geting a transfer. I wish you to say nothing about this. I will give my reasons more at length another time. Write soon.
Allen

P.S. Burke request me to ask you to assist his wife in geting a house to live in. She will have to leave where she is now living.

1. Donald M. Hood was quartermaster of the 21st Georgia Regiment. J. C. Nisbet claimed that Hood was "the soul of energy in caring for his regiment."
2. John Gibbs Goss (1826–84) was a teacher, minister, and well-to-do farmer in Antioch.

Camp near Port Royal Va.
Jan 12th 1863

Dear Boykin

I wrote to you yesterday. Mike came in this morning and I write again. Your principle enquiry is about Col. M. His case came to trial last week.[1] I was of the opinion that he would not be dismissed, but from what I can learn of the evidence he certainly will if he does not prove malicious prosecution. It is true that Col Mercer is guilty, but Boykin, the fact is malice and self interest is at the bottom of the whole affair. And if Col M. is the man I think he is, he knows it. I found it out when we officers made such a splutter at Bunker; but it was too late then. It will be several days yet before the trial is finished. Bowling will be dealt with very severely for his conduct. He hates me because I had him arrested and brought to the company last summer when he ran away and got a birth in the ambulance corps. I had quite a ripet to get him; went to Genl Trimble for an order. Snodgrass[2] went to Trimble and Ewell with a lie and had them (John and Tip) detailed after I had sent up a protest. This made me mad and I said I did not care if the whole company were teamsters. True I do regret that so many are on detached service, but could not expect any better when this affair eminated as it did. Susie writes that you will pay some attention to my negroes. No kindness that you could show would be more acceptable to me. Be shure and be very strict with them, more so than your own.

Mike tells me that I did not get Formby's place. I don't know what to do. I cant get off to come home to see to anything. I am bothered half to death. Knowing I could not get off I have been tolerably well satisfied untill the last battle. If a fight was to come off now I do not think that I could go into it with good grace. I've got one of the best Sharps rifles extant; and am so afraid they will take it away from me I don't know what to do. It is against orders for an officer to carry anything more than side arms, or an enlisted man a pistol. If Col. M. gets back and they try to take it away I will give it to Bagby as he gave the sargeants permission to carry rifles; as it is Maj. Glover won't let them have them. Billy Reid and Wince Harper were acquited by the regimental courtmartial. I did not prefer any of the charges. You will find out all the sentences soon enough. As the affair will gain publicity at home. I would be glad the truth was known. Give my love to your Mother, Father and Lizzie. What's the matter you never mention your boy. I can't keep my mouth shut about mine.

Allen

1. According to General Orders No. 135, Headquarters, Department of Northern Virginia, December 20, 1862, a court-martial was to meet in the camp of Ewell's division on December 24 for the trial of Colonel J. T. Mercer.

2. Major Charles Edward Snodgrass (1830–1900) was quartermaster of General Jubal A. Early's division.

Camp near Port Royal Va
January 12th 1863

My Darling Susie

Mike came this morning. Many thanks for your kind letter, the handkerchief and also for the boots, though it would have been equally as well for my feet and much better for my temper if I had never seen the boots. They are too small entirely for camps besides they are worthless. Certainly Holle is a very base man. They are not the style that I wrote for. Shall I trouble you again for another pair? If Mathews had leather he could make such as I want. He sent John such a pair as I would like to have only that the legs are not near large enough and three or four inches too short. Do not flater yourself, my dear, that I can come home. I see no chance and you will only be subject to bitter disapointment I fear. Berry says he wrote to Mrs. R that thare was no chance for furloughs instead of what Mrs. Nancy B.[1] said which was to the contrary. I do not know what to say about land. I will write some other time. I send you a copy of the Southern Illustrated News containing the portrait of Gen'l Lee.[2] The representation is not very good, but speaks well for Southern art. All the boys are following suit and sending them home. You can make shirts or drawers for me and send them when I write for them. I will make another application for a leave of absence sometime soon. It may be several weeks before I hear from it, possibly a month. I suppose you think of going into service. Come to this company by all means and mess with me. How is the boy? I know it will be an age before I hear from you again. Write me about twenty pages when you write. You know I never could write. I will write again soon. Goodbye my dear Susie.

Your boy

Ugie

1. Nancy W. Wilder Britton, wife of Private Thomas Britton.

2. A woodcut engraving of Robert E. Lee appeared in the December 13, 1862, issue of the *Southern Illustrated News.* The print was a crude mirror-image adaptation of a photograph taken about a decade earlier.

Near Port Royal Va
[Jan] 16th 1863

My Dear Susie
I write only a few lines. I have been waiting to see what would become of an application for a furlough that I sent up a few days ago. It was disapproved by our brigade commander while others were approved. It is my opinion in fact I have no doubt but the cause was that thare would be only one commissioned officer left with the company. So you see thare is no possible chance to come home. I will try and so must you to be content. All the fond hopes of which I have long cherished of seeing you again are vanished, and I see nothing but a dark dreadful future.

Thare came an order the day that I last wrote you to grant enlisted men furloughs to the amount of two from each company. Bagby and Talley have sent up applications; but I do not know what will become of them as we recieved orders last night to be ready to march at any time. Several reports are current in camps about the movements of the anemy. Some say they are crossing above here others that they are making demonstrations about Culpeper C.H.[1] The weather turned off remarkably cold last night. I dread a march or fight now much more than usual. The truth is I never will be content to go into another battle or do more duty. Possibly I may overcome this feeling in time. My dear you must try to get some land to cultivate from Mr. B. I will try and write to him soon. I was so much in hopes that I would get home. I have neglected it. Nothing more today.
Your boy
Ugie

1. Burnside attempted to flank Lee's position by crossing the Rappahannock upstream from Fredericksburg. As the Federal movement commenced, heavy rains set in, and the operation became known as the "Mud March." By January 22, 1863, Federal columns were at a standstill, and Burnside abandoned the operation and ordered the army to return to its camps.

Camp near Port Royal Va
Jan 17th 1863

Dear Sir [John T. Boykin Sr.]
I avail myself of the present opportunity of writing you a few lines. There is no general news here but what will be anticipated by the papers. The boys are down in Port Royal on picket. The yanks on one bank of the river and they

on the other. It is not customary for pickets to fire on each other in cases like this. The other day one of Genl D H Hill's men induced a Yankee to come over promising to trade tobacco for coffee, and then captured and carried him to Hill, thinking himself rather sharp. Hill sent the Yankee back and had the man bucked.[1] It is against orders to talk to each other on picket. But they sing, talk and curse each other. We had orders indicative of a march a few days ago, but I believe evrything is about quiet now. The weather is remarkably cold at present. No wind rain or snow, but old winter that chills you through before you know it.

Clinton told me about your not being able to get old man Formby's place for me. How ever much I may regret not geting it, and not having land, still I do not question your judgement or discretion in regard to it. Susie writes that Mrs. Lee's place[2] will be sold soon and hopes to get. This place if enough of it as I think it is good land would suit me very well even if I sold the Wisdom place.[3] That the prospect for peace is somewhat bright at present I believe is admited by evryone. But with a continuation of the war and the consequent depression in business and distress, I would much prefer that my family remained where it is, knowing that yourself and Boykin are able and willing to give Susie much valuable assistence in the general management of my business. I have never learned whether Susie proposes to get any land to cultivate from you or not. I was very much in hopes that I could come home this winter but do not think it possible now, or even after this. It is no use to fret if the military harness does chafe. So I endeavor to bear it with as much equanimety as possible. We have just recieved a small lot of shoes through the blockade. They are the English shoe and surpass anything of the kind I ever saw in my life. I would like that you could see them.

The health of the company is very good at present. There is some small pox in the regiment at present which can not be sent to hospital; no one seems to care anything for it. Most of the men have been vaxinated. Our surgeons treat it very successfully; give no medicine unless it is sometimes a gentle purgative and take great care that the patient does not take cold. I would be glad to hear from you soon about that land. I remain as ever,
Your friend and Ob't Sv't
Ujene Allen

1. Bucking was a common punishment in which the soldier was tightly bound and usually gagged.

2. Hannah Lee (born 1789) was the widow of Noah Lee. The Lee family owned a large plantation near Houston Community.

3. Allen and his uncle Hamilton M. Wisdom had jointly inherited the Wisdom property in Troup County upon the death of Eleanor Wisdom in 1861. On July 18, 1861, the day they departed for the army, the men recorded a deed whereby Allen purchased sole interest from Wisdom for $1,500.

Camp near Port Royal Va
Jan 20th 1863

My Dear Susie
Here I've been siting waiting for a letter from you several days, but narry time
did the letter come. Today being my birthday and alowing five days for you to
write and ten for the mails (this for good measure) I had settled down on the
idea that I would certainly get one, probably two or possibly three from you.
But instead of this the carrier thrust his head in my tent and bawled out;
"how many papers today lieutenant?" "Wait," said I. "Give me my letters
first." "No letters for you today; how many papers you say?" "Not a one; yes,
stop. give me three" He gave me the papers and hurried away leaving me
alone to read the news and meditate on my late as well as all human expecta-
tions. I told you this was my birthday. So it is, I'm twenty four today. I have
just been thinking of the boy who when told by his mammy that he would be
ten years old next [illegible]; jumped up and cried out; "heppe! I wish I wus a
hunderd."

The regimental court martial ajourned today. I have had quite an easy time
recently. The company has been on picket twice and has just returned this evening. I remained in quarters, done my writing, smoked my pipe of content-
ment as well as tobacco. I have also tried in vain to solve that knotty question
of getting a furlough. I wrote to Mr. B yesterday and will write to Boykin
soon. How do you do and what do you do evry day? Give me an insight into
your everyday life. It would be interesting to me. I do the same. Tell me all
about the boy. Does he talk any. You spoke of making me some shirts. I have
more need of them than drawers. The colars are not large enough. I have a
neck like an ox weigh a hundred and sixty nearly, ugly as ever. Good bye. If
you dont write I will.
Ugie

Camp near Port Royal Va.
January 22nd 1863

My Dear Susie
I will write a few lines, though I have nothing of interest more than we are
about to be transfered to another brigade. I hear that Genl. Trimble had been

promoted and will take charge of Genl. Jacksons old division. Col. Hoke is now brigadier and will be given a N. Carolina brigade and [we] will go with the 12th Ga to Brig. Gen Doles[1] brigade in D. H. Hills Division. The 4th and 44th Ga. are under him. The men hate this arrangement. This is especially the case with the 21st N. C. and our regiment. They have fought side by side in nearly all the battles and have the utmost confidence in each other. Genl Hoke and Col Hooper are gone to see Gen Lee now, to endeavour to devise some means for us to remain. Our men do not like to leave their comfortable quarters. I will regret it very much myself. We have had wind and rain since night before last. A great many troops are not prepared as well for such weather as we, while others probably are better. Did I ever tell you about my comfortable chair. It is of rather novel construction. The seat is hewn out of a piece of poplar and a stout young hickory is sprung the right shape and the ends inserted in auger holes in the seat and make a splendid back. If we go to Genl Hills division it will be like beginning evrything anew. You know it will be hard to go to where thare is no quarters this weather and nothing to make them out of. I hear that wood is very scarce up thare. He is just at the lower edge of the battlefield. You must direct your letters to Hamiltons Crosing Va naming only the regiment. Mrs. Crouch has that wagon note, pay it. Nothing more today. au revoir.

Your Boy

Ugie

1. George Pierce Doles (May 14, 1830–June 2, 1864) was promoted to brigadier general on November 1, 1862, and assigned to command a brigade consisting of the 4th, 12th, 21st, and 44th Georgia regiments.

On Picket near Morse's Neck Va
Jan 27th 1863

My Darling Susie

I recieved your letter of the 11th several days ago; but have not had an opportunity of answering it untill now. I told you in my last that we had been transferred to Gen Doles brigade. We moved the next day and not having my trunk and coming on picket yesterday prevented me from answering your letter sooner. Our camp is about one and a half miles from the river and about one from the battlefield. I have a very comfortable cabin covered with dirt for my quarters, though the men have nothing more than their tents.[1] There is one cabin to each company and this gives one more tent to the men. Wood is

so scarce that we will be compelled to hall it; you may know that we will not
fare as well as we did at our old camp. We will build chimneys to our quarters
and use economy. I think we will be tolerably comfortable. I prefer this to any
other brigade, except Trimbles. We keep up a heavy double picket all the
while. Our rations are cooked (and sometimes eat up) as fast as drawn. All
extra bagage is sent back and we hold ourselves in readiness to go into battle at
a moments warning. Furloughing is stoped. Evrybody seem to expect a fight.
Our camp is under the anemy's guns. I do not believe thare will be any fight
here unless the anemy turns our flanks. If the anemy crosses here or between
here and Port Royal he will get the crowning whiping of all. This is a settled
fact. We can not cross the river and the anemy having the best position can
cross on his boats when he chooses. If we have to fight I had rather fight here
than any place I ever saw in my life; trenches for the infantry covered by our
batteries. Circumstances render it necessary that we should be on the alert.

If Ethan is not entirely well you had better let Dr. Shaw[2] have him. True I
dislike to loose anything on him, but he is of no service and may never be. If
you get a horse be shure and get a good one. Let Mr. Boykin see that he is
good. Of course I approve of you geting a buggy. You can not do without
one. What do I live for if it is not to make you comfortable and happy. My
box has not come yet. I am afraid that some of the things will be spoiled. Our
wagons go to Guinnys Station almost daily after commissaries. I fear that
rations are not as plentiful here as in the "old 7th." Apples sell readily at two
and three dollars per doz and the poorest kind of cakes fifty cents apiece. We
buy a great many; anything to vary our beef and bread. I have two splendid
pair of shoes now and you need not trouble yourself about any boots. I paid
($30) thirty dollars for one pair in Richmond. Neither need you send me
your blankets. Shirts and socks are all that I care anything about now and do
not need them at present but may after a while when I can not get them. Be
ashured that I will avail myself of any [opportunity] to come home and can
not but hope that something will transpire so that I can. I have writen to Mr.
B. about Mrs. Lees place but I am afraid the place was sold before he recieved
my letter. I also wrote to your Pa not long since. Have you heard Mr. B say
anything about that Wilkerson note.[3] Unless you have special need for money
do not collect anything on good punctual men. Have you ever heard anything about what Asa Winn owes me. Get some one to see him and get his
note with interest on the account (about 25 days). Goodbye for the present.
Kiss the dear little boy for me.
Ugie

1. Lieutenant Thomas Hightower wrote to his wife on January 29, 1863, that the 21st Georgia's new camp consisted initially of "only a few pine pole cabins covered with dirt."

2. George W. Shaw (born 1835) practiced medicine in the Houston Community.

3. Jesse Wilkerson's note was for the purchase of a tract of land from the estate of Ugie's father Robert Allen.

Camp near Morses Neck Va
Jan 30th 1863

My Darling Susie

I write you only a few lines today. I have been looking for a letter from you a day or two and probably will get one this evening as yours of the 11th was the last. Lt Waller came in a day or two ago and says that Black was to start in a few days. I wrote my last while on picket. The day we came in it commenced snowing and although the ground was wet about twelve inches was on the ground yesterday morning. It is meting some but not as fast as I would like to see it. The boys of this regiment and 4th had quite an exciting and amusing snow battle yesterday and I believe are fighting again today. Let me tell you. There is a probability of Lt Henderson and Berry R coming home on detail to get recruits and catch deserters. While we were on picket the order came and Waller not being here Col Hooper sent in his name as one of the detail from the company as there was to be a man and officer from each company. Col Hooper told me he wanted to send me but knew the other party was not fit to leave here in command of a company. I tell you this confidentially and to give you his own words. It is very hard on me I think. It is just as I tell you. Col Hoopers reply however flattering does not heal my heart aching to see my darling Susie and boy. Let us hope that the war will soon end or some circumstance will transpire so that I can see you. I have not as yet recieved my box. I need it, as our ration is not as good as formally. I have no way to write as my house leeks from the rain and snow and will try to be more interesting in my next. My principle object being to tell you about the detail. As ever, Your boy
Ugie

11

FROM HAMILTON'S CROSSING
TO CHANCELLORSVILLE

Who can weigh the grief of a heart at the affliction of another
that beats a fond echo to every emotion of its own?

T HE month of January 1863 brought several welcome changes in the life of Ujanirtus Allen. Allen's long-running feud with Leroy T. Waller over the command of the Ben Hill Infantry finally ended when Waller left the company and Allen was promoted to captain, to date from May 31, 1862. Allen was also assigned to catch deserters and enlist new recruits in Troup County. He apparently spent most of February and March 1863 at home. In spite of the promotion and his trip home, Allen returned to duty in a morose state of mind. In the late winter and spring of 1863, he contemplated more seriously than ever the possibility of resigning his commision and leaving the company.

Friction between the 21st Georgia's colonel and the company-grade officers undoubtedly contributed to Allen's dissatisfaction. Mercer's drunken behavior at Gaines's Mill had earned him the enmity of many within the regiment. Shortly after the battle of Fredericksburg, on December 20, a court-martial convened to try Mercer on two charges, "drunkeness on duty" and "conduct unbecoming an officer and gentleman." Details of these charges are unknown, but they apparently stemmed from the Gaines's Mill episode and another incident in which a drunken Mercer punished his body servant by slightly cutting him with a knife.

The court-martial ended on March 6, 1863, when the court found Mercer not guilty of both charges. The court did censure him for "the mode adopted by him of punishing his servant." Mercer returned to camp a few days after his trial, but he apparently did not assume command of the regiment until early April 1863. On April 5, Lieutenant Thomas Hightower wrote home about conditions within the 21st Georgia, alluding to a group of officers that likely included Ugie Allen. "The worst of the officers," noted Hightower, were "very much beset" about Mercer's reinstatement. Hightower added that Mercer would probably make a few of the discontented officers "walk a chalk line as they took a pretty strong stand against him in the trial." Several officers resigned rather than serve under the "highly sensitive" Mercer, but Allen stayed with his company.

The coming of spring in 1863 brought renewed military activity in eastern central Virginia. In the last few days of April the Union Army of the Potomac, under its new commander General Joseph Hooker, undertook a flanking movement to dislodge the Confederates from their position at Fredericksburg. A large portion of Hooker's army marched north of Lee's line at Fredericksburg, eventually crossing the Rappahannock River and marching through the Wilderness of Spotsylvania to attack the Confederates from the rear or west.

Robert E. Lee responded to Hooker's move by sending Stonewall Jackson westward with most of the Second Corps to confront Hooker's Federals. George Doles's brigade, which had spent the last few days of April 1863 near Hamilton's Crossing, was one of the units with Jackson. At 2:00 A.M. on May 1, Doles's regiments left Hamilton's, marching westward on the Orange Plank Road. Although Doles's men skirmished for a short time that afternoon, they saw little serious action that day.

Around 6:00 A.M. on May 2, the officers in Doles's regiments formed their men in columns along the Orange Plank Road. With orders to move around the Union army and strike its vulnerable right flank, Stonewall Jackson's "foot cavalry" began one of the most famed marches in American military history. By 3:30 P.M. Doles's men had covered almost twelve miles and found themselves formed in line of battle south of the Orange Turnpike.

Jackson's long battle lines began advancing against the enemy shortly after 5:00 P.M. With a line of skirmishers thrown four hundred yards in advance, Doles's regiments "moved as rapidly as possible through the very thick wood." After advancing for approximately a half mile, Doles's men broke out into a large clearing where they came under heavy enemy musketry and artillery fire. Hoping to capture the Union battery that was playing on his men, Doles ordered Colonel Mercer to move the 21st Georgia northward to flank the cannon and enfilade the Union entrenchments. The Federals resisted for only ten minutes before their position collapsed. Advancing at the run, the men of the 21st Georgia surged around a Union cannon, planting their flag on the captured gun.

Following a brief halt during which the regiment reformed its line, the 21st continued forward at the double-quick. Mercer's men soon found themselves facing another line of Union breastworks. "By a slight change of position," the Georgians secured an enfilade fire on the Federals. With Mercer's men firing into their flank and Doles's other regiments advancing against their front, this second line of Union troops fell apart.

After overrunning the second Federal position, Doles ordered a halt at the edge of a field to reform his regiments. A portion of the 21st Georgia, including the regimental color-bearer, failed to hear Doles's command and continued toward a Federal battery. Colonel Mercer reported that his men charged through a "thick pine woods" to within three hundred yards of the Union guns before realizing they had no support. Extricating themselves from their dangerous position, the color-bearer and his comrades rejoined the regiment, which retired for the evening to a position just south of the Orange Turnpike.

The four Georgia regiments of Doles's brigade had acquitted themselves honorably in Jackson's May 2 flank attack at the Battle of Chancellorsville, capturing at least eight pieces of artillery and many prisoners. But the victory came at a high price; among the "many gallant men killed and wounded" was Captain U. C. Allen. Early in the engagement, probably while charging the first Federal line, Allen was severely wounded in the left knee. His close friend Private Thomas Britton remained with the stricken officer and eventually escorted him to a field hospital.

Only hours after Allen was wounded, his beloved corps commander also received a severe injury. On a reconnaissance in front of his lines around 9:00 P.M., Stonewall Jackson came under the mistaken fire of his own men. With two gunshot wounds in the left arm and one in the right palm, Jackson, like Captain Allen, went to the rear for medical assistance.

Richmond March 28th 1863

My Dear Susie

It is with heavy hart that I again attempt to write. Previous to this time when leaving all that is dear to me on earth I have with an iron will endeavored to crush all feelings of sadness or grief and spurn every thought but that of duty and almost immeasurable devotion to my country. But this is too much. I can do it no longer. It is too much that I should be torn from you this long and now seeing no hope, nothing but privations and dispair in the future. Perhaps when I mingle again in the busy scenes of camp these feelings may be for the

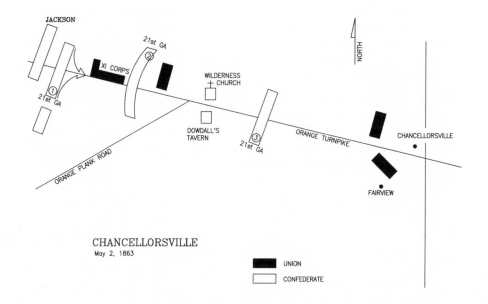

JACKSON

21st GA

XI CORPS

WILDERNESS
CHURCH

NORTH

CHANCELLORSVILLE

21st GA

DOWDALL'S
TAVERN

ORANGE TURNPIKE

21st GA

ORANGE PLANK ROAD

FAIRVIEW

CHANCELLORSVILLE
May 2, 1863

UNION

CONFEDERATE

moment forgotten giving sweet relief to my drooping spirit. I sometimes hope they may. What a thought! I shudder to think about it. Who could hope that the grief of a fond heart yearning for the society of another those feelings springing from Divinity itself should for a moment be overwhelmed by circumstances springing from the wickedness and heartlessness of man!

It may be a day or two before I go. Nothing could be done yesterday—thanksgiving. Tomorow is Sunday. I feel less like doing duty than I thought I would when I left home. I saw Lt. W. yesterday he says that he, through the assistance of our congeressman Tripp, has been reinstated.[1] I do not know it to be so. I hope he has on account of that money. I do not know that his reinstatement will affect my position. Neither do I know that it will not. If my position is preduiced in any manner it will afford me grounds for resignation or transfer somewhere. I understand there is a law passed allowing any brigadier to conscript any resigned officer before he leaves. I learn that everything is in a strange condition at the regiment. Evrybody is on the qui vive for Col M's restoration and many of the officers are trying to get other positions. They can not resign, and look for thunder and lightning if he does come back. If I find anything of interest I will write everything in detail when I get to the regiment. I have found the box you sent me here in the express office and sent it on to the regiment. Did I tell you that there was nice calico a yard wide in Atlanta. Thare is more goods in the Confederacy than there was 12 months ago. My paper is about out I wish I had another leaf. I hardly expect a letter from you earlier than an answer to this which will be quite a long time. I can not but hope that you have written. As ever,
Your boy
Ugie

1. Despite the assistance of Robert Pleasant Trippe (1819–1900), a Confederate congressman from Monroe County, Georgia, Leroy T. Waller eventually resigned his commission. On September 10, 1863, Waller enlisted at Hickory Flat, Alabama, as a lieutenant in Captain S. A. Moses' cavalry company. Waller apparently served with this command for the remainder of the war, performing guard duty and arresting conscripts in various Alabama and Mississippi locales.

Camp Near Hamilton Xing Va
April 1st 1863

My Dear Susie
I arrived at camps yesterday after a stay of four days in Richmond. I was quite anxious to get away from thare I could not but feel when I took the train that

would bring me in the military lines; like one being banished from the world and civilization. I found the company in better health than ever before. Compared to them the people at home look like invalids. There was considerable snow yesterday all gone now. I find the men with much better clothes and quarters than I anticipated. We are making vigorous preparations for an active campaign when ever the roads permit us or the anemy to move; which will be several weeks if the weather does not improve. The anemy spends much time in ballooning[1] and druming. We go on picket tomorrow and remain two days. News! News! Colonel John T. Mercer Knight of the Black Stud and Bottle, assumed command of the bloody 21st a few hours ago. I think that there will be some knashing of teeth among the officers. One just poked his head in my tent and made the melancholy inquiry, "what shall we do to be saved?" Let me tell you; I intend to be very circumspect in what I say or do. I have not committed myself to any one. I would not mind a little disturbance if it would open the door for me to get out of the army. I will write more some other time if I learn anything to write.

Did I tell you everything in the box you sent me was spoilt. My boots are the very thing. I think they are the best I ever had in my life. Evrything you sent me was all right. I sent you the "Illustrated News." I could not find the "Magnolia" office—tell Boykin so.[2] I drew $80.00 commutation for quarters and fuel in Richmond for the time I was absent. And as you furnished both to me you are certainly entitled to the money. I sent you a package by express from R. Please credit it to my account. I do not know that you need the articles, neither do know that you have enough. I saw no cap that I could well send to my boy. See if you can not make him one the same style of my old one and trim it with gold lace. You can get the patent leather at Hogansville or somewhere else. This is quite the go in Richmond.

Dick Waller got a resignation accepted at Richmond. He told me he was restored but would not be assigned to duty here but was coming up to the regiment in a day or two. I have nothing more today.

Goodbye

Ugie

P.S. Of course will expect a very long letter.

1. The Federals used hydrogen-filled balloons as observation posts.
2. The *Magnolia* was a weekly journal of "literature and general news" published at Richmond.

Camp near Hamiltons Crossing
Apr 6th 1863

My Dear Susie

I recieved your letter of March 27th two days ago and would have answered it
yesterday but we had no mail today (Sunday). We were out two days and more
on picket as I told you in my last returned yesterday. Be assured we escaped a
bad time. Yesterday we had the hardest wind that I have known since I've
been in service together with snow and sleet. There was several inches on the
ground this morning. I find that the army or at least our division is under
stricter dicipline than ever. I wrote you in my last that Col Mercer was again
in command. I do not know how he will be—strict enough I guess. I suppose
I can get along as well as any of the other officers who had the assurance to
tender their swords on a certain occasion. Let me tell you. Not long since
evry officer in the regiment sent a petition to the Secretary of War to relieve
the command of him. I am glad that I was absent at the time. If it were not
that I wished to quit the service or at least this branch of it by all means; I can
safely say that allthough I pay due defference to the good opinions of any one
I would not court his favor. I mean that I would not bootlick him as some do.

My dear, I do not know what to say about Boykins land. If I was at home I
would certainly buy it. I mean if I had a discharge. There is an order here to
conscript evry resigning officer. The power is given to a brigadier general. If I
could resign unconditionally and get a leave of absence and get away I could
do very well. If Hooper was here and Genl Doles also I might do something.
Col M will take command of the brigade soon Genl Doles being absent. Col
M would think that I was leaving from the hatred to him and would do everything against me. I have had an idea of approaching him on the subject, but
have felt unwilling to do so up to this time. Here is the idea; Capts Nesbett,
Hamilton, and Battle are absent and will probably never return. Col Hooper
left a few days ago and no doubt will not return. There is also a lieutenant
here who is doing all he can to get away. All this is caused by an unwillingness
to serve under Col M. Some others swore they never would do it, but are
about to renig. These things are calculated to cause him to bear down on any
effort that I could make. I can probably give you something more explicit in
my next letter. I can not get a substitute and buy Burks land also. If I do not,
no doubt his land would suit me very well. My dear I do not know what to
tell you. I see you can not do well without me. I am willing to serve my country and have done my duty so far as well as any man in the Confederate army
and feel that it would not be wrong for me to represent myself through

another. I concur with you in what you said about a cheaper place. I hear that Col M is writing to B tonight what can be the import of that letter! Tell Boykin that he can be of great service to me just now in gaining my object—quitting the service or at least this branch of it. You know if I do not get out I would like some other department where there was not so much phisical labor to perform. He might congratulate him on his restoration recommend me to his favor disclaiming any feeling on my part of an unfriendly character toward him. The truth is I acted on principle and believe I was right; others from impulse and selfish motives. Therefore I was caught in bad company.

I have wrote to you in a previous letter concerning the company. I would like for you to send me a receipt roll for the bounty that I paid the recruits last year. It is about my drawer. It is on white paper written with blue ink and duplicate. I want only one copy. Take care of the other one. Send me also my last years furlough (mine and Harpers). I wish to collect some money on it. Do not trust these papers by mail as they are both over fifteen hundred dollars. I think of nothing more that would interest you. As ever.
Your boy
Ugie

Camp Near Hamiltons Crosssing Va.
April 8th 1863

My Dear Susie
I received your letter of the 3rd Apr by Crouch this morning. He brought your ambrotype also. It is by far the best that I have ever seen of you. I do not care anything about the hat. The probablilty is I will [have] to send some of my clothes home or lose them as we will not have sufficient transportation. Previous letters will tell you about my box. I got everything you sent me. The knife is a very good one. You said it was a common knife and I bought two in Richmond. You got the package I sent you from R. didn't you? Billie Evans[1] has no substitute. Things are just as I told you in a previous letter. Uncle Billy's[2] letter is quite interesting. The boys are having prayer meetings evry night in the company. From what I can learn thare is quite a reaction throughout this brigade in regard to religion. I have sixty one men at the company now. George Glenn was examined for light duty or discharge the day I left Atlanta. If you hear where he is or what they done with him let me know it. The company is doing well in evry respect. Thare is much hard feelings

against Colonel Mercer. My idea is to get away from here. Everything is in his hands. I have had no intercourse with him up to this time, neither has any one else. I do not know how he will be. He is not a man easily approached. Lt. Waller came to Richmond and got the Secretary of War to accept his resignation instead of striking him from the rolls. An official notice has already been received at the company to that affect. He never came to the company. Let me tell you. Do not recieve anything but current bank notes for any debt due me previous to the war. I forgot to speek about this before I left home. You can readily see the justice in this. Gold and bank notes were the only currency previous to the war. The Confederate curency is not as valuable as that and you see that an old debt is never paid with the former. I have nothing that would interest you. I will write again soon. Kiss Bobbie for me. Goodbye. Your boy
Ugie

1. William Swanson Evans (1838–1914) was 2nd lieutenant of Company B, 4th Georgia Regiment.

2. William R. Welborn (born 1809), a physician in Franklin County, Georgia, was the brother of Susan's mother Stacey Rebecca Fuller.

Camp Near Hamiltons Crossing Va
April 12th 1862

My Dear Susie
I thought of writing yesterday but Bobbie Strong is here and will start home tomorrow and I think you will get this as soon as if I had written. Bobbie brought on a substitute for Berry but Col M has sworn by all that man can that he will receive no substitute in the regiment. So you see he will not be able to get him in. Mercer is ruling everything with all the vigor that he can devine. I have tried for a long time to see something to admire in him, but instead of admiring the man I cannot but despise him. There is some talk running through the company that he may appoint Boykin his quarter master. Tell B. that I say not to have anything to do with him. I will write Boykin a letter, I think. I will content myself but will avail myself of the first opportunity to leave it. If I ever get away from it for any cause whatever I will stay away until struck from the rolls. Or at least I think I shall. Other officers intend doing the same thing. I think I shall send some things (old clothes) that I have no use for here home by Bobbie Strong. I would like to have my tooth brush but care nothing for the clothes and hair brush. The flanel that I send is much worn but I might need some and could not get any. I would

only need a change of it. We have drawn a ration of shad and will probably draw more. We get a pound and a quarter to the man. Doles and Colquits[1] brigades have a fishery. Our mess have had more than we could consume in one day. Who wouldn't be a soldier and eat fish! You don't want fish or nothing so (8).[2]

General Doles has just returned from home. He says that our Gov Brown will make an effort to have our brigade transferred to the state service. He will offer six full regiments for us. It would cause a perfect jubilee in this brigade if we were transferred thare. I have no idea that the transfer will be made. I do not believe that they will give veterans for unaclimated fresh troops. From what I can learn our army is in splendid condition in evry respect. The anemy could advance now if he wished. By some it is surmised that we will cross and attact the anemy if he does not us. The soldiers are all remarkably healthy and in fine spirits. They spend much of their time in playing ball, jumping, wrestling and other athletic sports. Berry will endeavor to sell his substitute to some one else. I wish that I had not come back. Everything is quite dull in the way of news. I would be glad that I could send a longer and more interesting letter. You must write often. Write me how Bobbie is geting along the little saucy boy. Goodbye my dear.
Your Boy
Ugie

1. General Alfred Holt Colquitt (1824–94), a former Georgia congressman, commanded a brigade composed of the 6th, 19th, 23rd, 27th, and 28th Georgia regiments.
2. Allen's use of the numeral 8 is unexplained.

Camp Near Hamiltons Crossing Va
Apr 15th 1863

Darling Susie
I expected a letter today. No doubt it will come tomorrow. I will not depend on the mails as you probably will want to hear before a reply to your next reaches you. I do not write because I am overstocked with news. Wish I knew something that would interest you. The weather has improved much recently and it will not be long untill we will begin active operations here. Indeed we are expecting it daily. Much of our time is occupied in drill and other duties that increases the effeciency of the army. We had a brigade drill a few days ago—the first in several months. I doubt it would be interesting to you to see one man maneuvre four regiments. The men of the regiment have a scheme

on foot to present Genl Trimble a memorial (probably a sword) of their high regard. It has been raining all day. Genl Doles sent down and had Colonel M. to take his guard off. I predict that they will not get along together well; though hope they will. We are all geting along very well. Rations are somewhat short though we do much better than we have done before this. We make our flour into rolls and lightbread. We can make very nice bread equal to anything we see at home. When we make up the dough we set a small piece by the fire in a cup and keep water in it. It rises and serves as yeast to make up next time. So you see we can keep it as long as we want to. Try it. Keep trying it untill you succeed and you will like it. Tell me how is your health. Are you free from that burning and numbness. Tell me how Bobbie is doing. You want to hear me say something about coming home don't you? I know nothing to say. I wish that I did. You must write me a long letter. Thare are many things that would be interesting to me if you were just to think of them or rather think to write them. Goodbye for the present.
Ugie

Camp Near Hamiltons Crossing Va
April 17th 1863

Dear Susie
I received your interesting letter of the 10th yesterday. We are having better mail facilities than formerly, and I hope our correspondence will be more regular if we do not get in a march. Evry moment in the day is occupied now in duty. The officers have a drill besides two other company and batallion drills. I would wait untill a good opportunity presents itself before I bought a horse and then get a good one (a mare). You need not expect to get a good one with little money. It would be a good idea to get one from Tenn. or north Georgia. B. sold Ethan very well. I can say as much for the mule. Such mules will sell for four hundred before next Christmas if the war does not stop, which it will not. I think that Mrs. Garretts mule is worth $135 but prefer a good brood mare if I could get one. I think you are certainly the best financier that I have ever known. Out of ($121) one hundred and twenty one dollars for the beef paid the negroes, Jim[1], Hilt[2], Mr. Brewer and had a bonus of twenty dollars. Lt. H and myself have not sent those things yet, but will today if we can fix them up. I may send some things that I brought with me. I will send four flannel (nett) suits, 2 pr nett drawers 1 pr double do., 1 overshirt, 1 common

cotton shirt, 1 pr thin socks a bundle of collars and that gold lace. Let Mrs. Fears have half of it to trim a coat for Ol. Send her word the first chance that you can get it. I also send a little knife, fork and spoon captured at Fredricksburg to Bobbie. I think they will suit him to eat with very nice. You see how they are put together. The knife is inserted in the handle of the spoon and the fork over the blade of the knife and holds it together. I will also send a jacket that I have no use for. Susie you had better take up the bonds for that cotton I subscribed to the Confederacy they are at a high premium. Do not sell them for less than the market price. If they are worth thirty or fifty dollars you might as well save it as for some sharper to make it off of you. Let me be as equinomical as possible for no one can deny but that I have made great sacrifices for the country. I hope to be able to write more next time. Cant you give me four pages. Don't ask the same question. Goodbye for today. I may write the next in bivouac.

Ugie

1. Troup County court documents indicate that slaves were allowed to "labor or engage in business for their own benefit," as long as they did so on their master's premises.

2. George A. Hilt (born 1825 in Pennsylvania) was a mechanic.

Camp Near Hamiltons Crossing Va.
April 20th 1863

My Dear Susie

Your letter of the 14th came to hand today; like all others from you it was quite interesting. I have only one objection to it possibly you may find the same to this—too short. Why do we not pitch in and write longer letters as we formally did. Do you suppose there is less news, do we need practice. My last visit has certainly in nowise diminished our regard for each other but on the contrary has caused the sacred and unextinguishable fires on the alter of affection to burn with greater intensity, sheding a celestial light upon our path. I look back on my visit home as the brightest, happiest period of my life. How much more happy would I have been if it had not of been for the ever recuring thought that I would have to leave you.

We go out on picket tomorrow. The weather is not as good as it was when we went out last and I do not anticipate as agreeable time. There is nothing to prevent the anemys attacting us at any time, unless it is fear. We will not remain here inactive long. It is rumored that the anemy is going down the

Potomac. Possibly you will not get the package that I sent you. It contains only some collars and a pair of sleeves. Make the express company responsable. I shall send more clothing home than I expected. I think the chance is good for us to lose all of our clothing except what we wear. The government can neither furnish transportation or knapsacks. I wrote to George[1] myself not long since—am glad to hear that he is improving. You wrote that B. said he would give me any assistance that he could. I know of nothing to suggest only that he should be very cautious. We have fish frequently recently. Trout, shad, bass, rock herring and a veriety resembling the sucker. The bass and herring is my favorite. You know that they must be plentiful as I set myself up as a conoiseur. The bass is of the perch tribe only much larger. One apiece makes us a good meal. I had a fine super last night, herring and pure Rio coffee—only six dollars per pound. I write this by guess. The wind has blown out my dim Confederate candle[2] not less than a half dozen times, but I must write tonight. Ol is intent on a letter to his Juliana. He lights the candle and me my pipe.

Au revoir.

Ugie

1. George Fuller, Susan Allen's brother.
2. A "Confederate candle" consisted of cotton string, coated with just enough wax to make it stiff, coiled around a bottle or dowel.

Camp Near Hamiltons Crossing Va
April 25 1863

Dear Susie

I returned from picket yesterday. We had a very wet time—were out three days. We had an alarm several days ago though I believe it amounted to nothing more than the capture of our fishermen and saine by the anemy down at Port Royal. I do not anticipate remaining quiet very long. I can see no sense in two armies remaining face to face so long without doing something. It is quite agreeable to the most of us but when Genl Lee says march we are ready. Lt. H. and myself have sent off those things at last; we sent the box to his father. You can get my things and pay part of the express. Oliver T. F. sent some things also you had better take care of them until his family can get them as it would be an accommadation to him. I only wish that I had sent more things. Mercer has three officers under arrest. Its "hide out little ones yer dad's comin home drunk," with the officers and men of the regiment.

Col. Hooper will return. I've been trying to quit using tobacco for some time, but can't say that I will be successful. Wont you be glad if I am! Not more so than myself I do not suppose. We do not know how firmly we are tied in the coils of habits untill we endeavor to throw them off. Some one has truly remarked that habit is our second nature. Boykin writes me about the farm. You must keep me well posted. Do not neglect to say much about yourself and our little boy. Remember me to the negroes; tell them that I always like to hear of their doing well and being faithfull to their business and hope they will give a good account of themselves. I have long since ceased to speculate on the prospects of peace, if there be any. Old Abe is determined on prosecuting the war to extermination and we on resistence. I tell you thare is no hope of an early peace only through foreign intervention and mediations which is quite impossible. But as I said when I was at home the soldiers are quite sanguine of ultimate success. No one is despondent but the speculators and extortioners. Remember me kindly to Mrs. B., Mr. B., cousin Mary and Louise. Kiss Bobbie and accept the love of his Papa.
Ugie

Camp Near Hamiltons Crossing Va.
April 27th 1863

My Dear Susie
I received your kind letter of the 20th today. I wrote two days ago but know that my letters can not be too frequent, though they may be short. I would prefer writing longer ones, but the truth is I have never known such a dull time in regard to news or such as would interest you. I can not conceive what is the cause of the inactivity of the anemy. It may be that the condition of his army precludes his moving forward. Possibly it is demoralised by past reverses and the expiration of the enlistment of many of his troops. I have been thinking this evening that possibly thare may be trouble brewing between John Bull[1] and Abe. God grant that it may be so. I do not feel that I am selfish in this, for I can not but believe that this war (which would in all probability cease) is one among the greatest scourages that has visited the world in many centuries. This war may be the death knell of true republicanism and civil liberty. Again our position was such among the nations of the earth that the war is not only a great national calamity but is seriously felt by all civilized nations.

The words sadness, regret, and sorrow are inadequate to express my feelings in regard to your health. Who can weigh the grief of a heart at the affliction of another that beats a fond echo to evry emotion of its own. I wish my dear that I could be with you now. Try my dear and follow evry perscription of the doctor. You must have some one to stay with you. Hire some one to go after cousin Tudy. Write me from time to time how you are doing.

I have fine fish yet. They help out our rations very much. Tell Jim to watch the stock over at the Wisdom place and thrash Samples negroes good if he finds them doing mischief. Those negroes are put up to do what mischief they do. I know too well how things go. How is my little boy doing—romping and saucy as ever? I still have my idea in view nor do I expect to relinquish it soon. I will write again in a few days.

Your boy,

Ugie

1. In the early stages of the Civil War, southerners felt assured that demand for their cotton would compel world powers to intervene on their behalf. By the spring of 1863, hope for mediation by Great Britain ("John Bull") or France was fading. Influential British egalitarians resisted interference. Some historians theorize that British textile manufacturers were eager to see the southern monopoly on cotton production broken in favor of British plantations in India.

Camp near Hamiltons Crossing Va
April 28th 1863

Dear Susie

John Terry starts home this morning on a short leave of absence to attend to his mothers estate. I would have writen something like a letter but I wrote day before yesterday. There is heavy firing going on now, no doubt but the anemy is attempting to cross as a dense fog covers evrything.[1] I have been in hopes that the anemy would let us alone here but it seems that he is determined to have a fight. If we are engaged I will try and let you know how we get along as soon as possible if I am spared to do so. I have nothing of interest to write. Goodbye.

Your boy,

Ugie

1. The firing that Allen heard near Fredericksburg was a diversion to mask Hooker's movement around the Confederate flank.

Battlefield May 4th 1863

My Darling Susie

I received a shot through the left knee on the second, but hope that amputation will not be necessary. Ben Harper, Clinton & the 2 Gosses are also
wounded Arch Tyree, Forbus and probably others that I know nothing of. I
will write again when I can.

Your boy,

Ugie

EPILOGUE

It now becomes my painful duty to inform you . . .

UGIE Allen's short note to Susan dated May 4, 1863, was the last letter he wrote to his wife. Wracked with pain, and probably under the influence of opiates, Captain Allen was barely able to speak during his last four days of life. Although several surgeons examined him, all of them agreed that his weakened physical state precluded the possibility of an operation. On May 8, in the company of his friend Thomas Britton, Ujanirtus C. Allen died. Before returning to his regiment, Britton buried his friend at the field hospital at Chancellorsville, clearly identifying the grave with a wooden headboard. Two days after Allen's death, his much-admired corps commander Stonewall Jackson succumbed to pneumonia at Guinea Station.

A few weeks after her husband's death, Susan Allen journeyed to Virginia to claim his remains. Her family's tradition is that she traveled alone riding horseback and leading a pack mule for a portion of the journey. After reinterring her husband's body in the Baptist Church Cemetery at Antioch, Susan paid the substantial sum of $1,218.75 to place a large marble obelisk over the grave. The inscription reads, "In memory of Capt. U. C. Allen, Co. F 21st Regt. Ga. Vol. who was born Jan 29 [*sic*], 1839, and was wounded in the Battle of Chancellorsville May 2, 1863, and died May 8, 1863."

The Ben Hill Infantry, under the command of Edward "Ned" Henderson, served in the Army of Northern Virginia for the remainder of the Civil War. At Appomattox Courthouse, seven members of the company surrendered their weapons. Out of the one hundred fifty-five men who had served in the Ben Hill Infantry during the four-year conflict, fifty-nine had died.

On July 23, 1868, five years after Ugie Allen's death, his widow married a Confederate veteran named Wilson Washington Strickland. In addition to

Ugie's son Ujanirtus Robert Allen, the couple reared four children of their own on a Troup County farm. The younger Ugie Allen graduated from the University of Maryland School of Medicine and practiced in and around the Georgia communities of Antioch and Houston for forty-five years. He never married. Susan Allen, known to her family as "Little Granny," died on March 11, 1915, at the age of seventy-two.

Hospital near the battlefield,
May the 8th 1863

My dear Friend
It is with great sorrow that I have to state to you that my captain is dead. he died about one hour ago. he was perfectly rashional all the time, though he could not talk much, he would call me to him and say that he wanted to talk, though he couldn't talk with any satisfaction. he expressed some hopes of being prepared to meet his God and I do feel to hope that he is better off. it seemed to greave him to think that the wickedness of men was the cause of his death. I staid by him and dun all that was in my power to give him care. the reason why the Dr. did not amputate his leg was that the shock was so great that he was not able to stand it. Lieut Henderson happened to pass by in a short time after he was shot. he staid with us a few minutes. I will make a box to bury him in if I can get a hammer. there are plenty of planks at this place. I am in hopes that you have heard of his bad luck ere this. I will look for some one after him in a few days. I will put him away the very best that I possible can. Susan you are aware that Ugy was a particular friend of mine and I will say hear for your benefit that you must not take his death any worse than you possible can help. you can only say that there is thousands that are in your condition. as I have not the language to write a good letter you will please excuse me. I am as ever your friend untill death. I have wrote to Nancy twice sense the battle. Capt Allen sent a few lines to you last monday.
yours truly
T. J. Britton

I will give his pocket book and your likeness to Lieut Henderson when I go to the com.

At our same old camp
May the 10th 1863

To my Dear relatives in Georgia
I will write you a few lines this butiful Sabboth morning to let you hear from me. I would have wrote sooner if had of had time. I got hear last night about nine oclock from the battlefield hospital. I am well though I feel considerable worsted. I am sorry to have to state that Capt Allen is dead. he died last friday morning. I stayed with him and dun everything that was in my power to do for him as long as he lived. I made a box and berried him the best that I could. I hated very bad to give him up. I could not help sheding tears over him while I was a covering him up. he died just like a man a going to sleep. he was concious of his death. he prayed several days before he died. I have some hopes that he is better off. it grieved him to think that he had to die on the account of wickedness of other men, that is those who brought on this war. Ben Hooper was seriously wounded through the right side. he is doing tolerable well. Mike Clinton, Gorge Williams, Arch Tyre, Henry & Frank Goss, Sim Market, Henry Forbus, and John Matthews was slitely wounded and holes shot through several of the boys clothing. Gorge Williams & Arch Tyre is with the company. I am abliged to think that our com. was greatly blessed. we saw a very hard time and was very scarce of rashings on the account of bad management. I wrote a few lines to Nancy last monday & wednesday also, and I wrote a short letter to Susan the morning the Capt died. Bill Hunter from Coweta lost his left hand. it was cut off just below the elbow.[1] John Henry Stuart from Heard was shot through the throat the ball came out under one arm. he is doing tolerable well though he cant speak above a whisper.[2] Henry Forbus is with the com. also. I will close as the mail will leave in a short time. I desire an interest in all of your prayers. write soon. I am very anxious to hear from you as there was several sick the last time I heard. excuse my short letter and bad writing. yours respectfully,
T. J. Britton

1. William J. Hunter served as a private in the "Senoia Infantry," Company D, 19th Georgia Regiment. Hunter survived the amputation of his left arm, dying on January 30, 1890, in Coweta County of tuberculosis contracted during his Confederate service.

2. John Henry Stewart, a sergeant in the "Heard Volunteers," Company E, 19th Georgia Regiment, died in the field hospital at Chancellorsville on May 15, 1863, from the effects of his wound.

HdQrt 21st Ga Regt
May 10th 1863

Capt [J. T. Boykin Jr.],
I telegraphed to you a day or two ago that Capt. Allen was mortally
wounded. It now becomes my painful duty to inform you that he is dead. He
died day before yesterday morning.

He was a noble spirit and fell gallantly by my side leading his men in the
charge. There is no loss I more deeply deplore. The fall of such men checks
our exultation over our great victory.

We lost 87—less than any other Regiment in the Brigade. Write to me.
Yr's truly,
J. T. Mercer

Near Hamilton Crossing, Va
May the 13th 1863.

Mrs Allen,
The very unpleasant and painful duty devolves upon us to write you in regard
to the wound and death of your gallant, noble, and devoted, husband; which
you have hearn e're this, though we suppose none of the particulars have
been written you yet; which we will try to give you.

He was wounded in the evening of the 2nd inst. about 6 o'clock by a musket ball which entered his knee and caused his death. His system would not
admit of amputation, if it had I think he might have recovered. Never did we
regret to hear of the death of any friend or associate as much as we did of
Capt Allen's,—he was a warm friend and our esteem and friendship was
much strengthened by long association with him in service. We do earnestly
sympathize with you in your bereavement and in your loss of a true and
devoted husband, we also feel that our loss is great and irreparable, and that
the Confederacy has lost one of her brightest jewels—but we must remember
that the Lord giveth and that He taketh away—and hope that our loss is his
eternal gain.

After he was wounded I did not see him, though Thos Britton was left
with to wait and attend him which he done till his death, then buried him as
well as he could, at the battlefield hospital near Chancellorsville which is
some 18 miles from here—On the 6th Col Mercer went to the hospital to see
him and others of the Regt. who were wounded & he told Col Mercer to tele-

graph to Capt Boykin and he give us the telegram and we sent it to Guinea's to dispatch and the office was moved to Hamilton's Crossing which made it one day later—and we could not dispatch you till we left the battlefield on the 6th just 2 days before he died. Britton said that he did not talk but very little after he was wounded. He said at times Capt seemed to suffer a great deal of pain and then became quiet again in a short time.—but when he died, he died perfectly easy and without a struggle, he said just as one falling into a slumber.—He said he wrote you a short letter immediately after his death.— He took care of his things and brought them to camp with him. I am looking for Capt Boykin or some one else now every day to come after him and his effects here which we will take care of as long as we stay here; and if any comes we will send them all to you. The reason we have not written to you before is from the fact that we have been very busy since we have been back at camps.

Your friends,

Lts Fears & Henderson

Tribute of Respect,
Near Hamilton's Crossing, Va
May the 17th, 1863

At a meeting of the Ben Hill Infantry (Co F) 21st Regt. Ga Vols. this morning, the meeting was organized by calling Lt. E. M. Henderson to the chair, who proceeded to state briefly the object of the meeting: Lt. J. T. Bagby being requested to act as secretary, the object of the meeting being to take action in regard to the death of Captain Allen. The chairman then appointed a committee of three to draft resolutions. Whereupon they reported the following, which were unanimously adopted.

Whereas the Almighty has seen fit to remove from our midst our comrade and fellow soldier Capt. Ujanirtus C. Allen; who died on the 8th May from a wound received while engaged with the enemy in the battle of Chancellorsville on the 2nd Inst.—

He is another sacrifice on the altar of our country's independence; and though he fell while in the defence of his country and dearest rights, we deeply regret our loss of him and feel that as an officer our loss is great and irreparable. Therefore, Resolved 1st, That in the death of Capt Allen the Confederacy has lost one of her most gallant and efficient officers and society an

ornament. 2nd That we offer the family and friends bereaved our heartfelt sympathy and do condole with them in their bereavement,—but we should not forget in our bereavement that he was taken from us by "Him who doeth all things well." 3rd That a copy of the proceedings of this meeting be sent to the family bereaved—also and to the LaGrange Reporter for publication.
Committee:
Lt. O. F. Fears
Sergt. J. S. Horsley
Prvt. W. L. Birdsong
Lt. J. T. Bagby, Sect.

Camp 21st Ga Regt
May 21st 63

To Capt John T. Boykin
Dear Friend with pleasure I avail myself of the present opportunity for the purpose of writing you a short letter informing you that my health at present is very good, hoping at the same time when this comes to hand it may find you and family together with the neighborhood in the possession of good health. I have no news very interest at this time to communicate to you we are all doing tolerable well and our sick boys are improving slowly. It is the impression of the army here generally that there will be another engagement here soon but this is something that is very hard to tell. No won knows or can tell when we are going to have a fight here from the fact that there is never any noise made about it untill we get to cracking away at the yankees. this is a kind of business that I for one am getting awful tierd of and want to see this question settle very bad but see no prospects at present for a compromise any time. I see from extracts of northern papers of the yankees whose time is now out that are passing through Washington City on there way home wish all of them would go home and let us alone but this they will not do. I have a little news to relate to you and that is that the prospect is very good for us to get our regt transferred to cavalry service at least we have got our papers fix up and on the way Col Mercer is doing his best for us and seems very anxious to mount the Regt. I want you procure me a horse if we do get transferred or at least assist me in procuring one. I think that if we all get transferred we will be permitted to come home for about (3) three weeks in order to procure horses for the company. We are all very much hope up at the idea of being

transferred as the service will be lighter on us and we have been through enough hardships to be favored some I think. The promotions in our company has taken place but the 3rd Lt has not been Elected yet but I suppose will be in a few dazes. I understand that you had been as far as Richmond. I was sorry that you could not come on to the company. we all want to see you very much indeed. I have written several letters to you recently and have been somewhat supprise at you not answering them but since I heard that you had been as far as Richmond I could account for you not writting. Bob Wilkes is just from Richmond and informed that you had been there. I was very sorry and felt very sad when I heard that Mrs. Allen was so seriously affected upon hearin the death of her noble and gallant husband. I wish that it were in my power to say something that would be consoling to the feelings of his bereaved. Thomas Britton inform me that he profess to have a hope before he departed this life and seem to be perfectly resign to his death and the highest honor that we can pay to his death is to endeavor by the help of God to avenge his wrongs by imitating his noble and patriotick examples. as for his position in our company it can never be fill again as well as he fill it himself. on duty he was a strict disciplinarian. off of duty he was gentleman sociable and aggreeable to all and right here I want to make a remark in regard to some reports that went home against [him] from this company which I learned rendered him unpopular to some extent with some people at home. he in all his transaction with the company never did give any provocation for no such and had it not have been through the influence of another officer that once belong to this company there never would have been any hard feelings resting against him. this you know by experience as well as I but ever since he was promoted to the captancy & return to the company the boys all seem to like him the best in the world and never did any one get along better with their men than him and he has often remarked to me that he never did see a company as much changed in his life as ours in regard to him and he seem to be well please with his position much more so than he had for a good while before his promotion taken place and I believe that I have the best right to know his feelings in the respect than any one else here for he was more free to converse with me than any one else here. he had on hand some money I think about 150 dollars he had not draw and since he came to the company. his clothing is here with the company and if I can have my way I shall try and take care of it but we are allowed but very little bagage now. this is the reason I wrote to you to know what disposition to make with his things and we do not know wether they will hall them for us or not. there is some money due him from some of the boyes. when I see you I will tell you as nigh as I can how his business stands here etc. everything is near about straight with Qms department so far as he is concern. write to me soon and am very anxious to here from you. I close by subscribing your friend etc.

James T. Bagby

Camp 21st Ga Regt
May 29th 1863.

Mrs. Allen

I send you Capt Allen's trunk and all of his things by Mr. Cameron.[1] I would have sent them to you before this but have not had the opportunity to do so. I send you all the money that he had. I have collected some and there is some owing to him in the company yet. The boys that owe him are at the Hospital and as soon as they come in I will collect the money and send it to you immediately. His sword was stolen from him on the Battlefield the evening that he got wounded. All his other things was saved.

Very Respectfully your obt servt

E. M. Henderson

1. Benjamin H. Cameron (born 1804) was a wealthy Troup County planter.

June the first 1863
Camp near Fredericksburg Va

Dear Friend,

I attempt to write a few lines in answer to yours of the 27th which came safe to hand today. I will say in the outset that you cannot expect me to put up anything like a good letter from the fact that you no my deficiences. I think that it is the hardest undertaking that I ever met with to under take to write to you about the death of my Capt & good friend. It is a very heavy loss to our Com. as well as to you. Susie you must excuse me for not writing something about what he had to talk about when I wrote about his death. I was in no fix for thinking. you stated that you never heard of his saying anything only what he said when the Dr. spoke to him about his condition. he seemed a little alarmed when the Dr. told him what he thought of his case. I remember very well that he told him that his puls was always very weak even when he was well and that he would willingly loose his leg if he thought that it would do any good that was about the 3rd or 4th day as well as I recollect. Col Mercer was present at that time and I think that he ast the col to telegraph to you that he was wounded. he told him that he would do so and that him & Dr. Capers would do everything that was in there power for his good. they then called up other Drs and to get there opinion of the case. they decided that if they were to undertake to amputate his leg that he would sink under it. Dr Philpot[1] of the 4th, Dr. Ethrige[2] of the 12th & Dr Capers laid him on the table the morning after he was wounded, the evening before. I was present all the time. I saw that his case was a very bad one from there maneuvers. they saw that the shock was very great, and they could not get up reaction so they did not opperate on him. if they had I don't think that he could of bore it. I never could discover that he had any puls after he was shot, though he was perfectly rashinal all the time, it true that he would talk a little idol when sleep. he showed some anxiety to talk though he was in so much pain that he could not with any satisfaction. He sometimes would call me and tell me to talk to him. I remember that he told me onse to whisper something in his ear. I did so after studying a little. I then whispered, do you want me to pray for you. he answered yes. I told him that I would and that I had been praying for him. I told him that he remembered that I prayed for him in our little meetings while we was in camps. He said he did. He called on the Lord to have mercy on him very often while in his sufferings. he told me that he had been studying about his condition every sense he had been in service and more especially for the last 4 months. he said it was true that he would fly in to a passion at time, though he was always sorry for it. if he feard death, he didn't appear so. He said that there was one thing he hated, that was that he had to dye on the account of the wickedness of other people. I presume that he had allusion to those that was the cause of the war. I do feel to hope that he has gone to rest. I have just been up and had a talk with Dr. Capers. he said that he would write to you. I told him that I would be very proud if he would, so he taken your addres. he seemed to simpathise with you a great deal. Suda it will not be any trouble to find where he was berried. I put his name very plain on the head board and put a cover on top of the board. There are some 35 or 40 graves where he is berried. he is on the upper side of the grave yard at D. H. Hill's division battlefield hospital, about 2 miles east of the battle field. if any one comes after [him] while we are near this place I think they will let me go and show them the grave. Suda, as to his things, I don the best I could with them. I gave his pocket book, knife, comb & pencil to Lieut. Henderson just as soon as I got to the com. One thing I hate very bad, that is that I could not save his sword. he wanted me to carrie him back a little if I could, though I did not get him more than ten steps, as he was entirely helpless. after I had bound his leg and got the blood stoped I went to get it and some one had taken off. I can't tell whether it was any of our Regt. or not. there was other troops a passing while we was thare. I did not put his dress coat on him to berry him. the reason was it had been off from the time he was wounded. Suda, he did [not] say anything about no person, nor none of his affairs. I ast him if he wouldn't like to be at home whare he could be with you and have good attention. he said that he would. I was in hopes that he would say something about his family, though he did not. I went to him just before we started in to the battle and said to him, Capt. if I should happen to fall & he did not, that I wanted him to write to Nancy just as soon as he did to you. he said that he would sertain if he had the good luck to come out safe. he then made the same request of me. I am in hope that Dr. Capers will give you great satisfaction in his letter. if there is any possible chance for me to assist you in geting him home I will do it with great pleasure. if I had of known when I commensed that I would of wrote so much I would have commensed on a large sheet. excuse bad writing & spelling. I don't no of anything else that is worth writing.

your friend as ever,

T. J. B. [Thomas J. Britton]

1. William H. Philpot (1828–1904) of Talbot County, Georgia, enlisted as a private in the "Southern Rifles," Company A, 4th Georgia Regiment. He was appointed surgeon of the 4th Georgia in July 1861.

2. James Allen Ethridge (1828–93) of Eatonton, Georgia, enlisted as a lieutenant in the "Putnam Light Infantry," Company G, 12th Georgia Regiment. He was promoted to surgeon of the 12th Georgia on May 15, 1862.

Camp of 21st Ga Regt
Fredericksburg, Va
June 1st 1863

At a meeting of the officers of the 21st Georgia the following Resolutions, upon the death of Capt. U. C. Allen were submitted and passed—

Whereas, An Alwise God has seen fit to cut short the glorious career of our beloved companion in arms Captain U. C. Allen Co. F, 21st Ga regiment who, while gallantly leading his command at the battle of the Wilderness May 2d 1863, fell mortally wounded, and expired on the 8th of May and whereas we deem it meet and proper as a tribute of respect to the memory of our departed comrade to express our high appreciation of his eminent worth, and our deep grief for his loss Therefore it is—Resolved, that the death of Capt Allen is deeply and sincerely mourned by his brother officers, who consider that in him the country has lost a true patriot the army a noble representative and the regiment, one of its brightest ornaments—Resolved that while we hartly sympathize with the bereaved widow and friends of our fallen comrade, we would direct them for consolation to the cause and manner of his glorious death, Assuredly does he Sleep with the brave, who sinks to rest, By all their Country's wishes blest—Resolved that a copy of these Resolutions be sent to Mrs. Allen. Also that a copy be addressed to the LaGrange Reporter for publication

Thomas W. Hooper, Lt Col 21st Ga

J. B. Akridge Capt 21st Ga Rgt

T. M. Hightower 1 Lt 21st Ga Rgt

H. T. Battle Capt 21st Ga Presd Meeting

W. J. Holt Lt 21st Ga, Secretary

APPENDIX

ROSTER OF THE "BEN HILL INFANTRY," COMPANY F, 21ST GEORGIA REGIMENT

The National Archives' "Compiled Service Records of Confederate Soldiers in Organizations from the State of Georgia" is the principal source for this roster. Additional and some variant names appear in "Roster of the Ben Hill Infantry," published in the LaGrange *Reporter* on April 27, 1900. Survivors of the company compiled the list from memory. Henry W. Thomas published the same roster in 1903, in *The History of the Doles-Cook Brigade*. Other sources utilized include "Pension Applications of Confederate Soldiers and Widows Who Applied from Georgia" and Lieutenant U. C. Allen's list of twenty-seven men recruited in February 1862.

Demographic information on the soldiers is taken from U.S. census returns and from tax digests and other court records in Troup and Heard Counties, Georgia, and Chambers County, Alabama. If a soldier was not a head of household in 1860, property value and number of slaves are those of his parents.

Ainsworth, David Harrison "Harry"
Born 1840 in Tennessee. Residence Chambers County, Alabama, in household of Alexander Frazier. Illiterate. Farmer. No property; no slaves. Ainsworth's widowed mother Julia owned a plantation with 11 slaves in the State Line District of Heard County, Georgia. Private 1 March 1862. Wounded at Groveton (Second Manassas), Virginia, 28 August 1862; furloughed to Oliver Hospital, LaGrange, Georgia, March 1864. Farmer in Trinity County, Texas, 1870.

Akers, Reuben A.
Born 1836. Residence Troup County, Georgia, in household of John Akers. Farmer. Property value $16,500; 19 slaves. Private 9 July 1861. Wounded at Malvern Hill, Virginia, 1 July 1862, and at Kernstown, Virginia, in 1864. Died 22 October 1884 at Birmingham, Alabama.

Allen, Ujanirtus C.

Born 20 January 1839. Residence State Line District, Heard County, Georgia. Married; 1 child. Farmer. Property value $14,200; 13 slaves. Junior 2nd lieutenant 9 July 1861; 2nd lieutenant 3 December 1861; captain 31 May 1862. Wounded at Cold Harbor (Gaines's Mill), Virginia, 27 June 1862; wounded in left knee at Chancellorsville, Virginia, 2 May 1863. Died of wounds 8 May 1863.

Anderson, John R.

Born 1838. Residence Troup County, Georgia. Married; no children. Farmer. No property; no slaves. Private 9 July 1861. Wounded in head at Cold Harbor, Virginia, 27 June 1862. Died of wounds 29 June 1862 at Stark's House Hospital.

Arrington, Francis M.

Born 1836. Residence Coweta County, Georgia. No property; no slaves. The census taker in 1860 found Arrington residing in a Coweta County, Georgia, hotel. He listed his occupation as "hauling." Private 9 July 1861. Deserted May 1862; rejoined from desertion 10 June 1864; deserted 13 June 1864. Enlisted as a private in Company C, Veteran Battalion 2nd Regiment, Potomac Home Guard Brigade, Maryland Infantry, 14 February 1865. Discharged 25 May 1865.

Bagby, James Thomas

Born 1835. Residence Pool's Mill District, Troup County, Georgia. Married; 1 child. Farmer. No property; no slaves. Private 9 July 1861; 1st sergeant 3 December 1861; 2nd lieutenant 12 February 1863; 1st lieutenant 8 May 1863. Wounded at Second Cold Harbor 3 June 1864; captured at Cedar Creek, Virginia, 19 October 1864. Released at Fort Delaware, Delaware, 17 June 1865.

Bagby, Marshall Marcellus Yancey "Mount"

Born 1845. Residence Greene County, Georgia, in household of Elizabeth M. Bagby. Apprentice saddler. No property; no slaves. Brother of Thomas Bagby. Private 10 January 1862. Killed at Groveton, Virginia, 28 August 1862.

Bagwell, Madison M.

Born 1828. Residence Fayette County, Georgia. Married; 2 children. Illiterate. Farmer. No property; no slaves. Bagwell married Amanda Escoe, sister of Private Jeff Escoe. Private 16 February 1862. Captured at Petersburg, Virginia, 2 April 1865. Released at Point Lookout, Maryland, 24 June 1865. Farm laborer in Coweta County, Georgia, 1870.

Banks, Jeptha B.
Born 1824. Residence State Line, Heard County, Georgia. Married; 3 children. Mechanic. Private 4 March 1863. Wounded and captured at Winchester, Virginia, 19 September 1864. Exchanged 10 February 1865. In Wayside Hospital 16 February 1865 with femur fractured by gunshot. Farmhand at Antioch, Troup County, Georgia, 1870.

Bassett, Rufus H.
Born 1835. Residence Antioch, Troup County, Georgia. Married; no children. Farmer. Property value $304; no slaves. Private 9 July 1861. Wounded in abdomen at Groveton, Virginia, 28 August 1862, and died at field hospital the next evening. His widow, Mary Ann Smedley Bassett lived until 1902 and never remarried.

Bennett, Jesse E.
Born 1846. Residence Troup County, Georgia, in household of Teresa Bennett. Illiterate. Farmer. Property value $1,200; no slaves. Private 4 March 1862. Wounded at Fredericksburg, Virginia, 13 December 1862. Wounded and captured at Winchester, Virginia, 19 September 1864. Released at Point Lookout, Maryland, 19 July 1865.

Bennett, William
Born 1843. Residence Troup County, Georgia, in household of Teresa Bennett. Farmer. Property value $1,200; no slaves. Private 9 July 1861. Wounded and captured at Gettysburg, Pennsylvania, 4 July 1863. Transferred from Fort Delaware, Delaware, to Point Lookout, Maryland, 20 October 1863.

Betterton, John C.
Born 1844. Residence Pool's Mill District, Troup County, Georgia, in household of Leroy B. Betterton. Illiterate. Farmer and drayman. Property value $200; no slaves. Private 9 July 1861. Died from nervous fever at Culpeper, Virginia, 1 February 1862.

Birdsong, Washington F.
Born 1823 in Oglethorpe County, Georgia. Residence Antioch, Troup County, Georgia. Married; 3 children. Farmer. Property value $5,770; 5 slaves.

· Private 1 March 1862. Detailed provost guard 17 November 1863. Captured and paroled at Farmville, Virginia, 7 April 1865. Died at Antioch, Georgia, 1881.

Black, Whitfield J.

Born 1826. Residence Pool's Mill District, Troup County, Georgia. Married; 6 children. Illiterate. Farmer. Property value $1,300; no slaves. Private 9 July 1861. On detached duty April 1862. Admitted to Chimborazo Hospital, Richmond, 4 May 1863. Furloughed 27 May 1863. Attached to military hospital at Atlanta, Georgia, 1 December 1863. Absent without leave from Company F, 1 March 1864.

Bowling (Bolin, Bowlin), Daniel Asbury

Born 1834. Residence Houston, Troup County, Georgia, in household of Daniel Bowling. Farmer. Property value $5,310; 2 slaves. Private 9 July 1861. Detailed as teamster 13 June 1862. Wounded at Spotsylvania, Virginia, 12 May 1864. Captured near Washington, D.C., 13 July 1864. Died at Elmira Prison, New York, 2 April 1865.

Bowling, John T.

Born 1832. Son of Daniel and Rachel Bowling. Private 4 March 1862. Died at Lynchburg, Virginia, 15 September 1862.

Bowling, William D. "Tip"

Born 1839. Residence Troup County, Georgia, in household of Mary Bowling. No property; no slaves. Private 4 March 1862. Listed as "missing" during the battles of Front Royal and Winchester, 24 and 25 May 1862. Deserted 22 March 1865; took oath of allegiance to U.S. government and was given transportation to Springfield, Illinois, 29 March 1865. He was evidently accepted back in Troup County, where he applied to be reinstated as a voter in 1867.

Boykin, John Thomas Jr.

Born 3 March 1835. Residence Troup County, Georgia. Married; 1 child. Farmer. Property value $10,400; 11 slaves. (John T. Boykin Sr. owned property worth $56,000, including 45 slaves.) Captain 9 July 1861. Resigned 31 May 1862, and appointed recruiting officer in Troup County. Died at Antioch, Troup County, 25 June 1901.

Brewer, John H.
Born 1843. Residence Houston, Heard County, Georgia, in household of John C. Brewer. Student. Property value $8,000; 30 slaves. Private 9 July 1861. Killed at Groveton, Virginia, 28 August 1862.

Britt (Brett), John H.
Born 1830. Residence Houston, Heard County, Georgia. Married; 1 child. Tailor. Property value $800; no slaves. Private 9 July 1861. Discharged due to illness 27 January 1862, at Manassas, Virginia. Died at Chattanooga, Tennessee, February 1862, en route home.

Britton (Brittain), Leonidas Artimecy "Lon"
Born 1843. Residence Troup County, Georgia, in household of Lucinda Britton. Private 9 July 1861. Wounded at Sharpsburg, Maryland, 17 September 1862. Admitted to Jackson Hospital, Richmond, on account of old wound 15 June 1864. Absent from the company, sick, 31 August 1864. He used the surname Britton but was the son of Lucinda Walker Britton and her second husband Leonidas Scott.

Britton, Thomas J.
Born 1837. Residence Pool's Mill District, Troup County, Georgia. Married; 1 child. Farmer. Property value $300; no slaves. Son of John B. (died 1840) and Lucinda Walker Britton. Private 4 October 1862. Wounded at Cedar Creek, Virginia, 19 October 1864. Died at Belle Grove (Cedar Creek), Virginia, 1 November 1864. Half-brother of "Lon" Britton.

Burk, Francis Marion
Born 1837. Residence Tallapoosa County, Alabama. Married; 1 child. Blacksmith. Property value $50; no slaves. Private 4 March 1862. Wounded at Groveton, Virginia, 28 August 1862 and at Fort Steadman, Virginia, 25 March 1865. Captured at Richmond, Virginia, 3 April 1865. Admitted to U.S. Army smallpox hospital 27 April 1865.

Clinton, Michael
Born 1831. Private 9 July 1861; corporal 4 July 1862. Wounded at Groveton, Virginia, 28 August 1862 and at Chancellorsville, Virginia, 2 May 1863. Detailed on a gunboat at Kinston, North Carolina, 12 April 1864. Returned to 21st Regiment and wounded at Cedar Creek, Virginia, 19 October 1864.

Cooley, Henry S.
Born 1838. Residence Antioch, Troup County, Georgia. Married; 1 child. Farmer. Property value $2,205; 1 slave. Son of Effington D. Cooley. Private 1 May 1862. Killed at Winchester, Virginia, 19 September 1864.

Cooley, James Anderson "Doller"
Born 16 October 1842. Residence Antioch, Troup County, Georgia, in household of Effington D. Cooley. Property value $11,000; 10 slaves. Private 9 July 1861. Wounded three times and permanently disabled. Paroled at Lynchburg, Virginia, April 1865. Farmhand, Antioch, 1870.

Cooley, William Effington
Born 1836. Residence Antioch, Troup County, Georgia, in household of Effington D. Cooley. Property value $11,000; 10 slaves. Private 4 March 1862. Wounded at Winchester, Virginia, 19 September 1864. Captured at Strasburg, Virginia, 23 September 1864. Exchanged 17 March 1865. Farmer, Antioch, 1870.

Crenshaw, Henry W.
Born 1834 in South Carolina. Residence White's Hill, Troup County, Georgia, in household of James Crenshaw. Carpenter. Property value $670; no slaves. Private 9 July 1861. Died of typhoid fever at Sudley Church, Virginia, 14 October 1861.

Crouch, John A.
Born 1846. Residence State Line District, Heard County, Georgia, in household of Shadrach Crouch. Property value $6,000; no slaves. Private 22 March 1864. Killed at Petersburg, Virginia, 3 April 1865.

Crouch, Leander S. "Lee"
Born 1836. Residence State Line District, Heard County, Georgia. Married; no children. Mechanic. Property value $590; no slaves. Private 9 July 1861. Wounded at Sharpsburg, Maryland, 17 September 1862. Captured at Sutherland Station, Virginia, 4 April 1865. Released at Point Lookout, Maryland, 10 June 1865. Farmer, Carroll County, Georgia, 1870. Died in Troup County, Georgia.

Crowder, Asbury D.
Born 11 July 1840. Residence Chambers County, Alabama, in household

of Dr. Daniel G. Crowder. Private 9 July 1861. Wounded and captured at Winchester, Virginia, 19 September 1864. Died at Fort McHenry, Maryland, 5 June 1865.

Crowder, Charles George

Born 1847. Residence Chambers County, Alabama, in household of Dr. Daniel G. Crowder. Private 8 March 1863, Surrendered at Appomattox, Virginia. Farmer, Rock Mills, Randolph County, Alabama, 1870.

Crowder, John Clayton

Born 1823, in North Carolina. Son of Bartholomew Crowder of Chambers County, Alabama. Private 1 February 1864. Admitted to Jackson Hospital, Richmond, Virginia, 30 April 1864.

Dawson, Dempsey Eugene

Born 1836. Residence Antioch, Troup County, Georgia. Schoolteacher. Property value $600; no slaves. Son of Lemuel G. (died 1848) and Mary Glanton Dawson of Ridge Grove District, Chambers County, Alabama. First lieutenant 9 July 1861. Died of typhoid fever at Sudley Church, Virginia, 21 November 1861.

Dawson, Lemuel Hawkins

Born 9 December 1828. Residence Ridge Grove District, Chambers County, Alabama. Widower; 1 child. Farmer. Property value $12,677; 5 slaves. Son of Lemuel G. and Mary Glanton Dawson. Private 9 July 1861; quartermaster sergeant July 1861. Discharged by substitute 24 January 1862. Captain and assistant quartermaster, 47th Alabama Infantry Regiment, 1 June 1862. Captain and assistant quartermaster on staff of General George T. Anderson, 1 October 1864. Died in Chambers County, Alabama, 6 January 1911. Brother of Dempsey Eugene Dawson.

Escoe, Thomas Jefferson

Born 1836. Residence White's Hill, Troup County, Georgia. Farmer. Property value $1,350; no slaves. Son of Zachariah Estes Sr. and Nancy Escoe. Private 9 July 1861. Wounded at Hazel River, Virginia, 22 August 1862 and near Charlestown, West Virginia, 21 August 1864.

Estes, D. Zachariah

Born 1831. Residence White's Hill, Troup County, Georgia. Married; no children. Overseer. No property; no slaves. Son of Zachariah and Polly Estes and half brother of Jeff Escoe. Private 9 July 1861. Present at battles of Front Royal and Winchester, Virginia, 24 and 25 May 1862. Wounded at Groveton, Virginia, 28 August 1862 and at Summit Point, Virginia 21 August 1864. Died 5 August 1873.

Estes, James Phillip

Born 25 November 1840. Residence, White's Hill, Troup County, Georgia, in household of Tillman Estes. Illiterate. Farmer. No property; no slaves. Private 9 July 1861. Wounded four times. Paroled at Lynchburg, Virginia, 15 April 1865. Died 7 January 1920.

Estes, Reuben C.

Residence White's Hill, Troup County, Georgia. Illiterate. No property; no slaves. Private 8 February 1862. Died of pneumonia at General Hospital No. 2, Lynchburg, Virginia, 21 May 1862.

Fears, Oliver T.

Born 29 April 1839. Residence Chambers County, Alabama, in household of Samuel Fears. Overseer for his father. Property value $41,000; 32 slaves. Private 9 July 1861. Junior 2nd lieutenant 31 May 1862; 2nd lieutenant 8 May 1863. Member of color guard at battle of Winchester, 25 May 1862. Wounded at Cold Harbor, Virginia, 27 June 1862; wounded at Fort Steadman, Virginia, 25 March 1865. Died from wounds at Richmond, Virginia, 5 April 1865.

Forbus, Henry

Born 1833. Residence State Line District, Heard County, Georgia. Farmer. Property value $100; no slaves. Private 26 February 1863. Slightly wounded at Chancellorsville, Virginia, 2 May 1863.

Formby, Aaron T.

Born 1838. Residence Troup County, Georgia, in household of George W. Formby. Property value $7,340; 6 slaves. Private 9 July 1861. Wounded in the abdomen at Fort Steadman, Virginia. Captured at Petersburg, Virginia, 3 April 1865. Died of wounds 26 April 1865 at Fair Ground Post Hospital.

Formby, Henry D. "Dug"

Born 1831. Son of Richard and Ann Lee Formby. Private 9 July 1861. Wounded at Gettysburg, Pennsylvania, 1 July 1863.

Formby, George W.

Born 1842. Residence Troup County, Georgia, in household of George W. Formby Sr. Farmer. Property value $7,340; 6 slaves. Private 9 July 1861. Wounded at Fort Steadman, Virginia, 25 March 1865. Brother of Aaron T. Formby.

Formby, Lucius H.

Born 1845. Private 15 May 1862. Wounded at Groveton, Virginia, 28 August 1862. Surrendered at Appomattox, Virginia. Farmer, Franklin, Heard County, Georgia, 1870.

Formby, William A.

Born 1841. Residence State Line District, Heard County, Georgia, in household of Jackson H. Ponder. Blacksmith. Property value $2,600; no slaves. Private 16 February 1862. Wounded at Groveton, Virginia, 28 August 1862. Surrendered at Appomattox, Virginia. Died 1 September 1927.

Formby, William Thompson

Born 1840 in Virginia. Residence Troup County, Georgia, in household of Thompson Formby. Student. No property; no slaves. Private 9 July 1861. Killed at Groveton, Virginia, 28 August 1862.

Freeman, Jacob Clemmons Clark Jr.

Born 16 August 1846. Residence White's Hill, Troup County, Georgia, in household of J. C. C. Freeman Sr. Property value $2,897; no slaves. Private 21 March 1864. Wounded in right hip and captured at Winchester, Virginia, 19 September 1864. Exchanged 10 February 1865. In hospital at Greensboro, North Carolina, at close of war. Died 29 August 1925.

Garrett, George W.

Born 1833. Residence Troup County, Georgia, in household of Jesse H. Garrett. Overseer for his father. Property value $10,000. Private 4 March 1862. Wounded at Second Manassas, Virginia, 30 August 1862; wounded in knee at Winchester, Virginia, 19 September 1864. Received at general hospital, Howard's Grove Farm, Richmond, Virginia, 19 March 1865.

Garrett, Thomas R.

Born 1839. Residence Troup County, Georgia, in household of James T. Whitley. Farmer. Property value $1,000; no slaves. Private 9 July 1861. Killed at Groveton, Virginia, 28 August 1862.

Gilham, Thomas S.

Born 19 June 1834. Residence White's Hill, Troup County, Georgia. Married; 3 children. Farmer. Property value $4,482; 5 slaves. Private 9 July 1861. Died of typhus at Sudley Church Hospital, Virginia, 8 November 1861.

Glenn, George W.

Born 12 December 1837. Residence Heard County, Georgia, in household of William H. Glenn. Overseer for his father. Property value $35,000; 25 slaves. Private July 9, 1861. Blinded in right eye at Groveton, Virginia, 28 August 1862. Detached as enrolling officer for Heard County, 31 May 1863. Died 11 February 1895, Heard County.

Goss, Benjamin Franklin

Born 14 April 1842. Residence Antioch, Troup County, Georgia, in household of Rhoda Goss. Farmer, Property value $2,750; 1 slave. Private 9 July 1861; corporal 11 February 1862. Wounded three times. Captured at Winchester, Virginia, 19 September 1864. Took oath of allegiance to U.S. and enlisted in U.S. Army 15 October 1864. Returned to Troup County where he married Ann E. Linch on 25 November 1866.

Goss, William Henry

Born 1836. Residence Troup County, Georgia. Married; 1 child. Farmer. Property value $1,500; no slaves. Son of Rhoda Goss. Private 4 March 1862. Detailed as nurse in Gordonsville, Virginia, August–September 1862. Wounded at Chancellorsville, Virginia, 2 May 1863. Furloughed from Danville, Virginia, hospital 23 June 1863.

Green, Joseph Gibson

Born 1841. Residence Antioch, Troup County, Georgia, in household of Willis Green. Farmer. Property value $31,000; 25 slaves. Second sergeant 9 July 1861. Discharged owing to disability 5 October 1861. Moved to Cartersville, Bartow County, Georgia, after the war.

Green, Thomas

Born 1830. Residence Troup County, Georgia. Married; 1 child. Farmer. Property value $5,000; 5 slaves. Private 9 July 1861. Absent, sick, January–February 1862. Died in Troup County, 7 March 1862.

Hairston, Samuel B.

Residence White's Hill, Troup County, Georgia. Married; 1 child. No property; no slaves. Son of James M. Hairston; property value $18,515; 15 slaves. Private 9 July 1861. Captured at Gettysburg, Pennsylvania, 3 July 1863. Took oath of allegiance to U.S. at Fort Delaware, Delaware; released and enlisted in U.S. Army, 30 August 1863.

Haralson, Jesse Burgess Jr.

Born 16 February 1840. Residence White's Hill, Troup County, Georgia. Married; no children. Farmer. Property value $6,500; 3 slaves. Private 9 July 1861; sergeant 1 January 1863; junior 2nd lieutenant 8 May 1863. Furloughed at Petersburg, Virginia, February 1865. At the end of his furlough, he was unable to return to the 21st Regiment. He reported for duty at West Point, Troup County, and was assigned to duty with General N. B. Forrest. Captured at Selma, Alabama, 2 April 1865. Died 10 February 1924.

Haralson, Thomas Elijah Smedley

Born 7 June 1842. Residence White's Hill, Troup County, Georgia, in household of J. B. Haralson Sr. Farmer. Property value $6,500; 3 slaves. Private 9 July 1861. Discharged 29 January 1862. Enlisted in Company C, 14th Battalion Georgia Light Artillery, 15 April 1862. Surrendered at West Point, Troup County, 16 April 1865. Died 31 March 1918.

Harper, Benjamin

Born 1828. Residence Troup County, Georgia. Married; no children. Farmer. Property value $9,000; 8 slaves. Private 4 March 1862. Severely wounded in chest at Chancellorsville, Virginia, 2 May 1863. Furloughed for 60 days from General Hospital No. 16, 17 June 1863.

Harper, Samuel

Born 1830. Residence Antioch, Troup County, Georgia. Married; 5 children. Overseer. Property value $15; no slaves. Private 4 March 1862. On detached duty with Pioneer Corps, 27 October 1863–30 August 1864.

Harper, Winston W. "Wince"

Born 1833. Residence Houston, Troup County, Georgia. Married; 2 children. Property value $50; no slaves. Private 9 July 1861. Absent without leave 3 August 1864.

Henderson, Edward M. "Ned"

Born 9 October 1839. Residence Antioch, Troup County, Georgia, in household of Henry Johnson Henderson Sr. Farmer. Property value $30,990;

28 slaves. Sergeant 9 July 1861; 2nd lieutenant 3 December 1861; 1st lieutenant 12 February 1863; captain 8 May 1863. Wounded in left thigh at Winchester, Virginia, 19 September 1864. At home in Troup County on wounded furlough at close of the war. Died 22 February 1914.

Henderson, Henry Johnson Jr.

Born 1 January 1829. Residence Troup County, Georgia. Married; 3 children. Farmer. Property value $5,010; 4 slaves. Private 1 May 1862. Wounded at Cold Harbor, Virginia, 27 June 1862; wounded in left leg 22 October 1864. Died 26 April 1902, Troup County.

Henderson, Thomas B.

Born ca. 1820. Residence White's Hill, Troup County, Georgia. Married; 6 children. Carpenter. Property value $350; no slaves. Private 9 July 1861. Discharged owing to rheumatism 28 February 1862. Age on enlistment record, 35; age on discharge, 42. Living in Alabama, 1900.

Higginbothem, John Thomas "Hick"

Born 3 September 1840. Residence Chambers County, Alabama, in household of H. M. Higginbothem. Property value $2,100. Private 9 July 1861; sergeant 15 October 1862. Wounded at Groveton, Virginia, 28 August 1862; severely wounded at Winchester, Virginia, 19 September 1864. At home on furlough at close of war. Died 13 March 1913.

Horsley, Joseph Stafford

Born 24 December 1843. Residence Antioch, Troup County, Georgia, in household of Littleton Pitts. Orphan of Smith and Sarah Horsley. Student. Property value $7,576; 6 slaves. Third corporal 9 July 1861; fourth sergeant June 1862; orderly sergeant 1864; first sergeant 1864. Wounded at Cold Harbor, Virginia 27 June 1862; wounded at Snicker's Gap, Virginia 18 July 1864. Captured at Winchester, Virginia, 19 September 1864. Paroled at Point Lookout, Maryland, and transferred for exchange 15 March 1865. Died 17 November 1916 at West Point, Troup County, where he was a physician.

Horsley, Robert Green

Born 1846. Residence Antioch, Troup County, Georgia, in household of Robert Strong Sr. Orphan of Smith and Sarah Horsley. Student. Property value $7,576; 6 slaves. Private 21 March 1862. Captured in Jackson Hospital, Richmond, Virginia, April 1865. Released at Point Lookout, Maryland, 28 June 1865. Living in Texas, 1900.

Horsley, William Henry Harrison "Tip"
Born 1842. Residence Antioch, Troup County, Georgia, in household of Robert Strong Sr. Orphan of Smith and Sarah Horsley. Student. Property value $7,576; 6 slaves. Private 9 July 1861. Discharged at Sudley Church, Virginia, 2 November 1861. Reenlisted 4 March 1862. Wounded at Cold Harbor, Virginia, 27 June 1862; wounded at Cedar Run, Virginia, 9 August 1862. Severely wounded and captured at Winchester, Virginia, 19 September 1864. Released at Point Lookout, Maryland, 28 June 1865. Living in Texas, 1900. Brother of Robert Green Horsley.

Humphrey, John W.
Born 1844. Residence Antioch, Troup County, Georgia, in household of George W. Humphrey. Farmer. Property value $3,050; no slaves. Private 9 July 1861. Died at Sudley Church, Virginia, 24 November 1861.

Hunt, Henry
Born 5 January 1805, Hancock County, Georgia. Residence Heard County, Georgia. Married; adult children. Farmer. 9 slaves. Private 9 July 1861. Discharged owing to age at Manassas, Virginia, 30 June 1862. Captain of a militia company, 1864. Farmer, Heard County, 1870.

Ingram (Ingraham), Sam
Private 15 May 1862. Wounded at Sharpsburg, Maryland, 17 September 1862. Died in camp 15 February 1863.

Jackson, William
Born 17 April 1841. Residence Troup County, Georgia. Married; no children. Illiterate. Private 26 February 1862. Discharged owing to rheumatism at Charlottesville, Virginia, 18 June 1862.

Johnson, Augustus A.
Born 1841. Residence Troup County, Georgia in household of John J. Johnson. Farmer. Property value $890; no slaves. Private 9 July 1861. Discharged 20 January 1862. Enlisted in Company C, 14th Battalion Georgia Light Artillery. Surrendered at Macon, Georgia, April 1865.

Johnson, Brice Chisholm
Born 1846. Residence Troup County, Georgia, in household of Thomas P. Johnson. Property value $20,594; 18 slaves. Private 1 April 1863. Paroled at Lynchburg, Virginia, 13 April 1865. Living in Texas, 1900.

Johnson, Jasper Thomas (also appears as Thomas T. Johnson)
Born November 1826. Residence Antioch, Troup County, Georgia. Married; 1 child. Farmer. Property value $6,800; 5 slaves. Private 6 January 1862. Died at Manassas, Virginia, 19 February 1862.

Johnson, Jeptha V.
Born 1824. Residence Troup County, Georgia. Married; 1 child. Farmer. Property value $2,000; 3 slaves. Private 9 July 1861. Served through the war.

Lanier, James Jackson
Born 13 October 1836, Meriwether County, Georgia. Private 28 February 1862. Wounded at Groveton, Virginia, 28 August 1862. Captured at Cedar Creek, Virginia, 23 September 1864. Exchanged 17 March 1865. Died in Chambers County, Alabama, 21 September 1902.

McClain, James M.
Born 22 August 1843, Oglethorpe County, Georgia. Farmer. Private 15 May 1862. Wounded at Sharpsburg, Maryland, 17 September 1862. On detached duty in hospital 17 February 1863–31 August 1864. Paroled at Staunton, Virginia, 30 April 1865. Died 7 March 1915.

McClain, Samuel J.
Born 1820. Residence Troup County, Georgia. Married; 10 children. Farmer. Property value $600; no slaves. Fourth corporal 9 July 1861; fourth sergeant 5 December 1861. Listed absent, sick in general hospital, on a number of muster rolls. Died at Liberty, Virginia, June 1862.

McClain, William H.
Born 1839. Residence Troup County, Georgia, in household of Samuel McClain. Private 9 July 1861; appointed corporal; appointed sergeant. Killed at Winchester, Virginia, 19 September 1864.

McClurg, Henry J.
Private 20 February 1864; absent without leave 31 August 1864. Pension application filed in Colquitt County, Georgia.

McDonough, John D.
Born 9 June 1841. Private 15 February 1862. Discharged owing to disability

at Farmville, Virginia, 13 November 1862. Migrated to Texas in 1866, where he worked on railroads. Died 7 January 1910; buried at Greenwood Cemetery, Weatherford, Parker County, Texas.

McDonough, William B.
Private 16 February 1862. Captured at Winchester, Virginia, 19 September 1864. Took oath of allegiance to U.S. at Point Lookout, Maryland, and released 19 March 1865.

Manning, James
Born 1838. Residence Troup County, Georgia, in household of James Bonner. Farmer. No property; no slaves. Private 8 March 1862. Wounded at Snicker's Gap, Virginia, 18 July 1864. Died of wounds at home.

Market, Patrick Henry
Born 22 April 1843. Private 9 July 1861. Wounded in right wrist at Groveton, Virginia, 28 August 1862; wounded at Chancellorsville, Virginia, 3 May 1863; wounded in left knee at Snicker's Ferry, Virginia, 18 July 1864. At home, wounded, at close of war. Died in DeKalb County, Georgia, 19 April 1925.

Mathews, John W.
Born 1846. Residence State Line District, Heard County, Georgia, in household of James W. Mathews. Shoemaker. Property value $300; no slaves. Private 9 July 1861. Slightly wounded in hand at Chancellorsville, Virginia, 3 May 1863. Sick in hospital 23 May–31 August 1864. Farmer, Heard County, 1870.

Mobley, Wiley
Born 1836. Residence White's Hill, Troup County, Georgia. Married; 6 children. Overseer. No property; no slaves. Private 9 July 1861. Died at Pageland, Virginia, 11 September 1861.

Mobley, William T.
Born 1843. Residence Troup County, Georgia, in household of James Mobley. Farmer. Property value $100; no slaves. Private 9 July 1861. Discharged 1 August 1862, for disability owing to typhoid pneumonia.

Moon, Charles B.
Born 1839. Residence Antioch, Troup County, Georgia, in household of

J. W. Wilkes. No property; no slaves. Private 9 July 1861. Wounded and captured at Petersburg, Virginia, 3 April 1865. Released at Hart's Island, New York, 15 June 1865. Living in 1894.

Nichols, William M.

Born 1843. Residence White's Hill, Troup County, Georgia. Property value $1,000; no slaves. Private 9 July 1861. Captured near Paw Paw, West Virginia, 24 October 1864. Transferred to Camp Chase, Ohio, 29 November 1864; paroled at Camp Chase, 2 May 1865; received at Vicksburg, Mississippi, 12 May 1865. Living in Alabama, 1900.

Norman, James A.

Private 24 January 1862, substitute for Lemuel H. Dawson. Died of pneumonia 19 March 1862, at Richmond, Virginia.

Parker, J. Isham "Dock"

Born 1836. Residence Houston, Troup County, Georgia. Married; 1 child. Property value $50; no slaves. Private 9 July 1861. Listed absent, sick, on rolls for March, April, and December 1862. Died in General Hospital at Orange Courthouse, Virginia, January 1863.

Parker, Thomas

Private 9 July 1861. Wounded at Harpers Ferry, [West] Virginia, 12 September 1862.

Parker, William H.

Born 7 January 1844. Private 9 July 1861. Captured at Frederick City, Maryland, 9 July 1864. Released at Elmira, New York, 29 May 1865. Died at West Point, Troup County, Georgia, 1 October 1927.

Partridge, Henry T.

No property; no slaves. Private 9 July 1861. Died of typhoid fever at Sudley Church, Virginia, 9 October 1861.

Perry, William A.

Private 11 March 1862. Wounded at Chantilly, Virginia, 1 September 1862; died of wounds at Middleburg, Virginia, September 1862.

Phillips, Henry R.
Private 9 July 1861. Last appears on roll 28 July 1861.

Phillips, James H.
Born 5 February 1835. Residence Antioch, Troup County, Georgia. Married; no children. Illiterate. Farmer. Property value $290; no slaves. Private 26 February 1862. Wounded at Cold Harbor, Virginia, 27 June 1862; died of wounds 13 July 1862.

Phillips, William B.
Born 14 February 1835, near Wetumpka, Alabama. Residence White's Hill, Troup County, Georgia. Farmer. Property value $290; no slaves. Private 9 July 1861. Wounded at Cold Harbor, Virginia, 27 June 1862; slightly wounded in arm at Plymouth, North Carolina, 18 April 1864. Captured at Farmville, Virginia, 6 April 1865. Released at Newport News, Virginia, 26 June 1865. Died 10 February 1912.

Pitts, Samuel S.
Born 1845. Farmer. Private 9 July 1861. Wounded at Cross Keys, Virginia, 8 June 1862; wounded at Groveton, Virginia, 28 August 1862. Captured near Paw Paw, West Virginia, 24 October 1864. Paroled at Camp Chase, Ohio, 2 May 1865; received at Vicksburg, Mississippi, 12 May 1865.

Porter, David A.
Residence White's Hill, Troup County, Georgia. Married. Property value $475; no slaves. Private 9 July 1861. Wounded at Cross Keys, Virginia, 8 June 1862; died from wounds at Charlottesville, Virginia, 13 June 1862.

Porter, James
Private 9 July 1861. Died of pneumonia in General Hospital No. 2 at Lynchburg, Virginia, 24 May 1862.

Porter, John
Private 9 July 1861. Living in 1900.

Ramsey, Augustus Antoine
Born 1830. Residence White's Hill, Troup County, Georgia. Married; 4 children. Property value $10,095; 10 slaves. Son of Allen C. Ramsey. Private 9

July 1861. Discharged 8 November 1861. Enlisted 4 March 1862, in Company E, 41st Georgia Infantry. Wounded and captured at Perryville, Kentucky, 8 October 1862. Exchanged at Vicksburg, Mississippi, 12 November 1862. Enlisted in Forrest's Cavalry and died in service.

Reid, James L. B.

Born 1838. Residence Pool's Mill District, Troup County, Georgia, in household of Thomas Bagby. No property; no slaves. Private 9 July 1861. Wounded at Harpers Ferry, [West] Virginia, 12 September 1862. Sick in General Hospital 30 July–31 August 1864.

Reid, John B. Jr.

Residence Pool's Mill District, Troup County, Georgia. Private 9 July 1861. Captured at Winchester 19 September 1864. Paroled at Point Lookout, Maryland, and transferred to Aiken's Landing, Virginia, for exchange 15 March 1865. Hotelkeeper, Rabun Gap, Georgia, 1884.

Reid, John B. Sr. "Bailey"

Born 1806. Residence Pool's Mill, Troup County, Georgia. Married; 6 children. Overseer and brick layer. Private 9 July 1861. On sick furlough 8 December 1861; died at Richmond, Virginia, 17 March 1862. Troup County court records list him as a tax defaulter in 1862.

Reid, Thomas B.

Born 1830. Residence Troup County. Married; 1 child. Farmer. Property value $100; no slaves. Private 9 July 1861. Died at Manassas Plains, Virginia, 2 September 1861.

Reid, William Richard

Born 1842. Residence Troup County, Georgia, in household of H. M. Wisdom. No property; no slaves. Son of John B. Reid Sr. Private 9 July 1861. Wounded at Fredericksburg, Virginia, 13 December 1862. Under arrest awaiting sentence of court-martial at Staunton, Virginia, 4 August 1864.

Reynolds, John Leonard

Born 20 July 1842. Son of William Reynolds. Private 9 July 1861. Wounded at Fredericksburg, Virginia, 13 December 1862; wounded at Chancellorsville, Virginia, 3 May 1863; wounded at Winchester, Virginia, 19 September 1864. At home on wounded furlough at close of war. Farmer and minister, Dadeville, Alabama, 1870. Died 17 February 1912; buried Woodville Cemetery, Greene County, Georgia.

Robertson, Benjamin
Private 9 July 1861. Died of typhoid fever at Sudley Church, Virginia, 17 October 1861.

Rogers, Joseph L.
Born 1839. Residence State Line District, Heard County, Georgia, in household of Benjamin Caswell. Farmer. No property; no slaves. Private 9 July 1861. Wounded at Groveton, Virginia, 28 August 1862; died from wounds at Middleburg, Virginia, September 1862.

Rowland, Littleberry B.
Born 17 April 1830, in Greene County, Georgia. Residence Antioch, Troup County, Georgia. Married; 3 children. Farmer. Property value $6,200; 5 slaves. Private 23 February 1862; wounded at Groveton, Virginia, 28 August 1862; captured at Waterloo, Pennsylvania, 5 July 1863; paroled from Fort Delaware, Delaware, 14 June 1865. Died 28 January 1908.

Rowland, Samuel J.
Residence Antioch, Troup County, Georgia. No property; no slaves. Fourth sergeant 9 July 1861; third sergeant 5 December 1861; sergeant major January 1863; ordnance sergeant 20 April 1864. Surrendered at Appomattox, Virginia, 9 April 1865.

Rowland, William Henry
Born 18 March 1832, in Greene County, Georgia. Residence Antioch, Troup County, Georgia. Property value $175; no slaves. Third sergeant 9 July 1861; second sergeant 5 December 1861; first sergeant 12 February 1863. Wounded at Groveton, Virginia 28 August 1862. At home on sick furlough at close of war. Living in Atlanta, Georgia, 1900.

Rutledge, Lewis
Private 23 February 1862.

Sample, James Alec
Born 1828. Residence Troup County, Georgia. Married; no children.

Farmer. Property value $100; no slaves. Private 16 September 1862. Sick in general hospital 1 June 1864. Died at Lynchburg, Virginia, August 1864.

Sample, Thomas Jefferson

Born 1834. Residence Pool's Mill District, Troup County, Georgia. Married; no children. Property value $4,700; 3 slaves. Private 9 July 1861; fourth corporal 5 December 1861. Died at Richmond, Virginia, 18 December 1861.

Sharbuth, James

Private 9 July 1861. Discharged owing to disability 18 July 1861.

Skipper, Levi

Born 1834. Residence State Line District, Heard County, Georgia. Married. Farmer. Property value $100; no slaves. Private 4 March 1862. Died of pneumonia at Charlottesville, Virginia, 5 May 1862.

Skipper, Thomas

Born 1842. Private 9 July 1861.

Skipper, William

Born 1845. Private 4 March 1862. Wounded at Groveton, Virginia, 28 August 1862; wounded in thigh at Sharpsburg, Maryland, 17 September 1862. Present 31 August 1864. Paroled at Lynchburg, Virginia, 13 April 1865. Farmhand, Antioch, Troup County, Georgia, 1870.

Strong, Robert Harrison

Born 1825. Residence Antioch, Troup County, Georgia. Married; 3 children. Farmer. Property value $17,215; 14 slaves. Son of John Blackstone Strong and cousin of Private Robert Harrison Strong Jr. Private 9 July 1861. Living at Waco, Georgia, 1900.

Strong, Robert Harrison Jr.

Born 13 October 1839. Residence Antioch, Troup County, Georgia. Married; 1 child. Farmer. Property value $4,345; 1 slave. Private 9 July 1861. Lost right eye owing to typhoid fever and discharged 25 November 1861. Enlisted in Company E, 41st Georgia Regiment, 1 April 1864. Surrendered at Greensboro, North Carolina, 26 April 1865. Farmer, Antioch, 1870. Died 30 September 1923.

Strong, William W.

Born 1845. Residence Antioch, Troup County, Georgia in household of R. H. Strong Sr. Private 9 July 1861. Discharged at Richmond, Virginia, 15 January 1862. Reenlisted 4 March 1862. Killed at Groveton, Virginia, 28 August 1862.

Swint, Andrew J.

Private 9 July 1861. Captured in Loudoun County, Virginia, 16 July 1864. Died at Elmira, New York, 4 March 1865.

Swint, John

Born 1824. Residence State Line District, Heard County, Georgia, in household of Edwin Lewis. Private 13 February 1863. Captured near Harpers Ferry, [West] Virginia, 9 July 1864. Died at Elmira, New York, 18 January 1865.

Talley, James Thomas

Born 1835 in Newton County, Georgia. Residence Pool's Mill District, Troup County, Georgia. Married; 1 child. Illiterate. Overseer. Tax defaulter. Private 14 August 1861. Wounded three times. Surrendered at Appomattox, Virginia. Farmer, Franklin, Heard County, Georgia, 1870. Living in Troup County, 1899.

Tapley (Tarpley), Southey T.

Born 1821 (date also given as 1835). Residence Antioch, Troup County, Georgia, in household of Littleton Pitts. Merchant. No property; no slaves. Second corporal 22 August 1861; third sergeant 4 July 1862. Captured at Harrisonburg, Virginia, 25 September 1864. Exchanged 17 March 1865. Living in Alabama, 1900.

Terry, George W.

Born 13 November 1839. Residence White's Hill, Troup County, Georgia, in household of Julia Terry. 18 slaves. First corporal 9 July 1861. Died of typhus at Centreville, Virginia, 18 December 1861.

Terry, John

Born 1831 (date also given as 1823). Residence White's Hill, Troup County, Georgia. Married; 1 child. Farmer. Property value $512; no slaves. Son of Julia Terry. Private 9 July 1861; sergeant November 1861. Slightly wounded at Cedar Creek, Virginia, 19 October 1864. Captured near Farmville, Virginia, 6 April 1865. Took oath of allegiance to U.S. at Newport News, Virginia, and released 26 June 1865.

Todd, George
Born 1826. Residence Pool's Mill District, Troup County, Georgia. Married; 2 children. Tax defaulter. Private 9 July 1861. Detailed teamster 27 December 1862 to 23 April 1863. Present August 1864. Killed at Winchester, Virginia, 19 September 1864.

Tyree, Archibald W.
Born 1829. Residence Houston, Troup County, Georgia. Married; 1 child. Carpenter. Property value $2,350; no slaves. Private 1 May 1862; sergeant 1863. Detailed as nurse at General Receiving Hospital, Gordonsville, Virginia, 17 October 1862. Slightly wounded at Chancellorsville, Virginia, 3 May 1863. Killed at Summit Point, Virginia, 21 August 1864.

Ussery, Malachi G. "Mack"
Private 4 April 1864. In hospital at Charlottesville, Virginia, with impetigo, 17 August–8 September 1864.

Vance, James H.
Born 1843. Residence Hickory Flat, Chambers County, Alabama, in household of William Vance. Student. Private 9 July 1861. Wounded at Groveton, Virginia, 28 August 1862. Assigned to hospital duty 17 February 1863. Captured near Petersburg, Virginia, 25 March 1865. Released at Point Lookout, Maryland, 21 June 1865.

Vance, William
Born 1821 in South Carolina. Residence Hickory Flat, Chambers County, Alabama. Married; 6 children. Property value $100; no slaves. Private 9 July 1861. Died at Sudley Church Hospital, Virginia, 18 November 1861.

Wallace, Jonathan H.
Born 1827. Married. Private 9 July 1861. Severely wounded in thigh and captured at Fort Steadman, Virginia, 25 March 1865. Died of pyaemia (blood poisoning) at Douglas General Hospital, Washington, D.C., 23 September 1865.

Waller, Leroy T. "Dick"
Born 1834. Residence White's Hill, Troup County, Georgia. Married; 1

child. Property value $1,625; no slaves. Second lieutenant 9 July 1861; elected 1st lieutenant 3 December 1861. Resigned 12 February 1863. Died in Texas before 1900.

Waller, Stephen S.
Born 15 November 1844. Residence Chambers County, Alabama. Farmer. Private 9 July 1861. Captured near Paw Paw, West Virginia, 24 October 1864. Paroled at Camp Chase, Ohio, 1862. Died 10 March 1914.

Waller, Thomas
Private 9 July 1861.

Whatley, Cicero Columbus
Born 4 December 1835. Residence Antioch, Troup County, Georgia, in household of Vachel Davis Whatley. Property value $2,500; 5 slaves. Private 9 July 1861. Died of nephritis at Lynchburg, Virginia, 26 June 1862.

Whatley, Gipson Flournoy
Born 28 April 1833. Residence Antioch, Troup County, Georgia. Married; 3 children. Property value $5,825; 3 slaves. Son of Ornan M. Whatley. Private, Company B, 37th Alabama Infantry, 22 April 1862. Discharged owing to disability 30 July 1862. Private, Company F, 21st Georgia Infantry, 21 February 1863. Transferred to Company H, 21st Regiment and appointed first sergeant 1 January 1864. Captured at Winchester, Virginia, 19 September 1864. Exchanged at James River, Virginia, 18 March 1865. Residence Five Points, Chambers County, Alabama, 1891; member of legislature. Applied for pension from Randolph County, Alabama, 1916.

Whatley, Ornan Monroe
Born 1842. Residence Antioch, Troup County, Georgia, in household of Vachel Davis Whatley. Property value $2,500; 5 slaves. Private 9 July 1861. Discharged owing to disability 3 August 1861. Living in Troup County, 1900.

Whatley, Vachel Davis
Born 9 August 1838. Residence Antioch, Troup County, Georgia, in household of Ornan Whatley. Farmer. Property value $15,260; 12 slaves. Private 9 July 1861. Killed at Woodstock, Virginia, 9 October 1864. (Place and date of death also given as Mt. Jackson, Virginia, 23 September 1864.)

Whatley, Walton Bell

Born 25 October 1840. Residence Antioch, Troup County, Georgia, in household of Ornan Whatley. Farmer. Property value $15,260; 12 slaves. Discharged from 21st Georgia Regiment 1861. Taught school until June 1864, when he joined Captain Wilson's Company, "Home Guards." Died in Troup County, 23 July 1915.

Whatley, Whorton Houston

Private 9 July 1861. Served through the war.

Whitaker, James T.

Born 1844. Son of James M. Whitaker. Private 1 February 1864. Died of disease at Kinston, North Carolina, 20 April 1864.

Whitaker, William Arnold

Born 15 October 1846. Residence State Line District, Heard County, Georgia, in household of James M. Whitaker. Property value $100; no slaves. Private 1 February 1864, at LaGrange, Georgia; joined the company at Kinston, North Carolina. Surrendered at Appomattox, Virginia, 9 April 1865. Died 8 March 1920.

Wilkes, Leonard Henry

Born 1846. Residence Antioch, Troup County, Georgia, in household of Rebecca Wilkes. Property value $3,140; 1 slave. Private 15 February 1863. Captured at Winchester, Virginia, 19 September 1864. Exchanged at Point Lookout, Maryland, 13 February 1865. Drew a pension from the state of Arkansas.

Wilkes, Thomas B.

Born 10 October 1826. Residence Antioch, Troup County, Georgia. Married; 1 child. Farmer. Property value $11,000; 8 slaves. Son of John and Lydia Wilkes. Private 4 March 1862. Wounded at Cold Harbor, Virginia, 27 June 1862. Killed near Bethesda Church, Virginia, 2 June 1864.

Wilkes, Walker L.

Born 1835. Son of William M. and Rebecca H. Wilkes. Private 4 March 1862. Sick in General Hospital 15 November 1862–30 April 1863. Died of fever in camp.

Wilkes, William H.

Born 1842. Residence Antioch, Troup County, Georgia, in household of Rebecca Wilkes. Property value $3,140; 1 slave. Private 9 July 1861. Captured at Salisbury, North Carolina, 12 April 1865. Released at Camp Chase, Ohio, 19 June 1865. Died 20 July 1892.

Williams, Frederick

Born 1844. Residence White's Hill, Troup County, Georgia in household of Dr. G. M. White. Farmer. No property; no slaves. Son of Madison and Caroline Williams. Private 9 July 1861. Wounded at Groveton, Virginia, 28 August 1862. Paroled at Lynchburg, Virginia, April 1865.

Williams, George W.

Born 1838. Residence White's Hill, Troup County, Georgia, in household of James Smedley. Property value $100; no slaves. Son of Madison and Caroline Williams. Private 9 July 1861. Wounded 1 September 1862, at Chantilly, Virginia and 2 May 1863, at Chancellorsville, Virginia. Absent, sick, at General Hospital 20 June 1863. Died at Hagerstown, Maryland, 25 June 1863.

Williams, Israel A.

Born 1842. Residence Troup County, Georgia, in household of Jeff Williams. Farmer. Property value $5,500; 3 slaves. Son of Madison and Caroline Williams. Private 9 July 1861. Wounded at Cold Harbor, Virginia, 27 June 1862. Died of typhoid fever at Farmville, Virginia, 6 August 1862.

Williams, John C.

Fifth corporal 9 July 1861. Captured at Winchester, Virginia, 19 September 1864. Exchanged 18 March 1865. Living in Troup County, Georgia, 1900.

Williams, Thomas M.

Born 1837. Residence Pool's Mill District, Troup County, Georgia. Married; no children. Miller. Private 16 May 1862. Present 31 August 1864. Miller, West Vernon District, Troup County, 1870. Living in Troup County, 1900.

Winn, William

Residence Antioch, Troup County, Georgia, in household of Asa G. Winn. Property value $5,000; 10 slaves. Private 9 July 1861. Discharged 1861.

Wisdom, Hamilton McGee "Hamp"

Born 1814. Residence Houston, Troup County, Georgia. Married; 3 children. Farmer. Property value $11,000; 13 slaves. Private 9 July 1861. Discharged by substitute 27 October 1861. Captain, Company F, 37th Regiment, Georgia Militia, 9 April 1864. Migrated to Louisiana after the war.

Wisdom, Robert Allen

Born 1842. Residence Houston, Troup County, Georgia, in household of H. M. Wisdom. Student. Property value $11,000; 13 slaves. Private 27 October 1861. Substitute for H. M. Wisdom. Fourth corporal 21 December 1861. Wounded at Groveton, Virginia, 28 August 1862 and died the next day.

Wright, Samuel F.

Born 1840. Residence Pool's Mill District, Troup County, Georgia. Illiterate. Private 15 February 1862. Wounded at Groveton, Virginia, 28 August 1862; wounded at Cedar Creek, Virginia, 19 October 1864. Farmhand, Antioch, Troup County, 1870.

Yarbrough, Thomas

Private 15 February 1862. Died of measles at Lynchburg, Virginia, 9 May 1862.

Young, John Leonidas.

Born 1835. Son of L. H. and Rebecca Young. Property value $15,000; 14 slaves. Private 9 July 1861. Died of typhoid fever at Pageland, Virginia, 6 October 1861.

BIBLIOGRAPHY

Unpublished Primary Sources

Akin, Warren, Family Papers. Manuscript No. 2551A. Special Collections, University of Georgia Libraries, Athens.

Antioch Baptist Church Records. Manuscript No. 48. Troup County Archives, LaGrange, Ga.

Boykin Family Papers. Manuscript No. 15. Troup County Archives, LaGrange, Ga.

Carman, Ezra. "History of the Antietam Campaign." Manuscripts Division, Library of Congress.

Compiled Service Records of Confederate Soldiers in Organizations from the State of Georgia. Microfilm, Georgia Department of Archives and History, Atlanta.

Eighth Census of the United States, 1860. Nonpopulation Schedules: Agriculture. Record group 29, National Archives. Microfilm.

Gould, John M. Collection (Antietam Papers). Dartmouth College Library, Hanover, N. H.

Governor's Incoming Correspondence (Joseph E. Brown). Georgia Department of Archives and History, Atlanta.

Hightower, Thomas (Company D, 21st Georgia), letters. Civil War Miscellany. Georgia Department of Archives and History, Atlanta.

Mobley, William (Company F, 21st Georgia), letters. Civil War letters vertical file. Troup County Archives, LaGrange, Ga.

Pension Applications of Confederate Soldiers and Widows Who Applied from Georgia. Microfilm. Georgia Department of Archives and History, Atlanta.

Population schedules, seventh, eighth, and ninth censuses of the United States (1850–70). Record group 29. Microfilm. National Archives.

Population schedules—slaves, eighth census of the United States (1860). Record group 29. Microfilm. National Archives.

Richardson, Sidney Jackson (Company I, 21st Georgia), letters. Georgia Department of Archives and History, Atlanta.

Strong, J. B. "Antioch Families." Manuscript No. 5, Louise B. Hammett Collection. Troup County Archives, LaGrange, Ga.

Troup County, Georgia, Deed Books A–P, 1827–70. Troup County Archives, LaGrange, Ga.

Troup County, Georgia, Inferior Court Annual Returns Books A–V, 1827–80. Troup County Archives, LaGrange, Ga.

Troup County, Georgia, Inferior Court Loose Papers, 1827–1900. Troup County Archives, LaGrange, Ga.

Troup County, Georgia, Superior Court Loose Papers, 1827–1900. Troup County Archives, LaGrange, Ga.

Troup County, Georgia, Tax Digests, 1862–63. Microfilm. Troup County Archives, La-Grange, Ga.

PUBLISHED PRIMARY SOURCES

Adjutant & Inspector General's Office, Confederate States Army. *General Orders from the A. & I. G. O., Confederate States Army, from January 1862 to December 1863.* Columbia, S. C., 1864.

Allan, William. *History of the Campaign of General T. J. (Stonewall) Jackson in the Shenandoah Valley of Virginia.* Philadelphia, 1880.

Antioch. "Ben Hill Infantry in Camp at Wehadkee." Augusta (Ga.) *Chronicle & Sentinel,* July 11, 1861.

B. "Army of the Potomac, Colonel Mercer's Regiment, Camp near Centreville, Va., September 15, 1861," Rome (Ga.) *Weekly Courier,* October 4, 1861.

D. W. H. "From the Twenty-First Georgia." Rome (Ga.) *Weekly Courier,* December 26, 1862.

Emory and Henry College. *Catalogue of the Officers and Students of Emory and Henry College, Washington County, Va. 1857–1858.* Wytheville, Virginia, 1858.

Emory and Henry College. *Catalogue of the Officers and Students of Emory and Henry College, Washington County, Va. 1858–1859.* Wytheville, Virginia, 1859.

"From the Twenty-First Georgia." Anonymous member of the 21st Georgia Regiment. Columbus (Ga.) *Weekly Enquirer,* August 7, 1862.

Hamilton, Algernon Sidney. "The 21st Georgia at the Battle Near Port Republic." Augusta (Ga.) *Daily Constitutionalist,* July 4, 1862.

"Maryland Correspondence of the Southern Confederacy." Anonymous member of the 21st Georgia Regiment. Atlanta *Southern Confederacy,* September 25, 1862.

Myers, William S. "The Civil War Diary of General Isaac Ridgeway Trimble." *Maryland Historical Magazine,* XVII (March 1922), 1–20.

Nisbet, James Cooper. *Four Years on the Firing Line.* Edited by Bell I. Wiley. Jackson, Tenn., 1963.

———. "Stonewall Jackson." Richmond *Daily Whig,* July 3, 1862.

"Report of Casualties in Gen. Phil Cook's Brigade, Near Winchester, Va., Sept. 19th 1864." Macon (Ga.) *Daily Telegraph,* October 9, 1864.

Snead, Fletcher Tillman. "Casualties in Gen. Phil Cook's Brigade." Macon (Ga.) *Daily Telegraph,* November 2, 1864.

Tardy, Mary T. *The Living Female Writers of the South.* Philadelphia, 1872.

Taylor, Richard. *Destruction and Reconstruction: Personal Experiences of the Late War.* New York, 1879.

Taylor, Walter H. *Four Years with General Lee.* Bloomington, 1962.

The War of the Rebellion: A Compilation of the Official Records of the Union and Confederate Armies. 128 vols. Washington, D.C., 1880–1901.

Thomas, Henry W. *History of the Doles-Cook Brigade, Army of Northern Virginia C. S. A.* Atlanta, 1903.

Trimble, Isaac R. "General I. R. Trimble's Report of Operations of his Brigade from 14th to 29th of September, 1862." *Southern Historical Society Papers,* VIII (June–July 1880), 306–309.

SECONDARY SOURCES

Borritt, Gabor S., Harold Holzer, and Mark Neely Jr. *The Confederate Image: Prints of the Lost Cause.* Chapel Hill, 1987.

Bruce, Merle Massengale. *Early Marriages, Troup County, Georgia, 1828–1900.* Atlanta, 1982.

Carter, James Byars, M.D. "Disease and Death in the Nineteenth Century: A Genealogical Perspective." *National Genealogical Society Quarterly,* Volume LXXIV, No. 4 (December 1991).

Davidson, William H. *Pine Log and Greek Revival: Houses and People of Three Counties in Georgia and Alabama.* Alexander City, Ala., 1964.

Davis, William C., ed. *The Confederate General.* 6 vols. Harrisburg, Penn., 1991.

Eller, Lynda S. *Heard County, Georgia: A History of Its People.* Huguley, Ala., 1980.

Hall, David M. *Once upon a Time: A History of the Emory Chapel Community.* Auburn, Ala., 1976.

Harrison, Noel G. *Chancellorsville Battle Sites.* Lynchburg, Va., 1990.

Henderson, Lillian. *Roster of the Confederate Soldiers of Georgia, 1861–1865.* Hapeville, Ga., 1955.

Hennessy, John J. *Return to Bull Run: The Campaign and Battle of Second Manassas.* New York, 1993.

Johnson, Forrest Clark III. *Histories of LaGrange and Troup County, Georgia.* 5 vols. LaGrange, 1987–93.

Krick, Robert K. *Conquering The Valley: Stonewall Jackson at Port Republic.* New York, 1996.

——. *Lee's Colonels: A Biographical Register of the Field Officers of the Army of Northern Virginia.* Dayton, 1991.

——. *Stonewall Jackson at Cedar Mountain.* Chapel Hill, 1990.

Lindsey, Bobby L. *The Reason for the Tears: A History of Chambers County, Alabama, 1832–1900.* LaFayette, Ala., 1971.

McLendon, Dorothy, Lillie Lambert, and Danny Knight. *Family, Church, and Community Cemeteries of Troup County, Georgia.* LaGrange, Ga., 1990

O'Reilly, Frank A. *"Stonewall" Jackson at Fredericksburg: The Battle for Prospect Hill, December 13, 1862.* Lynchburg, Va. 1993.

Priest, John Michael. *Antietam: The Soldiers' Story.* Oxford, 1989.

Smedlund, William S. *Campfires of Georgia Troops, 1861–1865.* Marietta, Ga., 1994.

Smith, Clifford L. *History of Troup County.* Atlanta, 1933.

INDEX